The Light Garden of
the Angel King

Peter Levi, a classical scholar, archaeologist and poet, was born in 1931. He has translated two books for the Penguin Classics, Pausanias' *Guide to Greece* (two volumes) and *The Psalms*, as well as a collection of Yevtushenko (with R. Milner-Gulland) for the Penguin Modern Poets, and has edited Johnson's *A Journey to the Western Islands of Scotland*, Boswell's *The Journal of a Tour to the Hebrides* and Kipling's *Just So Stories* for the Penguin Classics. He also has edited *The Penguin Book of Christian Verse*. He is also the author of *The Pelican History of Greek Literature*. Among his latest books are *Shakespeare's Birthday* (1985) and *The Frontiers of Paradise* (1987). He is Professor of Poetry in the University of Oxford.

PETER LEVI

✻

The Light Garden of
the Angel King

JOURNEYS
IN AFGHANISTAN

PENGUIN BOOKS

PENGUIN BOOKS

Published by the Penguin Group
27 Wrights Lane, London w8 5TZ, England
Viking Penguin Inc., 40 West 23rd Street, New York, New York 10010, USA
Penguin Books Australia Ltd, Ringwood, Victoria, Australia
Penguin Books Canada Ltd, 2801 John Street, Markham, Ontario, Canada L3R 1B4
Penguin Books (NZ) Ltd, 182–190 Wairau Road, Auckland 10, New Zealand

Penguin Books Ltd, Registered Offices: Harmondsworth, Middlesex, England

First published by Collins 1972
Published in Penguin Books with revisions 1984
3 5 7 9 10 8 6 4 2

Typeset, printed and bound in Great Britain by
Hazell Watson & Viney Limited
Member of BPCC plc
Aylesbury, Bucks, England
Set in VIP Baskerville

For
George Pavlopoulos and
Takis Loumiotis

CONTENTS

PREFACE TO THE
PENGUIN EDITION

Without making enormous changes, I have made a number of corrections in this edition. Here and there I have recast sentences from present into past time, since otherwise the Russian invasion of Afghanistan had made them intolerably ironic. Still, this book remains isolated by what has happened; it belongs to the short modern period when the country was more or less open to travellers, during the short attempt at democracy before the disaster. I have not attempted to alter or darken the tone in which I wrote nearly fifteen years ago, though today one cannot avoid feeling deep sadness and bitterness. The Russians napalmed and bombed the villages of the Pech valley. Kamdesh has been destroyed. I must assume that most of my friends are dead.

Books are a kind of moral shadow-play. Questions of literary form are moral problems; they are a shadow-play of social and political issues. The classic form of the nineteenth-century travel book with its secure and discursive prose, its unruffled sobriety and impersonal good manners, probably comprehended a wider range of reality than the sharper, livelier style of writing which has succeeded it. Those amazed but calm glances of the Victorians were a uniquely suitable way of seeing wild landscapes and remote peoples. Major Leake and Lieutenant Wood and Dr Chandler and Darwin on the *Beagle* are not self-conscious observers, or if they are then just sufficiently so. Their lives were active and their scientific curiosity passionate, whatever was merely dangerous or adventurous in their journeys was laconically expressed, because in itself it hardly interested them. Physical excitement in their writings seems hardly more than a symbolic shadow of an intellectual tension, it is an implicit element that works by being dissolved and diffused. Modern travel writing is more sensuous and more restless, its motives are usually aesthetic and not scientific, more fuss is made about less and nothing is left out.

At one time there seemed to be a possibility of writing this present book as a long travel poem; I was thinking about the verse letters of Horace, about Byron, and in a confused way about Wordsworth. It turns out to be impossible, for physical reasons if for no others. I did write four or five poems in Afghanistan, they say very little about the country and they are extremely personal; I suppose what they express is something I would have been unable to work out in prose. When I arrived at Kabul I was still uncertain what kind of book I was going to write; I knew it would be archaeological, and about a journey, but how to answer so many questions in one book?

All my life I have wanted to travel in central Asia; the discovery of a Greek city at Ay Khanoum, on the banks of the Oxus, just inside Afghanistan on the Russian border, was the final straw. It was the first Greek city ever excavated in Afghanistan, and in order to visit it I engaged to write a travel book, and took the opportunity for some poking around at other archaeological sites. I should have liked to write with more authority about the Buddhist art of the first centuries A.D. which has so many classical elements, and about the Kushans, the successors to the Greek kingdoms in central Asia, but it was impossible for me to visit Pakistan or India to see the museums, and the southernmost part of Russia was also excluded. To put it in a nutshell, the question I most wanted to answer was what was the Greek occupation of Afghanistan like, and what became of these remote Greek kingdoms? The orthodox view among British scholars is that they perished in a wave of invasions by barbarous nomadic hordes in the century before the birth of Christ. And yet the earliest monumental art and sculpture of the Buddhists in northern India not only contain abundant and undigested Hellenic elements, but in their essential forms they are based on the Greek art of the Roman Empire; Afghanistan, which had once been Greek, became Buddhist at this time; by the sixth century A.D. it was perhaps the greatest centre of Buddhist pilgrimage. Had the Greeks died out utterly by then?

As an archaeological unity, Afghanistan is particularly unsatisfactory; as a political unity it was nothing but a chewed bone left over on the plate between Imperial Russia and British India. It has never been a cultural unity in any period, and it is not so today; nonetheless in 1970 it was a political reality, unified in some way by its religion, Islam, and by its special physical geography and remarkable climate. The centre of the country is

the tall ranges of the Hindu Kush, and even the lowest point I
visited in Afghanistan is several thousand feet above sea-level.
Virtually everyone, even in remote villages, can now speak
Persian, at least as a second language. For an individual traveller,
there is the narrower unity of his own experience and eyesight: a
unity of time. Today, with the Russians in possession of the
country, the summer of 1970 looks like an island in time, a ruined
paradise.

I am inclined to think that the form of a book expresses or fails
to express the world. The beginnings of a book, whether in life or
in imagination, are dreamlike, in the sense that the dreamer might
be responsible in his sleep. The invisible principles that criticism
can detect in a given literary form will reveal at a common-sense
level the writer's convictions about human society and about his
times. Most poets feel as if the only forms it was completely decent
to write in were the fresh forms of new poems. To make my own
feelings worse, I was intimidated as well as enthralled during the
time I spent in Afghanistan by getting to know the travel diaries
of Basho, so great an example one was ashamed to be planning
any other kind of book. I was also reading Malcolm Lowry's *Hear
Us O Lord from heaven thy dwelling-place*; between them Malcolm
Lowry and Basho seemed to exhaust the possibilities of honesty.

The best archaeological travel book I have ever discovered is
Leake's *Travels in the Morea*, but there are three or four other
extremely interesting books which are about Afghanistan: the best
is Wood's *Journey to the Source of the River Oxus*. Wood was a young
lieutenant of the greatest brilliance and promise who entered
Afghanistan, in those days an ill-defined territory, as a member of
the British mission to the court of Dost Mahommed at Kabul in
1840. He was sent north with a Dr Lord, who was to try to restore
the eyesight of the blind Mir of Kunduz; he seized the opportunity
to explore the upper Oxus, a territory as inaccessible to British
travellers today as it was a hundred years ago. Immediately
afterwards he resigned his commission in protest against the
disastrous policy of a British expedition to expel Dost Mahommed
and restore Shah Shuja; that expedition ended in the annihilation
of the British army of occupation. Apart from one survivor and a
handful of hostages, sixteen thousand men were massacred in the
Khord Kabul Pass between Kabul and Jellalabad in eleven days.
Wood left India and never returned to the army; late in life he
assumed a naval captaincy as manager of the Indus Steam

Navigation Company. His book was published in 1841 and 1872, the year of Wood's death, and then posthumously by the great geographer Sir Henry Yule.

There are three other indispensable classics of Afghan travel, Doctor (later Sir George) Robertson's *Kafirs of the Hindu Kush*, Robert Byron's *Road to Oxiana*, and Eric Newby's *Short Walk in the Hindu Kush*. One ought, perhaps, also to mention a most interesting pioneering work by the Hon. Mountstuart Elphinstone, *An Account of the Kingdom of Caubul*, which was substantially complete in 1814. Robertson was in Kafiristan, among the free mountain tribes who at that time had still never accepted Islam, in 1889 and again in 1890–91; he was a British political agent, an accurate but somewhat bluff and in some directions a maddeningly incurious observer. His adverse report on the Kafirs, with whom he found it difficult or impossible to negotiate, contributed to forming the British Government's frontier policy which, by the Durand treaty in 1893 and a supplementary agreement in 1895, abandoned the Kafirs to be massacred or forcibly converted by Abdur Rahman, in the interests of effective central government. They were, in effect, traded for the frontier Pathans further south, whose territory was annexed to British India. Still, to be fair to Robertson, he was a truthful reporter, and a visit to the same villages today confirms one's respect for him. He was humourless, but for a traveller alone among a wild and unpredictable people humour is a luxury. Robert Byron's is a more engaging style. The world, and to some degree central Asia, has changed since his visit, although if he had lived he would not yet be an old man; yet every one of his stories still rings true. Eric Newby's book is very recent but it already has the status of a minor classic, in my view rightly. Naturally these are not the only writers the country has attracted; it was the subject of Kipling's *Man Who Would Be King*, and Professor Gilbert Murray wrote a strange novel about it; it obsessed Matthew Arnold. These were not travel writers; yet there are some lines in 'Sohrab and Rustum' and 'The Strayed Reveller' that give a clearer, sharper, more accurate sense of what central Asia is like than any other sentences in the English language.

Afghanistan in 1970 was still sufficiently distant and extra-ordinary for it to be stupid to travel there alone. There were friends for whose company I longed most bitterly, and through whose eyes I knew I would have seen much more. But it will be

obvious from every page of this book that I was extremely
fortunate in the travelling companion I did have, Bruce Chatwin.
Most of our best observations and all the best jokes were his; and
it was he who was interested in nomads, he who told me to read
Basho, he who had done all the right homework in my subjects as
well as his own, who knew the names of flowers and who
understood Islamic art history. He was even stronger in the bread
and butter virtues without which we would have been doomed,
for a journey like this one ought to be indefatigable, extremely
patient, open-minded, friendly, and talented with the right kind
of gifts both of conversation and of silence. In Afghanistan there
were so many people from whom we received help that it is
impossible to name them all, but I would like to express at least
some stuttering formal thanks for the generosity of Mr Christopher
Rundle of the British Embassy, and for the great kindness and
hospitality of Dr Maurizio Taddei, Professor Paul Bernard, and
the other very friendly Italian and French archaeologists who
were working at Ghazni and at Ay Khanoum.

A few of the publications and discoveries since 1972 should be
recorded here: John Irwin's excellent work on Asokan pillars
appeared in four parts, starting in November 1973, in the
Burlington Magazine (vol. 115, p. 706), and continued in later
volumes. A Russian excavation at Takh-t Sangin in Tadjikistan
produced spectacular finds, and suggested the source of the
British Museum's Oxus treasure, acquired in 1897. The treasure
now found included a head of Alexander, an altar to the god of
the Oxus, and the grey clay head of a Greek prince. The English
publication was in the *Journal of the Royal Asiatic Society*, 1981.
When my own book was reviewed, most of its reviewers knew
even less about the subject than I did, and I think they were too
kind. The only unkind one was an Indianist specializing in war-
elephants and writing anonymously; he had neither read my book
nor ever visited Afghanistan; he is still mouldering in his museum.
By contrast, I got a splendid, charming and most helpful letter
from Peers Carter, British Ambassador in Kabul when I was
there. He pointed out numerous errors, most of which I have put
right now. On the problem of the upper Oxus, it is best to quote
him word for word:

I went up to the Pamirs in 1971, following the Askhan River to the
point where it turns south at Bazai Gunbad to the Wakhjir Glacier where

it, and therefore the Oxus, has its source. (It is now generally accepted that Curzon was right and that Wood made a mistake in going up the Pamir River instead of the Wakhan from the confluence at Qalai Panj.) I took with me my wife, a botanist from Kew, and Chris Rundle's successor. Incidentally, Tilman was also in the Chinese frontier area of Afghanistan in 1947.

I would like also to quote him on the golden oriole:

There were golden orioles in the Embassy gardens, too. They have a loud, clear, musical call which, according to Yakub Ali, the head gardener, says 'Dokhtar'e Sufi am' – I am the daughter of a Doctor of Divinity; and the bird's name, in Dari, is Dokhtar'e sufi.

PART ONE

❁

My Origins and Our Beginnings

CHAPTER
I

In Oxford just before Christmas it was dark in the mornings; and on Friday, the day the gardener comes, you could hear him sweeping the lawn in the dark. I was trying to learn Persian (an unsuccessful attempt) and working my way through Tarn's *Greeks in Bactria and India*, a necessary standard book about which everyone complains. The days and the book were full of dark grey gloom and rain, and early in the evening the air became black. I remember the appearance of the pink Christmas lights in St Ebbe's and, passing through Christ Church one night when it was foggy, the long line of isolated gaslights in the quadrangle. There was a performance of John Blow's *Venus and Adonis* at the Playhouse. I went to Eastbourne to see my mother; the air was clearer, but every morning there were seagulls in the garden. The sea was very cold and green-brown and the air had a brownish tinge. Someone sent me a postcard of a Persian painting which I idly propped up on my desk lamp. It began to work on me without my noticing it and, rather without thinking, I jotted down a short paragraph in a notebook as follows:

In that country it always snows for an hour or two a day; it is a pagan Christmas morning, they don't know there that it's solstice because they have no understanding of the stars. A single star (all they notice) is enough to navigate by. Long-necked gazelles and willow trees as fresh as salad. The people travel on bay mules. The palaces are abandoned and there are storks on the blue minarets, but the gardens are not overgrown. The road towards the White Tower along which caravans pass for one week in every year, and again in autumn for a week, like migrating birds or nomads with their flocks, crossing the whole of Asia at walking pace.

I must evidently have been trying to project an imaginary Afghanistan to see whether it made a coherent model. The reason for recording this strange jotting here is its curious combination of inaccuracies of fact with accuracy of feeling. It is not surprising that a Persian fifteenth-century miniature should be a wonderful tangle of fantasy and accurate observations of Afghanistan, but it does seem remarkable that such a picture, decoded at a distance of centuries and of thousands of miles by someone who has never seen Asia should still convey (as to me it does) just what Afghanistan is like. It is difficult for a European to arrive in Kabul without passing through Iran; even by air you will usually have to change planes at Teheran, and if you are coming to Asia for the first time you would be crazy not to stop in Istanbul as well. To descend on a remote city out of the air without a slow arrival is to deprive yourself of any chance of understanding where you are going.

My friend Bruce had travelled in Asia and been in Afghanistan before, for me it was still the remotest place I could imagine. When I was nine or ten I founded a society of little boys who wanted to go as Christian missionaries to Tibet; it lasted about three or four weeks I think, a long time in those days. Later when I was learning to be a school-teacher in London, when I was already a Jesuit, I used to go to gaze at the departure announcements at Victoria Station that read Paris, Warsaw, Belgrade, Athens, Istanbul. Even the name Istanbul was a magnet to me because that was where my father's family came from, and I had never been so far east. My grandfather was a Jewish indigo merchant and carpet dealer in that city before the eighteen eighties, when he moved to London and set up a carpet business in Houndsditch near the Bevis Marks synagogue. My grandmother had twenty-one children, and at that time sixteen of them had already been born. My father was one of the five born in England; quite late in life he became a Roman Catholic, but that was before I was born, so that my own Jewish origins seemed remote and mysterious to me. The older I have grown the more important they have become. I did not know anything much about the family's life in Istanbul, except that I had an elderly aunt in St John's Wood before the war who used to make rose-petal jam from the cabbage roses in her garden, but when I was a schoolboy my father's letter-headings still had the magic rubric 'and at Constantinople'.

So I set out for Istanbul by air on the seventeenth of June, hopelessly re-reading lesson eight in the Persian grammar and trying to forget other languages. As we approached Turkey there was a huge, dramatic sunset, and Asia could hardly have been more sinister; we dived into clouds of black, stormy mist. The atmosphere on the ground was thick and wet, and there was a mixed smell of fish, salt water and low clouds; then suddenly the walls at first sight like the walls of Rome, and those rococo details of architecture which one remembers with a start are associated with the origins of the rococo style in Europe.

The world began to fall into a different focus. What I have to write now about Istanbul is only preliminary to something else, and I was there for a very short time, much of which I spent in the dusty and leafy area of the archaeological museum; for the purposes of this book it is the focus that is important. First, to find the people one met as intelligent and as sleepy as one had always imagined, and to have the concrete experience of one of the great historic centres of the Islamic world. As you imagine it from Greece, Istanbul is still the owl-haunted ruins of Byzantium; what you see when you get there is a dense and living city with the most magnificent skyline in the world, walls far finer than the walls of Rome, and a commercial life like that of late Victorian London. The extent of Asia begins to amaze you, and this is the first step. Then consider the migrations of the Turkish people, from the remote pastoral life of the Mongolian steppe until this point.[1] Yet while the Sultan was besieging Istanbul, and the Ikons of the Virgin wept in their churches, Cyriaco of Ancona was reading the Sultan Livy in his tent;[2] and a few generations after the city was taken by the Turks a mosque was built directly opposite Hagia Sophia which deliberately challenged comparison, and which I believe the architects of that heavenly building would have accepted as its rival.*

It is not the equal of Hagia Sophia, which even as a dome in the distance is absolutely victorious. From close below, the great Greek church is so much buttressed that apart from a few splendid and ragged details it is hardly as impressive as the clean-lined sixteenth-century mosques. But the whole point of it is the inside; by extending the principle of buildings like the Roman Pantheon, the architects of Hagia Sophia reversed its effect, and weight and monumentality became this soaring lightness. It is a kind of transfiguration in architecture. Its present condition is terrible, far worse (with all its accretions) than that of comparable

* The Sultan Ahmet mosque, often called the Blue mosque, built 1609–16; the architect was Mehmet Aga.

buildings in the west. Nor is it possible to think of it without thinking of its history. From outside you look across at the Blue mosque; nothing could be more composed, more handsome or more brilliant. Has there ever been another such case of so daring a site so magnificently filled?

By way of contrast, the Istanbul Museum ranges over the entire Ottoman Empire, but everything in it speaks of Greek supremacy. The head of a Samian kouros and the best terracotta figurines from Lindos are in Istanbul, so are the mass of sepulchral carvings from Palmyra, a statue of a Hellenistic prince from Tripoli in Libya, an inscription in Greek from Herod's temple at Jerusalem, two Byzantine pulpits from Saloniki; in fact a wealth of classical detritus which says as much about the geographical spread of Greek influence as it does about the Turkish empire. But I would personally trade the entire museum for a single object, the upper jaw and living eye of a bronze serpent which is all that survives of the triple heads from the twisted serpent column at Delphi, brought here by Constantine. The lower part of that column still stands where it was found, on the site of the Byzantine race-course;* when it was first made and stood at Delphi, it was nothing less than the thank offering of Greece for the victory of Plataia, when the Persians were defeated and driven away in 479 B.C. If it is true that the Ottoman princes who destroyed and rebuilt Byzantium were in some way Hellenized, if it is true that there were remotely Hellenic elements even in the lives of the central Asian Turks, Plataia is one of the reasons why.

What is left at Istanbul does not, of course, represent any single historical moment exclusively. In the development of the city, my grandfather comes halfway between the present time and the birth of André Chénier, who I suppose was the best Istanbul poet since Paul the Silentiary. The atmosphere of André Chénier's Istanbul still clings to certain quarters. There still exists a mahogany and pink marble hotel where a travelling Englishman, strayed somehow from the grand tour, once told a friend of mine that he carried his own table linen and his own Tiptree's jam in a small travelling case. There is also a nineteen thirties hotel with the sympathetic title of Park Oteli, which has an Odeon type of décor in shades of coffee cream, and a string band. All night you

---

* At some time in the Middle Ages it had been pierced and piped to make the mouths of the serpents spit milk, wine and water. At Delphi the heads used to balance a golden tripod on their foreheads.

hear the ships whooping and hooting in the mist, and in the morning they serve rose-petal jam for breakfast. One morning I had a long conversation in French with a Jewish carpet repairer in a small shop which I wanted to think was like my grandfather's, and was invited to the synagogue. He turned out to have worked in Scotland – '*C'est très correct*,' he said, '*les gens sont plus civilisés.*' And there was a pleasing conversation with a museum guard about a Hellenistic tomb known as the Alexander sarcophagus. We were standing outside the museum and I had offered him a cigarette, which he hastily put out when a tourist bus arrived. 'Look,' he said, 'Russians! When they see the Alexander coffin, they say, Ah, Alexander! He Russian! Tee, hee, hee!'

From Istanbul another huge aeroplane flew through the afternoon to Ankara, and through the early evening to Teheran. We crossed endless strings of glittering tawny hills with stubble-coloured thistles; from high in the air the landscape seemed extremely wild and barren, but from ground level it was all fine pastures and rolling downs. At Ankara airport there was a storm brewing and both the sky and the land were picked out with a subtle variety of colours. There is nothing that so distinguishes places as the qualities of light; today, the difference between industrial and non-industrial atmospheres is so great as to make other differences seem minimal. In Athens the sharp classical light, in London the equable glow of eighteenth-century summer, and in New England the pure clarity of pioneering days are a memory for which we have only the uncertain evidence of art. But the change of light is what a traveller first notices. The first awakening in a foreign village is an impression that remains. Of course, the light alters; it is modified by what seem irrelevant circumstances, as much by snow as by the sea, as much by trees and crops as by a desert of sand and rock. As you get used to it you stop thinking about it. From Ankara to Teheran it becomes more and more intense until it reaches a kind of absolute at the Elburz mountains; European eyes are hardly capable of distinguishing anything more brilliant. Yet in Afghanistan on the first days there was a crisp blaze which was as different from the quality of light on the great eastern Iranian plain as Iran was different from Ankara, and Ankara from Istanbul. When the summer was over, England seemed to be only half-lighted, but infinitely subtle and varied, just as much a revelation as Ankara on a stormy afternoon with its clothy texture of colours three months before.

Above Teheran the air was like thick black silk, and the spectacular and endless pattern of lights on the ground seemed to promise a great city. By daylight, alas, it was shapeless and hideous, though admittedly still endless. I have never before arrived in a city about which I knew so little; by the time I had encamped on the roof of the British archaeological institute after a maniacal taxi-drive ending at a blank wall, and was searching by torchlight for more conventional objects in my baggage among a welter of ropes, compasses and binoculars, I felt I was close to the ultimate desert. The sky was like a star-eaten black blanket, and so far as I could read them its constellations were unfamiliar. Lawrence speaks somewhere of drawing 'strength from the depths of the universe'; Malcolm Lowry speaks about the deadness of the stars except when he looked at them with a particular girl; I had neither feeling. The founder of the Jesuits used to spend many hours under the stars; it is hard to be certain whether the first stirrings of scientific speculation or prescientific wonder about space and stars in their own nature were some element in his affinity with starlight, or whether for him they were only a point of departure, but in this matter I think I am about fifty years more modern than Saint Ignatius; stars mean to me roughly what they meant to Donne's generation, a bright religious sand imposing the sense of an intrusion into human language, and arousing a certain personal thirst to be specific. I fell asleep with this complicated thought and woke much mutilated by mosquitoes.

British archaeological institutions are much the same all over the world; some of them are at first sight extremely comic, but they are sympathetic places. For quite a long time I was a member of the one in Athens, where I became some kind of classical archaeologist. I had spent years on and off writing a commentary on Pausanias, the author of a comprehensive guidebook to contemporary Greece in the second century A.D. The archaeological problems of Persia and Afghanistan are a far cry from mainland Greece; the story of the Greeks so far from home had hardly been more than a tenuous and romantic whisper until the last few years.[3] But the question of what was the substance of Greek influence in Asia was in my mind from beginning to end of this journey, and for months before and after. I was not much

interested in Alexander's campaigns but in what became
Greeks and their kingdoms, above all in whatever connection
Greeks might have with the Buddhism of the Hellenistic peri
and the first centuries A.D., when Buddhism first deeply penetrated Afghanistan and reached China. The answers that I
discovered, more often by reading and conversation than by
visible evidence, were scattered and disjointed, but at some level
they are the subject matter of my book. Like everything European,
they are a mixture of Jewish, Greek and Barbarian elements,
which were intermingled a long time ago.

Persian archaeology is connected to Greek as a kind of counter-
weight. The Greek military occupation of Persia did not last long,
even though the interpenetration of Greek and Persian art is older
and lasted longer; the Romans could never control the Parthian
nomads who succeeded the Greeks or the revived Persian Empire
that succeeded the Parthians.[4] But while Rome was still a small
city, when the old Persian Empire fell to Alexander the Great, he
continued eastwards beyond the boundaries of modern Iran to
the edges of the Persian Empire in India. He spent several years
on that expedition, which was to some degree a solid conquest,
and at least much more than an extended raid, but what he left
was a remote extent of physically wild territory precariously
pinned down by Greek garrisons. The lack of archaeological
evidence makes it difficult to estimate what effect the Greeks had
on their environment in Asia; the only certainty is that in the end
Asia swallowed them. After Alexander's death, his successors in
the east could hardly hope to hold down the whole range of his
eastern territories. The military governor of the Greek garrisons
in the north-east declared himself independent, and founded the
kingdom of Bactria; to the south-east the Mauryan Empire of
north India occupied what was once the most eastern Persian
province and Alexander's remotest conquest. Persia itself was
overrun by the Parthians in the second century B.C.; the power of
the Seleucid* dynasty shrank westwards to Mesopotamia, and
finally into Asia Minor.[5] The Bactrian Greeks were now isolated
in the east, their history was eventful but comparatively brief.
Their kingdoms expanded astonishingly and soon split; the rulers

---

* The Seleucids were the family of Seleukos, one of the Macedonian generals
who had served under Alexander and who carved up the Greek world between
them after his death. The Seleucids made several attempts to assert their authority
in the east.

at war with each other and with their non-
As late as 30 B.C., when nomads not unlike the
dy overrun the important and wealthy Greek
ldle Asia and Afghanistan, there was still one
the Khyber Pass; but Greek India, like the
was politically short-lived. It lasted, that is,
... british India, only that what seems iron-shod in
...ent history in the past seems shadow-footed.

The role of the Parthians in Persia is very important; they were the forerunners of wave after wave of invasion by nomadic pastoral tribes pressing downwards into Asia from Siberia. They not only sealed off the Bactrian Greeks from the Mediterranean[6] and so perhaps contributed to the necessary conditions for the spread of Buddhism, but they successfully fought off the Roman Empire and handed on to the revived Persian Empire a genuine native tradition which to my eye is one of the most interesting in the whole history of civilization. It is this sudden sealing off from the Mediterranean in a world which at the same time has been percolated by the essential juices of Hellenism as well as by other influences, including those of the central Asian landscape, that makes a first visit to eastern Persia so heady, and I admit in my case, so dizzying.

In 1968, the British archaeologists in Persia had excavated what is probably the site of Hekatompylos, a Persian and Greek town which became the first capital city of the kings of Parthia. Hekatompylos already existed somewhere near Damghan when Alexander the Great passed eastwards in the fourth century B.C., and it was on this road that King Darius was murdered by his own soldiers.[7] A hundred and fifty years later, Alexander's successors had lost it and eastern Persia was in the hands of the nomads. Like the Turkish tribes that followed them after a thousand years and like their cousins who invaded Afghanistan and northern India the Parthians were a relatively simple and pastoral people, with an uncompromising culture of their own that had developed among the uncultivated pastures of what is now southern Siberia. The Russians have excavated some Parthian sites which have revealed the lives of these people when they were still living outside the bounds of the old Persian Empire. There is one in particular at Koy-Krylgan-kala,[8] to the east of the Aral Sea, where the central monument of a great encampment was a massive circular castle consecrated to the use of the dead.

There are a whole series of sites on the lower Oxus where this kind of tall funerary tower dominates a fortified camp and is central to it.

At Koy-Krylgan-kala the urns for the ashes of the dead were shaped roughly like the bodies of human beings, although one of them has the ears of a horse. They include crude pottery masks of human or divine faces. Men's and women's coffins were on separate sides of the building. There was a well and there were numerous small figures of Anahita, the Iranian water-goddess. Customs varied, particularly on the lower Oxus, but often in these dead men's castles the dead were not burned but exposed until they were consumed by sun, air and vultures. The bones were collected as the ashes were, and the castle was left to them. These were the people to whom Parthian Hekatompylos belonged. The bodies of the dead had been exposed and rodent tooth-marks were found on their bones, which were mingled with the bones of pony or perhaps wild ass, and also of deer and fox, in a tower inside the city. Unfortunately, the site has been often flooded and badly eroded, and it is never going to be possible to recover the street-plan; but some fragments of Hellenistic pottery have been found on the surface, and the evidence of coins suggests a date of about 70 B.C. (There was also a carbon date of about 240, with a wide margin of possible error.) The excavation is still in progress, but it looks as though the longstanding problem of the whereabouts of Hekatompylos is solved.

Because the Romans never conquered the Parthians, their information about Parthian geography was not good, and ours because it largely depends on theirs is not much better. When Greek cities were overwhelmed their names easily changed back to the native pre-Greek names; probably in many cases what perished was a Greek cantonment and what survived was the original native city.[9] Doura-Europos returned to being Doura, Orrhoe became Edessa and then Antioch, it returned to being Orhai in Syriac and Edessa in Latin. In 1970 no more than one Greek inscription had ever been found east of the Euphrates later in date than the first century B.C.[10] The Greek alphabet survived, but only to express native languages in writing. In fact it survived curiously long; as late as the eighth century A.D. the runic alphabet of the earliest written Turkish, which we know from tombstones scattered here and there in southern Siberia and Mongolia, arose partly from the Aramaic script which was the official writing system of the Persian Empire, and partly it seems from a local form of the Greek alphabet.[11]

Still, not everything Greek was lost, there were mysterious recurrences and many indirect influences; the trade-routes were not perpetually closed and Greek, or Macedonian, or in some way Hellenized, commercial influence survived every political change until the Islamic period. It is not surprising further west that the Syro-Roman law book that has reached us in Armenian, Syriac and Arabic versions, has a local Greek as well as a Roman substratum.[12] More surprisingly, there is a bronze pot in the British Museum from Wardak, near Kabul, which contained Buddhist relics and was inscribed and dated in the mid second century A.D. The inscription is in Aramaic lettering, but the name of the month is Artemisios, a Macedonian month name.[13] Nor is this unique; there is a similar inscription on a vase from Swat recording a Buddhist dedication by a Greek local governor.[14] Even the descendants of Arsakes, supposedly untamed Parthian kings, took such titles as 'king of kings', 'the benefactor', 'the just', 'the illustrious', 'the philhellene'. Their identification was at once with the ancient kings of Persia and the Hellenistic princes of the Mediterranean. It is hard to find out how much of the rich eastern trade of the Roman Empire was at that time in Greek hands, but it is significant that a certain Maes, also called Titianos, who is the source of one of the few classical accounts we have of central Asia, should be a Macedonian silk merchant of about A.D. 100, with agents in eastern Turkestan.[15]

In the trade connection between the late classical world and the east, the role of the city of Alexandria was probably central; there was a sea trade-route to the north of the Indus and far beyond. But one must try to distinguish the goods acquired in trade, which might often be uncharacteristic luxuries, from the typical material evidences of a civilization. It is all too easy to confuse a stray coin or a pretty foreign scent-bottle with 'new styles of architecture, a change of heart'.

It may seem bewildering to deal only in passing with these innumerable unconnected hints of Greek penetration and persistence, but it would be unfair to organize them into a one-sided general argument. One should be content at this stage to say that there are some traces of Greek elements in the life of central Asia persisting after the end of the Bactrian kingdom, and that some of these elements are Macedonian, so that they can reasonably be attributed to the influence of Alexander's Macedonian garrisons. They are a very minor theme in the archaeology of Iran. The city of Teheran, for example, is entirely modern, but it extends in one direction to a suburb called Rayy, the site of the Raga of the old Persian Empire which is the Rages of Toby's journey in the Bible, where Toby found 'a great crowd of his nation' and lent money to a member of his tribe. Seleukos refounded it as Europos.

The principal attraction of this suburb today is the tower of Toghril Beg, an austere almost kiln-like twelfth-century polygonal tower of baked brick on a circular brick emplacement.[16] It is quite undecorated except that its ground-plan is toothed like a cogwheel or a star, its doorway is huge and decorated with a running key pattern in the same baked brick. There are long stone waterspouts which suggest it must originally have had a tall conical roof like the brilliant Mongol tower at Varamin, but the tower of Toghril Beg is a hundred and fifty years earlier (1139–40) and without a trace of turquoise or of cobalt amongst its fine, plain bricks. It is a Seljuk Turkish memorial, and it still stands in a ragged, pleasant garden with a cemetery atmosphere. We saw it after a day among the raving colours and delicious clover and stubble smells of Varamin, where I encountered the forms of classical Islamic architecture for the first time. We arrived at Rayy almost numb with pleasure and sunstroke. I can only say that the tower of Toghril Beg imposes itself with complete authority; it is not possible to distinguish in memory the harshness of the material, the formal austerity that seems so indestructible, and the silence of the garden.

Lying in a corner there were the dark stone bases of two columns, crudely and inexactly executed. They consist of a round stub of shaft a few inches high and a foot or so across rising from a square stone; the stub extends almost to the edges of the square, but not quite. These slightly unlovely objects loudly suggest provincial Hellenistic architecture; indeed, an archaeologist whom I asked about them thought them too good to be Parthian, and regarded their manifest irregularity as a traditional local characteristic. I suspected then and believe more confidently now that they were part of a Hellenized Parthian building; bases like them were found at the Kushan temple of Surkh Kotal to the north of the Hindu Kush, and I was lucky enough to discover one myself on what was certainly a Kushan mound west of the Kunduz river on the edge of the Oxus plain. The two at Rayy

may possibly have come from the Parthian temple on the local
mound, which I could discover very little about. It was not for
want of an inspection on the spot, but the mound is sordidly
situated, has a complicated history and is surrounded by a fearful
obstacle course of concentric water-channels. We negotiated these
gracelessly but without falling in, but by these antics we accu-
mulated a Bacchanalian crowd of local youths and little boys.
The mound was steep but did not deter them, there was evidently
not much to see, and what there was seemed entangled in more
modern buildings. We disgracefully lost interest.

At Teheran the Jewish communities of my grandfather's day
are still flourishing and do not seem to have altered since Rayy
was Rages. I do not know if members of my family travelled so far
east as Teheran, but it was where the carpets came from, and
since my grandfather had to organize his own caravans, it is
possible that he was there.* The best of the carpet trade at
Teheran is still in Jewish hands, the shop-fronts are modern-
looking but the interiors cavernous and full of dark and ancient-
looking stacks of a variety of textiles. The merchants are old
gentlemen in shirt-sleeves whose second language is an eccentri-
cally sweet Levantine French. The ceremonious intimacies make
any transaction very much a matter of I and thou, and the system
for moving money from one country to another, which depends
on the mutual credit of persons known to each other in business
in different cities, passes nowhere through anything so impersonal
as a bank, although the network does include family money-
changers who are like family solicitors. From a carpetseller I got
a recommendation to a dentist; he seemed to work with nothing
but small metal toothpicks and a drug that tasted of apricots, but
he was the most painless and effective dentist I had ever been to.
If we are to speak of foreign business communities there was
another anciently established community even more striking than
that of the Teheran carpet merchants. At Isfahan in the Armenian
church museum the portraits of old members of the community
include Russian, Chinese, Persian and British Indian styles, and
an etching of a certain Father Abraham by Rembrandt. Why not?

We stopped in Persia for only a week, largely in order to get
used to the heat. I wanted to visit Persepolis, but the air service

* His official description of himself on my father's birth certificate is 'indigo
merchant'; the routes of the carpet trade, the silk trade and the indigo trade until
modern times were closely related.

was overbooked and the nightmare of fourteen or sixteen hours in a coach was more than we could face; it limits one's possibilities as a traveller not to like the smell and motion of coaches but personally I loathe them. We did succeed in reaching Isfahan, which is not so far south. We came in and went by air, and watched the great oasis spread its startling greenness and its cool-coloured glittering domes like an exact design against the desert. The desert was scoured with tracks that seemed to lose themselves among big dunes with outcrops of rock. Today the architecture of Isfahan is without any rival of its own kind. Every shape has the severe, sweet functional lines of brick and claybrick, but the flower-spangled and cobalt-inscribed glazes invest the mosques and the courtyards with a sense of pleasure and solemnity together which I have never experienced elsewhere. I do not want to write in detail about these unique and marvellous buildings; they deserve a book of their own, with exact ground plans and construction drawings. It was as if someone who had never before seen flowers on a tree had at Varamin seen a cherry tree in an album of old botanical drawings, and here for the first time an orchard of flowering apple and pear. The notes that I kept are full of incompetent sketches, and it is strange to find a passion for Seljuk brickwork recorded like the beginning of a love affair.

These are some notes about roses: 'roses smelling of warm roses and apricots, the warm smell they retain about dusk, giving off warmth and a kind of refined honey, a smell of apricots and honey and a touch of dry tea'. I find other notes about the relation of domes to carpets and dome-patterns to carpet-patterns,[17] with a resolution to see the dome of the dancing dervishes at Konya. Then comes an unexplained reference to the doctrine of the secret Imam, the mysterious pole of the universe. Among a chaos of architectural details and motifs I have found a handful of notes written on the roof of the Masjed-i Jameh, in an absolute of heat, silence and isolation, about the strangeness of forms and textures, and the vastness and variety of the roofscape, its bubbles and dunes and igloos which from below were great domes and vaults, its hooded crows, the sun and air as if over an icefield or a desert. I recall some smallish tiles of alabaster that seemed to be lying around loose; seen from below these are the yellow skylights in the winter gallery where Tamburlaine used to walk among the thick pillars.

A formidable dusk seemed to sweep in from the desert over a

wild-looking ridge of rock. The evening smelt of warmth and dust and petrol-fumes, with a sharper, colder smell from the desert itself. The river at Isfahan smells strongly even from some distance, but the smell of dust and of sand is even stronger. The moon over the aerodrome was brighter than the aerodrome lights. When the plane floated in it was like a green and white illuminated moth. We stopped for a very short night at Teheran, and by 4.15 a.m. were on the road again as it lightened. Perhaps because I had not bothered to sleep, I still have a sharply vivid recollection of that cold moment and that empty street. Bruce was croaking and joking. We had just arranged our luggage in a long line in the road to see if it was all there, when what should appear but a water-cart to water the road, which squirted us and our luggage, piece by piece.

I slept in the aeroplane and was woken by a steward to be confronted with a dead-looking omelette and a piece of Madeira cake. We were passing over the eastern Iranian desert. The landscape was withered and empty. It lay in great whirls and chopped tawny limbs. It was the metamorphosis of the skins of dead lions. I saw salt lakes full of scum. Of all the rivers in Afghanistan only the Kabul river and its tributaries run down into the Indus and reach the sea. All the others founder in the sand: and this includes even the Oxus, the *Amu Darya*, in the hushed Chorasmian waste. The Aral Sea, north across the border, is no more than a salt lake. I badly wanted to watch the desert but I fell asleep again. Bruce was identifying the mountains, and between sleeping and waking I saw that they were capped with snow.

CHAPTER
2

Kabul is high up, lost among mountains; it is an untidy town surrounded by wheatfields like rough mats and by grey and black mountains still fretted with snow at the end of June. As you come down out of the air you see the tents and flocks of nomads around it. When you reach the ground the mountains take on their height, and the snow on them is a long pattern of streaks and smears; it looks like Kufic writing stamped on the intense background of the air. The heat is Indian. You enter a curling, sprawling settlement around the edges of four or five hills; it has almost no bourgeois suburbs, in fact it still has some of the characteristics of a mountain village or a fur traders' post; you see pelts and furs hanging up for sale in the streets. There is a comic Wagnerian royal palace which used to have sentries in Nazi helmets and swastikas, because the Afghans believe they were the ancestors of the Aryan race, but no buildings of any architectural merit, although Kabul has trees and private gardens on a generous scale. The town is 6,900 feet above sea-level, but at mid-summer this height is expressed in nothing but a little breeze. The characteristic smell is a mixture of balsam poplars and crudely refined petrol. In all Afghanistan only Kabul has most of its main roads asphalted.

Unfortunately the seventeenth-century bazaar was destroyed and Kabul castle (the famous Bala Hisar of military histories) dismantled and left in ruins, by two British punitive expeditions in the nineteenth century.[1] The only old quarter of Kabul that still exists is built in an ancient traditional style, but it consists mostly of late nineteenth-century merchants' houses in terrible condition. The houses are simple but solid: timber frames filled in with stones and clay. This is a style that reached the frontiers of the Roman Empire, and as a formula for military construction it spread as far as Scotland.[2] In central Asia just as in iron age Britain, it is native. To penetrate this area you cross toxic runnels of every kind of filth, and stagnant waterpools of an astonishing bright colour like polished green stone. The flies swarm on everything, particularly in the foodshops and on children's faces, and it was odd to see swallows swooping idyllically over a peasoup sewage pond. At certain points in the alleys we passed through huge medieval-looking doors with metal bosses which must presumably have locked one street or quarter from another at night. It was partly for shade and partly from curiosity that we explored this area, but I own that having once seen it I never entered it again. It is only in the last decadence of what was once a practicable and decent way of life that human beings are so degraded by their surroundings.[3] For the genuine roots of the popular culture of the past, as of the future, one must look elsewhere. It is a sad thing to say, but in Kabul there was no obvious basis for the future, except perhaps among the students, whom we hardly saw because the university had been on strike for several months. That is how things looked in 1970.

The life of the wider streets is less appalling. You see a wide variety of dress, some of it in deep, pure colours faded with age and sun. Shopwindows and stall displays are obsessively decorated in exactly the same spirit as the designs of Islamic textiles or a sixteenth-century minaret; it is the same instinctive feeling for strong motifs and repeated contrasts, self-conscious in the one case and quite instinctive in the other, that makes everyday life in Kabul so invigorating to the eyesight. There are cold drinks you can buy in the street coloured like those imaginative liquids that used to advertise chemists' shops before the war. The bottles are stopped with marbles and shriek like mandrakes as they open; they are iced with muddy-looking snow. There are street traders selling small pebbles of lapis lazuli from Badakhshan. The pelts of snow-leopards hang outside fur shops. The first day I was in Kabul I saw three men riding on one bicycle, one in a fur hat, one in a Persian skullcap, and one in a turban.

The people belong to a variety of races. The ruling race, the Afghans in the strict sense, are Pathans, but these mountains still contain the descendants of many other conquering or migrating peoples. The Pathans are probably the Sakai who overwhelmed the Greeks.[4] Tajiks are more semitic to look at, less tall and more thickly built; they were the peasants of the Persian Empire, and they seem to have come eastwards from eastern Iran. The Nuristanis come from the old Kafiristan, which is eastern Afghanistan; it means land of unbelievers.[5] Its name was changed to Nuristan, land of enlightenment, at the time of its forcible conversion by Abdur Rahman, almost in living memory. Kafiristan was once a far wider area of mountains, including Gilgit and Chitral on the Pakistani side of the border, where pagan religion has not died out even now. The Nuristanis are the oldest inhabitants, and they are closely related to the ancestors of all Indo-European peoples. Their territory is a tangle of high mountain valleys which are often completely isolated and can never be penetrated except on foot.

The most recent arrivals in Afghanistan are the Hazaras, by far the most innocent and cheerful-looking people in Afghanistan. They are eastern Turks from central Asia,[6] but as farmers they have been pushed into the uppermost valleys, and in Kabul they do the heaviest jobs, some of which would be done elsewhere by animals. They have no political influence, and the Nuristanis have little, but the explosion of the Nuristanis, who are natively a very intelligent people, into Islamic Afghanistan is just starting. There are also Uzbeks from near the Russian border, who are delightful but somewhat poppy-drugged people with amused eyes and sweeping moustaches. They are the finest riders, and in the old days they were proverbial for the magnificence of their dress and jewellery; it is still said that some of the richest men in Afghanistan are Turkoman nomads; this is poetically but perhaps not literally true. There are many Turkic-speaking tribes in Afghanistan, but you will not see them in the streets of Kabul.

The most important monument of antiquity at Kabul is the ragged fortress called the Bala Hisar. It stands on an unexcavated mound with a basis of natural rock, to the south of the Kabul river; no one knows how old it is, and the problem cannot be solved except by investigating the lowest level of the mound. Kabul became the capital city of an Afghan dynasty only in the late eighteenth century, but it owes its importance to a Mongol king who loved it in the sixteenth, the emperor Zahir ud din Mahomed, called Babur.[7] He was one of the descendants of Tamburlaine, whose loins produced five generations of quarrelling princes in Russian Turkestan inside a century.

Babur's father was a king, but he lost his father's kingdom as a young man, and for several years he was a landless prince. In 1504 he took Kabul. It was the turning-point of his fortunes; before his death he had taken Delhi and founded the Moghul dynasty in India, but the Kabul he created remained his favourite possession.*

The walls of the Bala Hisar have been surveyed by French archaeologists, but without excavation it is not easy to talk about the history of the site.[8] The earliest pottery is said to be pre-Kushan, that is Greek or earlier, and it may be so, but the evidence of this kind of pottery on this kind of site has to be treated with reserve. There have been no stratified excavations in Afghanistan until recently of any sites which could give us an accurate pottery sequence; and the pottery itself is often of a very confusing kind; there are vessels still being made which are all but indistinguishable from Kushan and possibly earlier pottery.

For this reason we went to look at the surface shards on the ground outside the castle; we did not learn much, although we did see fragments of a fine, unglazed ware which I think was early Islamic. They came from a brick-red, puff-cheeked vessel of some size, with a frieze of cream-coloured waves or spirals. The same pattern is still being made near Kabul, but the colours are not so strong today. The ground below the castle turned out to be in some sense a military area, and the Afghan Army, like the mastiffs on the outskirts of nomad camps, has a highly developed sense of territory, so the expedition ended in our being suddenly attacked and belaboured by an enraged private soldier who was luckily unarmed except for his military belt. This odd little incident of fantasy was over almost before it had begun and it remains unexplained, except that the time was mid-day and the heat terrific. Kabul castle was held by a British army in the eighteen forties,[9] and no doubt several times refortified, but its best walls belong substantially to the generation of Babur, or to his uncle's reign at Kabul a little earlier. In certain outlying walls attached to the castle, much withered now but still easy to make out, and in what is left of the old walls of the city, the walling of the fifteenth or sixteenth centuries stands on the heavy foundations of more ancient walls, and the same foundations have been traced with more difficulty under the fortifications of the Bala Hisar. From the north side of these fortifications you can make out

---

* Babur seems never to have forgotten the beauties and glories of Samarkand, but Uzbek pressure in Turkestan was too much for him and he never came back to reign there; his grave is at Kabul, and perhaps all Afghanistan, in its physical presence, is his appropriate monument.

through binoculars some typically Timurid turquoise and cobalt decoration inlaid into the brickwork.

The question whether Kabul was ever a Greek city is a difficult one. The ancient cities in Afghanistan seem all to have depended on the important trade routes between India and Russian Turkestan; M. André Foucher has shown[10] by a 'recherche faite à vue de nez' that the principal route southwards, unlike the modern road, passed down the Panjshir river from the modern Charikar and the ancient Kapisa, the capital city,[11] to Jellalabad and the Khyber Pass. This route by-passes Kabul, so that it is questionable whether Kabul was at all an important city in the Greek period. There are a certain number of names of Greek cities for which we have still to identify the right archaeological sites and Kabul may be one of these. My own opinion is the old-fashioned one that Kabul was Ortospana, a lost city which we know from Strabo was a crossroads somewhere in this area.

What writers have neglected is the importance of Gardez, which is certainly a Greek site, which lies directly south of Kabul on an easy road, and which has easy access southwards across the Pakistan border to the Indus and the sea. The alternative site for Ortospana is a feeble claimant; it is a mound called Eskanderia,[12] halfway to Charikar east of the road north from Kabul. This mound has now been largely demolished, but if its name really refers to Alexander the Great, as does seem possible, the connection is simply legendary, like the local name recorded by Sir Henry Yule as an alternative for Wood's Lake Sar-i-kol in the Pamirs which is the source of the Oxus, and to which we can be certain Alexander's soldiers never penetrated.[13] The fame of Alexander spread in the east at a late period, neither through histories nor through mysterious survivals, but by an Islamic version of the Alexander romance.[14] The case for a Greek Kabul is compelling; one could almost say that if no mound existed at the crossing of the Kabul river on the crossroads of the direct road from Kapisa to Gardez, and the road from Ghazni and the west to Jellalabad, it would be necessary to invent one. The problem will never be solved unless one day the Bala Hisar is excavated.

By way of contrast, after the bizarre adventure at the castle, we went to stay with a friend in the British Embassy compound. The compound is enormous, a conception of Lord Curzon's, very green and guarded by centenarian Gurkhas. The houses are numerous and nestle in bosky avenues; they give the impression of having been supplied by Harrods about 1910. The residence itself is so grand as to be comic; it boasts the largest pediment and pillars between Delhi and the neoclassical opera house at Ulan Bator. The gardens are marvellous, although a former ambassador used to tell people that nothing grew in them which would not grow in Dorking. To my delight they were regularly visited by mynahs and two or three hoopoes. These are supposed to be the typically Greek bird, even Aristophanes takes their dignity seriously, but one seldom sees them now in Greece. Their obvious elegance and dandy colours make them easy to recognize and I know of no pleasanter or more cheering bird. No doubt superstitiously, I began to notice that at every single site in Afghanistan where the Greeks had been there was a hoopoe.

The embassy gardens were a world so different from the one outside the gates that they seemed just as proper a subject of study as any other; I find that my diaries are full of notes about them, for instance about a gardener whose job in the afternoon was to pick up windfalls of mulberries and apricots. 'At a certain moment of mid afternoon when everyone has forgotten the time, all the servants congregate squatting on the lawn, to watch some grey speckled turkeys graze, then they ceremoniously pen the turkeys in again and go back to their various jobs.'

Very late in the year and on my last morning in Afghanistan, I went to swim in the embassy pool. The sun was sharp but the water bitterly cold and there were shadows. An old Hazara gardener stood there beaming and urging me to go in. He started to chat when I climbed out. 'Cold is very good,' he said. 'In my village we have deep, deep snow as high as houses, here only as high as knees. In my village we have five months of winter, here only three. Here no good. My village much winter, very good.' I asked him why he left and would he go back. 'Here, much money, after money, I go to America. There much, much winter, much, much snow.'

On the late afternoon of the day we were battered at the Bala Hisar we decided to make a formal visit of respect to the grave of Sir Aurel Stein. He was never allowed to travel widely in Afghanistan as he was believed with some justice to be a British spy, but he died in Kabul, and his grave is in the small foreign cemetery among Russian engineers and European boys who died young.

MARK AUREL STEIN
OF THE INDIAN ARCHAEOLOGICAL SURVEY
SCHOLAR EXPLORER AUTHOR
BY HIS ARDUOUS JOURNEYS IN
INDIA CHINESE TURKESTAN PERSIA AND IRAQ
HE ENLARGED THE BOUNDS OF KNOWLEDGE
BORN AT BUDAPEST 26 NOVEMBER 1862
HE BECAME AN ENGLISH CITIZEN IN 1904
HE DIED AT KABUL 26 OCTOBER 1943
A MAN GREATLY BELOVED

He was the greatest of all explorers of central Asia. He was an intrepid traveller who seems to have thought little of losing all his camels in a salt-marsh or several of his toes in a blizzard. He was widely and by strict standards fabulously learned, a perfectly accurate observer and a wonderful photographer of the old school. He was an extremely able, plain writer. His scientific curiosity was like that of a natural scientist. As an old man he would live in a tent in preference to a house, and would never let his boots out of his sight. By origin he was a Jew from Budapest, and his first name in full was Marcus Aurelius, Mark Aurel; he died in 1943 at the age of eighty-one. It appears from a remark he lets drop in *Alexander's Track to the Indus* that among his early friends on the north-west frontier was a young captain of native infantry called Dunsterville, the original of Kipling's Stalky, and that the two of them were wandering about together among inaccessible hill country in the winter of 1898. The graveyard where he lies has many strange tombs, but several are the tombs of archaeologists. There is no better company any scholar or archaeologist or any traveller could wish to keep than that of Sir Aurel Stein.

Finally, and in my case with awe and almost with disbelief, we visited the memorial and tomb of Babur. Bruce warned me that five years before it was already in ruins, with the curved marbles of its arches being used for water-channels. It was therefore a great surprise to both of us to find that the memorial, which is a very fine grey marble pavilion, had been completely restored. It was built by Babur's grandson Shah Jahan in 1640, and the tomb, which is black, pink and green marble and alabaster, by Abdur Rahman about 1880.[15] The site is an old and disused garden out of sight of the city, on a hillside above the Kabul river with mulberry trees and one or two enormous planes of such a girth and with such limbs they may have stood here since Babur's death. The mulberries probably date from 1640. What I have called the memorial is really a mosque, open on three sides like the simple wooden mosques in many villages.[16] The material is Kandahar marble. The inscription over the main entrance reads as follows:

ONLY THIS MOSQUE OF BEAUTY, THIS TEMPLE OF NOBILITY, CONSTRUCTED FOR THE PRAYER OF SAINTS AND THE EPIPHANY OF CHERUBS, WAS FIT TO STAND IN SO VENERABLE A SANCTUARY AS THIS HIGHWAY OF ARCHANGELS, THIS THEATRE OF HEAVEN, THE LIGHT GARDEN OF THE GODFORGIVEN ANGEL KING WHOSE REST IS IN THE GARDEN OF HEAVEN, ZAHIRUDDIN MUHAMMAD BABUR THE CONQUEROR.

(It continues with a list of the victories of Shah Jahan.)

There is not much more to be said about the grave of Babur. There were Persian graffiti carved with knife-points in the lower trunks of the big planes, a soldier in khaki was reaching into the shadows for mulberries, an officer had slung his hammock for the afternoon between the branches of a plane. I sat on the other side of it trying to draw the grey marble mosque. No memorial would be adequate. Babur's autobiography is so intimate and so pure that he is perfectly present even through the medium of a foreign language. He wrote in one of the Turkish dialects of central Asia; a Persian translation was made in India at the court of Akbar in the late sixteenth century. The toughness of Babur's life is quite easy to imagine, but there is also a delicacy about him. Here is his only reference to the death of his father, killed in a landslide: 'It has been mentioned that the castle of Akhsi is above the ravines; the king's house is on a ravine. The Mir flew from the mountain-side with his pigeons and the house of his pigeons, and he became a hawk.' Here on the other hand is the death of an enemy:

He put him a few questions but got no good answer. Indeed Darwesh Muhammad's was a deed for which no good answer could be given. He was ordered to death. In his helplessness he clung to a pillar of the house; would they let him go because he clung to a pillar? They brought him to doom, and ordered Ali Mirza to the Greek Sarai there to have the firepencil drawn across his eyes.

The narrative of which most of Babur's writing consists is a straightforward and bloodcurdling account of fighting. It has an innocent objectivity; there is no invisible influence of a classical literary form as there is for example in the narratives of Julius Caesar, and there is no popular technique like those of Herodotus, there is not even any influence of epic. The closest analogy (but more classical because Spain was more classicized) is perhaps in Bernal Diaz del Castillo's *Conquest of New Spain*. For Babur's individual sensibility there is no analogy.

They dropped such a large stone on Abdulqasim, little Beg's elder brother, when he went up under the ramparts, that he spun head over heels and came rolling and rolling without once getting his legs under control, from that great height down to the foot of the glacis. He did not trouble himself about it at all but just got on his horse and rode off. A stone flung from the double watercourse hit Yarali so hard on the head in the end it had to be trepanned. Many of our men perished by their stones.

It is not a negligible quality in a writer to be plain without being callous. Babur's realism is almost boyish, but there is an adult and most acceptable restraint that underlies these tough descriptions; he is more like Isaac Babel than any other modern writer. In spite of obvious differences Babur and Babel in fact wrote about much the same people under essentially similar conditions. It is important to Babur's work that it was written after a repentance and a plunge into orthodox Mohammedan life, while the religious quality of Babel's short stories is mixed into an interim morality and an unsatisfied hunger for the face of Ariel, the god of the others. But a similar life in another age demanded the same responses as humanly decent, and these responses determined the virtues of a kind of prose. Here is Babur in love with a boy. The names Babur and Baburi mean Tiger.

I did not feel badly about my first wife, but I had not been married before and I was so modest and shy I used to see her only once in every ten or fifteen or even twenty days. Later on when even my first inclinations did not last, I got more bashful than ever. My mother used to send me to her once in a month or more, by driving and driving me, and pestering and pushing.

In those idle days I found a strange inclination in myself, and as the poem says I maddened and hurt myself for a boy in the camp-bazaar, he was called Baburi, and even his name fitted. Until then I never wanted anyone: I had not even heard or talked about love or desire, neither at first hand nor at second hand. In those days I used to write Persian poems of one or two couplets . . . He used to come to my presence but I was so modest and shy I could never look at him straight . . . One day in that period of longing and passion I was walking with friends along a lane and I suddenly came face to face with him; I was so confused I almost ran away . . . I used to wander on my own over hill and dale, and sometimes I went into the gardens and mooned about in all the lanes.

Babur is not like anyone else. His morals are conventional although notably kindly. He violently disapproves of the practice of keeping catamites, hates betrayal and cruelty and hates talking about them at any length, admires princely virtues and human accomplishments with a personal intensity. But what makes him tick seems to be a rooted passion for everything that grows, and for all the qualities and products of gardens. In his physical descriptions of fields and crops, he stands at the crest of a great wave of humane Islamic geographers who had described cities and places in civilized detail since before the tenth century; in his own taste, he is in measurable distance of those richly formal seventeenth-century gardens of Shah Abbas at Isfahan which survive both in paintings and in fact; other princes in his time wrote poems and had fine gardens; but his taste was bred more in the desert than theirs; his devoted planting of fruit-trees and roses and big plane trees, at difficult moments and at every moment of his life, is so far as I know unique. In spring he identified sixteen kinds of wild tulips on the hills around Kabul. These were his personal researches: he was unwilling to record even a musk-rat without a special note if he personally had never seen it. He was a connoisseur of the varieties of melons, he praised equally an abundance of waved red and white stone, presumably ribboned jasper, or of violets, and he remembered an individual apple tree he once sat under for as many years as his first lost battle.

There are two images in which I like to summon up Babur: one is a rhinoceros hunt. By this time Babur was a great king and a conqueror, but not yet emperor of India. He and his friends were hunting rhinoceros far to the west of their modern range in a low, overgrown jungle of reed-beds and scrubby trees; he was almost certainly seeing the animals for the first time, he was hunting on horseback with bow and arrow, and burning the jungle in several places to shift the rhinoceros from one patch to the next. A big female with whelps suddenly broke cover and went crashing across country, and it seems that Babur was so astonished that he simply sat his horse and watched her go. The other image is of the young Babur at the time when he first got decent arms and equipment, north of the Oxus. He had always wanted to go to northern China, and in fact nearly went in 1501. The gifts he received were

a Moghul cap, embroidered with gold thread, a long frock of Chinese satin, ornamented with flowered needlework, a Chinese breastplate of the old fashion, with a whetstone and a pocketpurse . . . All the younger Khan's men had dressed themselves out after the Moghul fashion. They had Moghul caps, frocks of Chinese satin, embroidered with flowers after the same fashion, quivers and saddles of green shagreen.

The sharkskin must also have been Chinese; it is odd and moving to think of a young Turkestan prince, practically born on horseback, wandering about the steppe with a little crowd of young men, dressed up in flowered Chinese silk robes and antique Chinese armour. Silk seems to have been exported cream-white from China and dyed at Bokhara or Samarkand; the flowered needlework was surely Turkoman silk embroidery, probably a riot of deeply coloured chrysanthemums. We see Turkestan and the mutual penetration of Chinese and Turkish arts somehow through the wrong end of a telescope, but when you combine these images with poetry in two languages, sober religion, personal delicacy and a breathtaking, epicurean architecture, then our own renaissance falls into a different position in history.

It is not possible to discuss the role of Babur and the Mongols in Afghanistan without raising the problem of the famous silk road and of Chinese communication with the west; the same theme is equally important for the Greeks and of course for the Buddhists. The first historical questions about it in modern times seem to have been asked by a certain Joseph Hager of Pavia in 1805.[17] The explorations of Aurel Stein revealed many traces of organized caravan routes between China and the north bank of the Oxus from the period of the early Roman Empire; from the Oxus it was possible to make directly for the west overland, but at least equally practicable to make southwards for the Indus and the sea, crossing the passes of the Hindu Kush. Both routes were used, and it was not only silk that was carried, nor was all the traffic in one direction.[18] Chinese influences on the west and the search for Chinese luxuries have often been studied, but by the same tracks Buddhism travelled eastwards into China, and the institution of public medicine and hospitals travelled with it; so did grapes and the use of wine, lapis lazuli, which gave the Chinese a new word for blue, and cobalt, so that the first Chinese blue glazed pottery, which has been found in the ninth-century tombs, was made with imported cobalt used at the same time to decorate the Islamic wares of western Persia and Mesopotamia. The lotus came to China along this road; there is even an influence of Turkish folksong on eighth-century Chinese poetry.[19]

What is now Afghanistan is a network of passes between China and central Asia, India and the west, so that the conflict and the intermingling of cultures here was bound to be extraordinary. But Afghanistan itself has not been a rich seedground; it is interesting chiefly because waves that flowed through it to mingle elsewhere left a little water behind in these mountains, and things that suffered metamorphosis and became creative elsewhere survived for longer here in a purer, more barren form. Babur went on to conquer Delhi and found the Moghul dynasty; he returned to Kabul because of the gardens and big trees and because it was cool in summer. The Greeks also expanded to the south, where in the kingdom of Gandara if they survived they accepted Buddhism and took some part in bequeathing and transmitting it to the entire eastern world.

Apart from the tomb of Babur and the ruined castle, the most impressive antiquities at Kabul are the Buddhist monuments in the Logar valley south-east of the city. These are a series of stupas, like the stubs of enormous domed towers; some of them are almost complete, others have left nothing but a rimmed mound like a lunar crater. There must once have been a big Buddhist monastery on the slopes of the hills, and there are plenty of fragments of its pottery to be seen in the fields. The first Buddhist stupa ever to be investigated by an archaeologist, so far as I can discover, was the 'Tope of Maunikyaula', which was visited and recorded by Mountstuart Elphinstone in 1809.[20] It was a tall beehive dome like the great tombs at Mycenae (at that time already attracting attention but still unexcavated), with a stepped base and a low engaged colonnade of pilasters. 'There was nothing at all Hindoo in the appearance of this building; most of the party thought it decidedly Grecian.' The conjecture that it might be Buddhist was first offered by a Mr Erskine, in a paper to the Bombay Literary Society in 1821, and in 1830 it was opened by 'the Chevalier Ventura, a general officer in the service of Renjeet Singh, who found it to contain, besides religious relics, many ancient coins of great interest.'[21] It is worth noting the man and the moment, because the study of Buddhist monuments and of the schist relief sculptures we now call Gandaran art immediately took root among the officers and officials on the north-west frontier. The first art collection of this kind that can be traced in the west was brought back by Dr Leitner of the Punjab service in about 1870;[22] during the same decade an officer called P. V. Luke, the engineer of the first field telegraph in the Khyber Pass, was photographing Buddhist antiquities in Afghanistan.

The question of what these enormous monuments were for is also the problem of their origins. The oldest date that can be put to a stupa is about 255 B.C., for a brick dome at Sanchi in Pakistan, rebuilt with elaborate stonework in what appears to be a wood-carving style in the first century B.C.,[23] carrying an inscription on one of its gateways which records that the carving was done by ivory-workers. Several other first-century stupas have stone imitations of wooden fences; this tendency to make the same object on a bigger scale or in a harder material is not so extraordinary as it sounds. One of the chief formal sources of Gandaran art is the imitation of Hellenistic stucco from Alexandria in the local schist;[24] near Kunduz north of the Hindu Kush the same art was transferred into white limestone which was harder still.

Stupas become more elaborate as time goes on; they acquire stages, colonnades and gateways, and in the end the huge discs of their sacred stone umbrellas and their massive substructures so increase that the original body of the dome itself hardly survives in their design. They always contain relics, presumably the relics of the Buddha himself, and the art associated with them is sacred: it is the convention of Hellenistic narrative scenes represented in relief applied to the life of the Buddha. Certainly in some and probably in many cases the strip cartoon effect of these reliefs is the result of their being copied from ancient book illustrations. The dominating and unifying position of the Buddha in each scene seems to reflect the position of the ruler in Roman imperial representations. But the origin of the stupa must be looked for in another direction: the first stupa must be a version of the familiar mounds or barrows of the dead, a tall mound built to contain relics, standing within a sacred area surrounded by a wooden fence. The Buddha of the earliest Buddhism was a human teacher like others; the emphasis on divine and magical elements came comparatively late and belongs to the period of the Roman Empire in the west and later. The stupas came with the later stage.

On a very hot day later on in the summer we climbed to the Menare Chakar, a stupa in the form of a tall column, on the hills above the Logar valley where the old road from Kabul down to Jellalabad and India turns towards the Lataband Pass. The valley itself, close as it is to Kabul, is a series of biblical and Virgilian farms and villages. The walls there are mudbrick ornamented with circles and stars and geometric patterns, with sometimes all the ornaments of a fine fantasy gateway sketched in mudbrick relief on the walls of a farmyard, around a simple wooden door. One richer farm had a fretted gallery of wooden pillars and windows above its gate. It was the most richly ornamented farmhouse I ever saw in Afghanistan, and some glimpses of poorer ruined houses in more or less the same style suggest that this may be what a rich house in early nineteenth-century Kabul would have looked like. The farms quickly die out into rough pasture and desert; from above, when you climb the small mountains fringing the strip of desert on the far side, the farms look like strands of dark green seaweed on a sandy beach. You pass some tattered nomad tents, camels sleeping or grazing, and an Islamic shrine with pink and white votive rags. From close below the mountain the thick pencil of the Buddhist column stands out against the sky; from a distance it seems not to be on the summit, but it was certainly built to be seen from close below crowning the ridge above the monastery.

That was a dusty month. When you drive up here from Pakistan in the winter, everything is white; the snow-world begins as you leave the gorge and emerge on this plain. But now the snow had gone the way of the wild tulips. The temperature was about a hundred and still increasing. The mountain is made of a glittering dark schist, crossed by narrow paths and at one place a broad droving track that climbs very slowly. I saw a hoopoe, and an unfamiliar blue flower. There was a tinkle of sheepbells, and you could hear the buzzing of a single bee, otherwise there was absolute silence. The column looked for a moment like a pillar with an urn on it in an eighteenth-century nobleman's park, at some wild point on the Welsh border. But it is far more subtle and strong. Indeed the subtle grandeur of this column, the effect of solidity and sublimity at once, and its economic richness of design, give it an individual quality which in my view raises it to the category of a very great work of art. It is sixty feet high and at least its eaves were once stuccoed. It is perhaps the most impressive surviving Buddhist monument in central Asia.

We climbed down through a noon landscape where nothing moved. Shepherds and sheep lay sweating and stinking in the shade of the first trees. Young children as naked as fishes and as dark as Indians were sliding about in a village watertank. On the outskirts of Kabul a tall man was carrying a goat across his shoulders, we passed a boy on a bicycle with a cartridge belt, and a young man with a rifle galloping on a donkey. Suddenly we were in traffic, in a crowd, in Kabul, and people wore European suits.

PART TWO

Bamiyan

CHAPTER
3

After a few days of the rich contradictions of Kabul the first
journey we made was to Bamiyan, the most famous Afghan
Buddhist site, in the passes of the Hindu Kush. I had been
reading Buddhist scriptures, I was most curious about the origins
of Buddhist art, and I have a passion for ruined monasteries. In
several ways, at least in their early historical development,
Buddhism and Christianity are obviously parallel phenomena. I
was devoured by thoughts that were not impersonal. Neither
Buddhists nor Christians have ever, so far as I know, converted
a nomadic people. When Buddhism spread into Afghanistan the
nomadic invasions were still to come; admittedly Buddhism
survived and took root under the Kushan Empire, but the
Kushans, who were cousins of the Parthians, had already settled
down and become permissive. It seems never to have advanced
westwards into the kingdom of the Parthians or into the revived
Persian Empire of the Sassanians, where Buddhists would have
had to compete not with paganism but with monotheistic fire-
worship, Judaism, and Orthodox and Nestorian Christianity.
Buddhists and Nestorian Christians reached China, and fire-
worship and Buddhism co-existed in the Kushan Empire,* but
Buddhism and Christianity seem hardly to have met at that time
except on trade routes, and neither of them could mingle with the
severe tribal religions of the nomads. Both the invading Mongols
and the invading Arabs were monotheists of some purity and
ferocity; it is very hard to separate their uncompromising spirit
from their untamed lives, but if ever the history of monotheism
can be written, that is if a genuine historical explanation of its
development could be given, I believe it will be seen that
monotheistic belief represents a particular stage of human development marvellously preserved, and must repurify itself continually

* There are traces of fire-worship in the popular beliefs of Nuristan and Swat,
and traces of Buddhism in the local superstitions of West Pakistan, to this day.

in order to survive. In its origins monotheism perhaps has more to do with the visible sky and the idea of a justice like the sun and a single darkness, than with any political institution.

The pure teachings of Gautama Buddha are like snow-water. He was a saint of philosophy, like Socrates and Epicurus; he and Socrates lived within the same hundred years. The earliest cult of the Buddha was much more rarefied than what came later; he was venerated for his teachings as a great enlightener, just as Socrates was venerated in the west, and the Buddhism of this period can be studied only in inscriptions and literary texts. But veneration led to pilgrimage, from the third century B.C. onwards there were more and more monumental domed mounds to hold less and less likely relics of the Buddha, and from the time of the birth of Christ wave on wave of somewhat Greek-looking figurative art; Buddhism had become a popular religion not intolerant of superstitions. Its great centres were domed mounds (*stupas*) and the lavishly decorated monasteries. Probably the best preserved of these monasteries is in north-west China,[1] but the monastery at Bamiyan in Afghanistan is on a vast scale and is naturally of great archaeological interest. It consists of several colonies of hundreds of cells cut into the rock of a cliff-face, with two or three colossal statues standing in niches in the cliff. The cliffs command a broad, rich valley, and Bamiyan is the most important settlement on the ancient routes across the Hindu Kush, from Balkh and Samarkand to Kabul.

On the road northwards from Kabul to Bamiyan, the first archaeological site is Khair Khane, an easy spur of hill overlooking the Kabul plain. We passed it often; it offers nothing much to see, but we always stared respectfully at it, because of the marble sun-god of the fifth century A.D. in the Kabul Museum which was found there.[2] He is sitting on a throne with a small figure of dawn driving a two-horse chariot below his feet. He has two Indian retainers and seems to belong to the revival of Indian paganism which so eroded the Buddhist world. It must be admitted that the incisiveness and crispness of the pagan sculptures of this class, and a certain absence of subjectivity, perhaps because of the hardness of the material, suggest most strongly that they belong to a victorious movement. There are some from Khair Khane and others from Gardez; the best of them have an archaic vigour like the treasury friezes at Delphi.[3] The finest of all is an unpublished group from Gardez in which a six-armed Siva has pinned a

centaur with a trident and beheads him with another hand; the
centaur is down on one knee and trying to draw a sword. He has
a moustached Indian face and one should remember that centaurs
belong to Indian as well as Greek mythology. Khair Khane was
excavated in 1934, but it remains something of an archaeological
mystery.[4] There are still huge thistles on the hillside like prayer-
flags, but in the next few years it will probably be swallowed up
by Kabul. (Or that is what I wrote twelve years ago, and with
normal development it would be happening. Since then the place
has been a battlefield and a frontier.)

The road to Bamiyan is certainly an ancient (I do not dare to
say the ancient) route from Balkh and Samarkand to India.[5]
Bamiyan is sheltered by high mountains and has to be approached
by winding and sometimes precipitous valleys. In the eighteen
forties a British expedition with artillery took a month to reach it
from Kabul. Between Bamiyan and the Oxus the passes are called
Akrobat, Dandan Shikan, and Kara Kotal, which means White
Point, Tooth-breaker, and Black Col. Beyond that lie six days of
'narrow defiles and stupendous cliffs'.[6] It was once an ideally
sheltered and remote Buddhist kingdom. No Greek remains of
any kind have been found there; the Greeks must certainly have
held this route through the mountains, and so must the Persians
before them, but if there was an early settlement at Bamiyan, it
has not been found.* In the nineteenth century the site of Bamiyan
even in May is said to have been unrelievedly grim. 'Desolation
is not the word for this place; the surface of the hills is actually
dead; no vegetable trace is to be seen . . . Such is the horrid
aspect.'[7] If this was a truthful description, then the digging of a
network of irrigation canals in the later nineteenth century has
been like the creation of a paradise from a wilderness.

At Charikar, we left the road to the north in a beaten-up Volga
taxi, to follow the Gorband river upstream. Charikar is on the
edge of a very rich plain of fruit gardens and crops where the
Gorband, the Salang and the Panjshir run together. Far away
across the treetops, close under the mountains as Pliny describes
it, you can see the site of Kapisa.[8] It is hard to make out at all
except in a kind of haze of agricultural wealth, but the site is a low
hill where the Gorband and the Panjshir rivers meet. We
attempted to reach Kapisa on three different days and every time

* Shahr-i-Golgola, the citadel of Bamiyan, has not yet been thoroughly
excavated.

got lost among the vines and the mulberries and the mudbrick walls. The Greek akropolis was the hill called Borj-i Abdullah.[9] The Begram treasure, part of which is shown in the Kabul Museum, comes from a village not far away in the plain. It was found there by chance, and it must represent everything small enough to be hidden from a Kushan palace of the first or second century A.D. Like Isfahan, it merits a book on its own.[10] There are Chinese and Indian luxury objects, Romano-Greek and Egyptian bronzes, and some astonishing local work of very high quality in which Hellenistic and native elements come together in a new style. One can find the backward-peering heads of the Siberian horses and the forward heads of Greek horses in the same carving. One of the strangest luxuries of all is a series of twelve- to twenty-inch figures of clear or blue glass dolphins, in a country where almost no one can ever have seen the sea.

We took the same route in reverse as the Chinese pilgrims to Buddhist shrines in the sixth century A.D., and along much the same road. The Gorband valley is a sugarcane of sweetness winding through deserted hills. Everything seemed on that day to be an effect of the wind; you could smell clover from half a mile away through the window of the car, and balsam poplars from an infinite distance. Even the snowglitter of the higher and the snakeglitter of the lower peaks seemed to be a function of light multiplied by wind. A string of camels passed by treading delicately, and the nomad tents were straining at their ropes. Inside the valley it was first hotter as the hills enclosed us and then cooler as we climbed to their level. We passed a caravanserai in ruins, some fortified farms, a big castle, and then suddenly an entire cliff top fortified, with round corner-towers crumbling in the sun. There were old clay walls completely honeycombed by small birds, some tiny birds like treecreepers, and a pinkish nude-looking finch-sized creature. People were fishing in the Gorband with big poles of white poplars; we found out that they were using mulberries for bait. School-children were moving everywhere along the road, because the previous night the Prime Minister had made a speech forcibly reopening schools after a long strike; in this strike the entire school system had followed the lead of the University of Kabul; after eight weeks this speech had got the schools to run again, but the university remained closed.

At Chardeh a Hazara boy of about twelve had been teasing the village idiot, who was retaliating by flinging him headlong with gleeful cries and then beating him. This event was repeated several times, since although the child was in tears he attacked and insulted the idiot again and again. So up the street and down it he was flung, to general merriment. People came out of cottages and peered from roofs, all laughing. The scene seemed all the stranger because we were eating lunch in a teahouse, I think for the first time, and there were birds hanging in cages in a mulberry tree over our heads. Parked beside us was the first Afghan bus I had ever inspected from close up. It was an open lorry elaborately, vividly, obsessively decorated in turquoise and white, with some romantic insets of mountains and cottages by moonlight, and two green and yellow budgerigars on a spray of mulberry, outlined against a huge moon.

The iconography of Afghan lorries repays study. They have a lot of scenes of transport: trains and even aeroplanes. They show crossed hearts and hands shaking each other, and romantic natural scenes that look like north Italy or Scandinavia. They have splendidly fearsome lions, sometimes lurking in jungles of vivid green, sometimes fighting each other or subdued by a prince, who may be an unarmed wrestler, and sometimes guarding the Afghan flag. The lorries travel into Pakistan, and most of their imagery derives from the postcards of the British India of the twenties and thirties. The framed prints in the teahouses belong to the same art-world, although both for better and worse, they have less popular quality, not being spontaneous. In fact I have observed exactly the same series of strange northern scenes, and funny sentimental girls, all so far as I can discover made in Peshawar, hanging in the taverns or teahouses in Afghanistan, in Teheran and Isfahan, in Istanbul, and in the remotest villages in Greece. I admit I had never thought about their origins until I saw them in Afghanistan, vaguely supposing them to be Italian, since in rich sentimentality of feeling they so resemble Italian religious art. The influence of postcards is as important for the teahouse prints of girls as it is for the scenes on lorries; I possess some old postcards which demonstrate this, though for the postcard influence on the iconography of lorries I rely on Mr Bruce Chatwin. But how on earth did British Indian taste in romantic pictures reach Greece? What is the distribution system? Is not this phenomenon as far-fetched as anything in the history of art?

We bumped and rattled upwards towards the Shibar Pass. The

mountains were sand-brown, red-brown and green and brown; in the distance they lay against a sky so blue you seemed to see them through a blue mist. The snow-peaks showed a startling charcoal and white above the chaotic sprawl of the lower mountains. At eight thousand feet the river was only ten feet across, giving off a delicious smell of water and growth and mint, and we were high enough for the crops to be still unripe in July. Spray and wind tempered the sun. Somewhere over nine thousand feet, giant sorrel began, and I saw a wild rhubarb like red cellophane growing out of the rocks on the mountainside. Men had been collecting it; they were carrying it down in enormous heavy bundles on their backs, grinning like schoolboys as they went by. Just below the pass itself a last big fort straddled the valley and an empty village like a deserted customs station dropped slowly to pieces. This pass is the watershed between the Oxus and the Indus, between the streams that reach the sea and those that expire in the desert or the huge salt lake of the Aral Sea.

The top of the pass was a silent world; it was the first time we had been in high pastures, and at once it was easy to understand how bare grazing land like this could seem a promised paradise to the nomads of Turkestan. Skylarks leapt and warbled just as if we were in north Oxfordshire, and a herd of sheep was moving across an unlimited limestone landscape with weird outcrops and bony flanks; farther off stood reddish earth-coloured rock mountains, with snowy ranges quite close behind them. The high pastures were governed only by a strong wind and a molten sun; we found a number of small bright flowers, including a very bright blazing yellow flower like an asphodel, which turned out to be Eremurus.

We returned to the car reluctantly and headed down the pass. We came at once to a wild, single-turreted castle ruin, and moved down one of the tributaries of the Bamiyan river, through a long, slow succession of deep red gorges and tottering rocks. At the main river we turned upstream, but we were still among ravines. The colours were a bruised carmine, an ochreous buff, and plain rock-grey. Finally we came out into a broader valley, below the powerful cliff castle of Shahr-i-Zohak. Its name means Red City, and the ruins are red claybricks, on a red cliff. It has triple fortifications and the cliff has been deliberately sheered off below it, two or three hundred feet above the river. Genghis Khan's grandson was killed here in the siege of Bamiyan in 1222; it is believed that the Khan himself destroyed Shahr-i-Zohak, overran the Bamiyan valley and massacred its people. This is still a predominantly Hazara, that is a Mongol area: it is a region where things take a long time to change: there were Buddhist kings at Bamiyan down to the last decades of the tenth century.

The Arabs had never taken Bamiyan and we know that about A.D. 827, Bamiyan had a Buddhist king. About 970, a Turkish governor of Balkh declared himself independent of Bokhara; he marched south, with a slave general called Sebüktegin, heading for the dependency of Ghazni; the king of Bamiyan attacked him but was trapped in a gorge and imprisoned; this king also was Buddhist. Sebüktegin became king at Ghazni and soon afterwards Islam had completely and irrevocably engulfed Afghanistan, even the mountains, except for Nuristan.

Bamiyan is trees, rivers, caves. The small hotel stands above it on a southern cliff, with a tiny airstrip behind it, and behind that again to the north the snowy range of Koh-i-Baba. The sun set exactly at the end of the valley, like a clear yellow liquid draining out of a pale blue sky. The valley was dusky and peaceful. Two heavily built Buddhas tower in niches in the northern cliff-face, each of the figures being well over a hundred feet high. Once they were red and gold, now they are the same clay as the cliff. They stare like tranquil magical robots at the snow and sky behind the hotel. The wind was noisy but the river was roaring louder still. The cliffs opposite darkened; they were honeycombed with several hundred black monastic caves and chapels.

In the morning, the Buddhas are in shadow and you see a whole parade of almost nude brown hills faintly dusted with green and deeply picked out into shadows. The Buddhas are not naturalistic; they are more like the seagull-eyed image of the virgin of which Robert Lowell speaks,[11] *non est species, neque decor*. The faces have been cut away and the restored pieces have a coldness, the feet a solid stance. No statue which has had its face removed can express justice or law or illumination or mercy, but there is a disturbing presence about these two giants that does express something. I do not know if it is 'expressionless, expresses God' or not.

The grottoes are really like a honeycomb, like the holes of birds or of wild bees. The valley floor is meticulously farmed, with close woods of white poplar, deep green colours, and a number of toy forts containing farms. Early on that first morning a boy in the fields was playing a flute, and most days we used to hear him. It had a double octave, and at first I thought it was a double flute, but later we saw boys with flutes more than once, and it was always a simple wooden pipe, I think made of poplar. We climbed, like all tourists, from gallery to gallery through the monks' caves, and stood on the head of Buddha listening to the swallows below our feet twittering round his faceless face. Was Buddha put here to contemplate or to be contemplated? Rather to contemplate, because the monks stared out of the same cliff at the same mountains and snow. The labour of constructing these sophisticated architectural forms in solid rock and on such a scale must have been enormous: it was presumably done by slaves. The Kushan Empire depended essentially on slavery; Gandara Buddhism seems in its origin to have had a strong upper-class flavour, and the Buddhist scriptures are written in a court language which the people were unable to speak.[12] Buddhist art and literature go closely together, and in spite of historical differences and local influences, for perhaps seven centuries there was a coherent universe of Buddhist religious art spreading from India and Afghanistan to the furthest west. Its monuments are inwardly convincing even without its literature, and without much comprehension of its imagery. The Sassanian grandeur of the painted decorations at Bamiyan belongs as closely to this universe as the imagery of daytime life belongs to the coherence of sleep. In the same way a Sanskrit poet in the first century A.D. describes the Buddha as taking 'the cross-legged posture, which is the best of all because so immovable, the limbs being massive like the coils of a sleeping serpent'.[13]

I found myself in an odd state of mind during these days. I had been reading some Buddhist writings with a kind of joyous attention, and for several months I had been studying Buddhist art in the museums in London and in Paris. I was deeply impressed, as anyone must be, with the goodness and peacefulness of Buddhist religion, and for some time I had thought of certain historic analogies with Christianity which in fact hardly hold water and are not interesting enough to write about. I felt a passionate identification with the Buddhists of these mountains in their history and I could not bring myself even to visit Shahr-i-Zohak because I felt that I hated military monuments and that all that carnage was somehow not the point of history. Bruce was far more scientific about Bamiyan; he had been there before and was interested chiefly in finding nomad tombs in the upper pastures. We toiled together through gallery after gallery of finely carved smoke-blackened grottoes, and tried to comprehend the swelling silken lines of the clay statues. There were Hellenistic as well as Sassanian elements, transmitted who knows how, but reminiscent of that most anomalous of all the relics of early Buddhism, the *Questions of King Milinda*, which is apparently a Sanskrit version of a lost work of Buddhist propaganda written originally in Greek.

In the land of the Bactrian Greeks there was a city called Sagala, a great centre of trade . . . Its king was Milinda . . . And the Elders went to Sagala, lighting up the city with their yellow robes which shone like lamps, and bringing with them the fresh breeze of the holy mountains . . . 'Now listen, O you five hundred Greeks, and O you eighty thousand monks . . .'[14]

This legendary assembly is not completely unlike the real life of Bamiyan in the fifth century A.D., when a passing Chinese pilgrim, on a visit to the original shrines of Buddhism, happened to be present when the five-year assembly of monks fell due to be summoned by the king.

They come as if in clouds and when they are all assembled, their place of session is grandly decorated. Silken streamers and canopies are hung out in it, and water-lilies in gold and silver are made and fixed over the places where the chief of them are to sit . . . The king himself . . . waits on them himself . . . uttering vows at the same time along with all his ministers.'[15]

The same witness records avalanches and land-slides in the mountains. 'The snow rests on them both winter and summer. There are also among them venomous dragons, which when provoked spit forth poisonous winds and cause showers of snow, and storms of sand and gravel.' By the seventh century we hear that the manners of the people were 'hard and uncultivated', that superstition flourished as well as the highest forms of Buddhist devotion, and that there were 'more than ten convents and more than a thousand priests', which sounds like a decline in numbers.[16]

It was the small shrines and hermitages that were unforgettable. On some of them the painted stucco had survived; there was a tiny closed chapel of blue and white roundels of almost claustro-phobic intensity. There were single round domes and systems of multiple domes in the rock, in one place a lantern roof carved into rock beams, tall, steep stairs like mine-shafts, and at least one absolutely night-dark chapel with no outlet except on to the dark stairs. You could hear chopping in the valley, and the desultory flute. Everything smelt of stonedust and scree, with a sharp whiff of spurge here and there on the slopes, but as you crossed the valley a plantation of white poplars crowded together with dark and white clover growing in the grass underneath them. One or two men and a few young boys were fishing in the river by casting a net. They had two trout, which looked extremely surprised to be caught. But except in early morning and late evening light there was something deader than deathly about those volcanic, sand-coloured cliffs and wild-looking passes. 'It is not death, it is not life I cherish. I bide my time . . .' 'Those who act from faith are akin to those who act from greed . . . Those who act from intelligence are akin to those who act from hate . . .'

We visited the Valley of the Dragon, a long, stony, mysterious canyon with stone-voiced birds. To get there we passed through Bamiyan village, which seems to specialize in metal-working. You could buy a suit of the kind of brown and cream tweed Stravinsky might have worn in the nineteen twenties, and we noticed a lorry decorated with a Taj Mahal and a tiger leaping on a spinach-coloured polar bear. The valley we wanted is a few miles west of the village. It opens like any other, curving away under cliffs smeared with volcanic ash. We became rather frenzied as it was much further than we thought; we were walking in a yellow blaze of disappearing sun and the canyon filled up with a greenish subaqueous coldness. We saw vultures, I was spitting out dust, and we heard a raven grunting. By the time we came to the final bend we were galloping along like a pair of nervous ostriches. The end of the valley was blocked with a slaggy mass of volcanic rock, which leaked a thin sulphurous water-stream covered in green filth that lost itself at once in the boulders. We could see a single vulture circling high up in the last of the light. The final barrier was a great scaly ridge of grey rock, cracked at the very top in a long smooth fissure like a giant knife-cut, narrowly split right along its length.

We climbed up to a small shrine with a blue prayer-flag, and some giant horns of wild goat. The legend is that the Prophet's nephew, Hazrat Ali, rescued a girl by turning a dragon into stone; you can see his blood and his shape in the red and white volcanic ash and the springs are dragons' tears.[17] The story as it was told in the nineteen thirties includes roaring and flames and a shaking of the ground, and then a dark cloud that hung over the valley for many days; it certainly suggests the memory of a volcanic disturbance, although hardly of the prehistoric disturbance that formed these rocks. I should have said already that Bruce and I are both petromaniacs, and it was the rocks which we found thrilling, rather than the legend that attracted us. The place was thoroughly awful, in the same sense in which Scott used the word awful of the polar wastes. It was intensely and objectively numinous, but there was absolutely nothing to be seen except the cracked rock, the shrine which was a tiny hut, the goathorns and the prayer-flag. It was the goathorns almost more than the rocks and the place itself we had come to find.

One can hardly speak of a goat cult surviving now anywhere in Afghanistan, yet in remote regions the horns of goats are peculiarly honoured, and very often attached to Islamic shrines. There was, for example, a splendid saint's shrine in Bamiyan village with fine markhor horns attached to it. The valley is a very popular place of pilgrimage. The crack in the rock is long but narrow, one could stand with a foot on each side: it seemed a strange place to find goathorns. I have read the publications of a German Hindu Kush expedition in 1955 that discovered some very strange practices and beliefs to do with wild goats among the Dardic tribesmen of Gilgit, Pakistan.[18] A hunter on the night before he goes after wild goat must not sleep with his wife. If he observes this law a fairy comes to him in his sleep and tells him on what mountain he can find an ibex or a markhor. After the kill, he must throw away some pieces of liver in the name of his special fairy. Ibex and markhor belong to supernatural flocks and until the fairies kill one it is impossible for any human being to slaughter it. The fairies perform the real kill and eat the real meat; then they put the skin and bones together again and bring it to life and give it to a hunter that they choose, but the human killing is really only a dream-kill and the human feast on the meat is only dream-eating.

Bamiyan is a long way from Gilgit, but the goat-owning goddess covers a wide territory and has been found as far away as the Caucasus. In this valley and at some shrines in Badakhshan there is more evidence of strong religious feeling about the horns of wild goats than can easily be explained. What is the meaning of the rock drawings of goats that the nomads make to this day? Perhaps nothing is left but an inarticulate sense, yet I did find in a shop at

Ghazni an undatable stamped terracotta bowl with a running frieze of goats like the nomad goat drawings, cavorting in a circle round the upper half of a crudely modelled female figure with a bow. I do not claim anything about this bowl. It was in a small antique shop at Ghazni; if I had to guess at its date I should suppose it was pre-Islamic and post-Kushan. Its provenance may not have been local and it may of course have been much earlier than I thought. I do not believe it was a fake, since it was cheap, and I never saw another like it.

From the high point where we stood, wanting not to leave it, we saw people and flocks moving on the scratches of paths on the tops of the downs or cliffs or dunes. We could hear the very last birds. Darkness fell before we got back to the village. It dropped on us more or less as we crossed a one-pole bridge, feeling foolish and wobbling. As we came back into the village, potteries and forges were belching volumes of smoke which flames hardly penetrated. The smoke was coming out of caves, and we could see fires and people and animals moving about in what must once have been more of the monks' grottoes. As we left behind this small troglodytic colony on the outskirts of the village, it darkened absolutely. The small circles of oil-light in the booths of the bazaar were wan and unwelcoming and the hotel seemed a long way off. Unchained mastiffs stirred as we passed. The first copper star nailed itself into the sky. Then more copper stars and some silver stars.

CHAPTER
4

We set out on a short day's walk in the upper pastures, towards the snowfields on the crests of Koh-i-Baba behind the hotel, to the south of the Bamiyan valley. By the time we got home we had walked thirty-five or forty miles. It was nearly the hottest season, but Bamiyan is extremely high above sea-level, the air is snow-cooled and the valleys are crag-shadowed, so the season was less mature and the dangers of sunstroke and exhaustion less obvious than in the plain north of Kabul. The effects of high altitudes are not what one imagines. The fearsome crags and freezing cold and mist that set everyone gasping in north Wales had coloured my ideas too sombrely. Thin mountain air in blazing sun is pleasant to breathe, it sharpens smells and refreshes eyesight. I think we both had the illusion of infinite energy, of the thin blood of a bird, and the rarer the air the deeper the sky. We moved south across the airstrip and into an empty valley behind Shahr-i-Golgola.[1] The heights of Koh-i-Baba disappeared, and the valley climbed slowly. Its sides were tall, sandy downs, peppered with vegetation. At first we followed a track with the wheelmarks of a jeep or a lorry, and if you looked closely you could see scattered flocks and children gathering fodder on the tops of all the downs.

We walked ankle-deep in artemisia; it gave off a sharp, sun-heated smell which seemed to have been undisturbed for many years, even by cattle. After about an hour we came suddenly on a line of four mounds. We looked and neither of us spoke, being unwilling to believe our eyes. It was too good to be true, after so many enthusiastic conversations, that you only had to move an hour into the hills to come across unexcavated and uncharted burial mounds. There was no possibility of dating this small group, but they were certainly man-made barrows. If it were possible to find these mounds higher up, where snow lies for so much of the year that the ground is always frozen, we should be able to recover complete burials perfectly preserved by the action of ice. Deeply frozen burials like this have in fact been found in Russia, and there could be no better way of solving the problem of what stage of development each of the peoples of the nomad invasions had reached when they crossed the Hindu Kush. We know that the nomads were accustomed to use the mountain pastures in summer, as indeed they do to this day, although they are restricted now by the lines of late nineteenth-century national frontiers; but no burial has yet been found in these upper grazing grounds or on the high passes anywhere in the Hindu Kush.*

If we are to think about the past in central Asia, we ought to think of most of the time and most of the territory as the grazing grounds of nomadic herdsmen. As early as the Greek period it was possible for one Greek prince to frighten off another by threatening to let in or call in the nomads,[2] and the Chinese walls in the east, the long boundary walls found by Aurel Stein in Seistan and the Roman frontiers farther west seem all to have been designed to keep out the uncontrollable peoples of the steppe; Aurel Stein at one time imagined that these *limites* might have been a connected system.[3] But the nomads were not simply barbarous; one should remember that Persepolis itself in the fifth century B.C., and still more Pasargadae slightly earlier, is not so much a palace as a huge, petrified royal tent.[4] The Odeion that Perikles built at Athens, the first roofed theatre the Greeks had ever seen, was modelled on the captured tent of the Great King, which he left with his general and lost at Plataia.[5] Marco Polo describes semi-permanent royal tents of the same kind about two thousand years later,[6] Jesuit missionaries in the seventeenth century drew a groundplan of the encampment of the king of Persia,[7] and anyone who has seen the trappings of even quite a poor Kazak tent, and the magnificent formalized eagles and flowers of its material, will easily imagine how impressive one of the great nomad encampments of the Middle Ages and the age of the invasions must have been.

There is a strange terracotta rhyton† from central Asia in the form of a centaur holding a long-horned baby goat, which

---

* The only burial mound excavation I know of in Afghanistan was the opening of four of the mounds south of Kunduz aerodrome by M. Casal. They were Hunnish and had been robbed; there were signs that they had been rich and a Byzantine gold coin was left in one of them.

† A drinking vessel in the shape of an animal or an animal's head; common in Greece from the fifth century.

I used to pass every day on the way to the library in the
Ashmolean Museum at Oxford. I had often wondered about it
and I should still not like to sit an examination about its formal
origins. It is extremely Greek in conception but not in detail,
the stance and the modelling are naive, and the barrel shape
of the body has something in common with small goat and
horse rhytons found with the Begram treasures and now in the
Afghan national museum at Kabul. It was found by Aurel Stein
with other treasures on the river Ishkoman in Gilgit, at a point
possibly on one of the routes of the invading nomads.[8] Of
course, that could also be a trade route, and one cannot argue
to a general cultural situation from isolated trade goods. The
bronze double-lugged cauldron with a horse's head attachment
found with it and the similar cauldron with an eagle's head are
certainly stray imports. But there was a small bronze ornament
from the top of a pole which I have seen in a private collection
and which is believed to have come from the Russian border
north of Herat, which was not imported. It was a four- or five-
inch statue of a woman with a stringed instrument seated on
a kind of bronze turnip decorated with strapwork rather like
the Delphic omphalos; her hairstyle and what could be made
out of her dress make it almost certain she was Kushan, and
the fineness and severity of this figure, which is unique at least
outside Russia, suggest that she was made about the time of
the invasion or before it. The only analogies were with ivory
figures in the Begram treasure from the lost palace of Kapisa,
and with the Asian-faced sphynx from the same treasure which
may possibly be Parthian.[9] We are hardly at the beginning of
the study of these people, and we ought not to underestimate
them. When more of the burial mounds are opened, it is likely
that much more material of the same kind will come to light.
One should remember the spectacular physical beauty of the
material culture, essentially nomadic, of the fifth century B.C.
which has come to light in frozen graves of the Altai mountains.

The four burial mounds in our valley seemed more or less
undisturbed, although one had been partly washed away and
another cut into to make a canal. I found a tiny deep blue
convolvulus growing on one of them, and a crop of vetch covered
the valley floor in a ragged carpet. The noise of the bees in the
wormwood was very loud as soon as one stopped walking. Bees or
cicadas buzzing in an absolute silence seem to be one of the

characteristic sounds of high-altitude pastures; a boy had been playing a flute on the downs as we came near; we often heard him, as he was always distant and never visible, like a wooden-voiced cuckoo.

As we climbed higher, instead of becoming bare the valley turned into greener, fresher crops more tightly hemmed in, carefully weeded, with the snow-water and springs harnessed into a complicated network of irrigation that covered every workable inch of the ground. We passed houses and isolated hamlets and lines of trees with their roots in the canals. We stopped to rest at a natural gateway of tall rocks where agriculture seemed to end; Bruce sat down to draw a rock and I went back to wash my dusty and possibly flea-infested trousers in a clear goat-pool. The water was waist-deep, and while I was walking about in the pool, a boy came past with a flock. He took my activities as the most natural thing in the world, and I suppose in fact that nothing is more everyday in central Asia than washing oneself in a goat-pond with most of one's clothes on. Bruce had a more exciting time; he watched a hawk over the rocks chasing a lark. The lark lost a feather, which floated idly to the ground while the hawk pounced to no purpose and the tiny lark sheltered in a cranny twittering with fear and triumph.

Above the rocks the fields were sparser but the valley continued. The hills became steeper and had patches of red rhubarb on their inaccessible sides. We left the last thin group of poplars and the last water and climbed round to the west up a stony inclined natural stadium towards a barren green-dusted horse-shoe rim. It must have been noon, our water was cold, but the brandy had gone hot in my pocket and had a delicious toffee taste. We climbed through a sort of grove of wonderful yellow eremurus, like redhot yellow pokers. Bruce was tired but untroubled by the height, which was now above nine thousand feet, but I was so tired I was almost paralysed, and my heart jackhammering in a most alarming way. We dragged ourselves unendurably along, two hundred feet at a time; as the slope became steeper we looked back and down on the first big outcrops of rock. We flung ourselves down among a whole mass of blazing yellow flowers. They were the embodiment of blazing heat and sparse air, but rooted and higher than my head. For several nights afterwards I dreamed about them. When we came out on to the top we saw a man far away at the same height on another hill, walking with the utmost ease, and up to 9,500 feet there were the eroded results of several attempts at cultivation on the steep slopes.

We were at ten thousand four hundred feet, on a narrow col between valleys, very close to the snowy crests; we had reached a long rib of rock not more than a mile below the summit, at any lesser altitude it would hardly have been half an hour's climb even for me. Snow lay below us in wide drifts where the main ridge confronted the north wind; for the last fifteen hundred feet of climbing the air had seemed to be burning and freezing at once. Below our feet the westward valley wound away downwards out of sight, round what seemed to be a rock shaped like a romantic ruined castle. We decided to leave the summit and the sky to the angels and the eagles and found a goatpath down to the rock. It was really a rock but the pinnacle on it really was a ruined castle. Only the lowest of a curtain of five or six tall claybrick towers was standing to any height; the ruined clay was like a deceased row of candles, but there was enough left of the stubs for us to get a clear idea of what it had once been. We scrambled up the enormous boulders which had smashed it and which still lay among it where they had fallen. The boulders were a knobbly hard rock, which was dreamily easy to climb on and carried a deep orange lichen of great beauty. The row of towers had once half-blocked the valley but it had always ended on the tall rock where the bottom-most tower still stood commanding the natural path. It was quite hidden from below as well as above, so that it occupied a position of surprise and defence. It had never held a large garrison and had no obvious water supply; the nearest spring was about a mile away below it and out of sight; the snow drifts were quite close but the snow on Koh-i-Baba is scarcely permanent. This castle turned out to be quite unknown to archaeologists.

It consisted of a line of towers on high towering rocks; the towers were mudbrick and not quite round, the stub of the keep was ten-sided and there were some square features. The castle stood on a substructure of stone wall bonded with a coarse grey cement, and had tall shooting-slits, one of which was arched. We saw very little pottery; the few fragments we did find were like the pottery of Shahr-i-Golgola, the principal Buddhist fortification at Bamiyan itself. Very fortunately, Bruce made a drawing of the ruins although his notebook was subsequently lost. We took no photographs because a camera had seemed too heavy to carry that hot day and we had set out without any more serious intention than a climb up to the snowfield and a look at the upper pastures. From the drawing and from what we remembered M. Leberre of the French archaeological mission, who had been working for many years on the ruined castles of the Hindu Kush, was able to place it as a seventh-century fortification.[10] It must have been a part of the considerable outer defences of the Bamiyan valley; its style had something in common with the far grander castle of Ghandak. The site was at just ten thousand feet, which may for all I know make it the highest castle in the world. It can have had no possible purpose, hidden away at such a height, except to control movement in the highest grazing grounds. We felt certain at the time that there was a negotiable route south over the crest of Koh-i-Baba, but the maps of this area[11] are unreliable, and without having explored the route we have no right to claim it existed.

In the last years of the independent kingdom of Bamiyan, the Buddhists must have led a hard and frightening life. 'And if,' says the scripture, 'you should hit on the idea that this or that country is safe, prosperous, or fortunate, give it up, my friend.'[12] They must have read that with a pang. Perhaps the political atmosphere of those years or one should say, those lifetimes, is best summed up in the description of a certain King Prabhakara-vardana in the sixth century as 'a lion to the Huna deer, a burning fever to the king of Indus, a troubler of the sleep of Gujarat, a bilious plague to that scent-elephant the lord of Gandara, an axe to the ivy of Malwa's glory'.[13] Political conditions apart, life must have been hard but cannot have been unattractive. In the Buddhist heaven there are no mountains and all the rivers are fordable, but perhaps that is an Indian Buddhist heaven.[14] It is the rivers and the mountains that have made these valleys behind Bamiyan a kind of earthly paradise. Until we continued down from the ruined towers we had no idea of such richness. It was a more than Alpine profusion and it went on getting better as we walked. We descended by a series of tributary streams until we met the Bamiyan river, following the water down in a long curve, as one stream flowed into the next.

The best of this country was high up, but not in the very highest fields. The roar of wind with perhaps a faint note of water had died away when we left the col, and we were in a world of peace, warmth and richness. Meadowsweet hung in thick white clouds among grain crops, with a tall butter-yellow fennel that over-spanned the dark green. I remember lucerne and bean-flowers, a fine cranesbill, blue and white vetch and tall yellow vetch. Sorrel grew to an enormous height, like the sorrel I remember when I was eleven years old, crawling among long grass at school to avoid cricket. We found a rather evil-smelling campanula of a pale, waxy violet with an orange centre, and shaped like an overgrown, formalized harebell. There was a pink and white clover-coloured vetch and there were lush deep green stretches. We lay down in a small meadow of tiny white vetches and deep grass stuck with hundreds of orchids and patrolled by a peagreen bug. The orchids were a deep violet etched with deeper violet. It was here we saw some big rocks of a granite-like stone with fine black and white speckles, and that was why we stopped; the rocks were a good shape and had the same ferruginous lichen as the boulders in the ruins. I wanted nothing so much at that moment as to set up a hermitage and watch the four seasons of the year passing over these rocks for ten years. We both felt great sympathy for that late medieval Chinese emperor who appointed a particularly fine rock to be lord of the marches (how much more civilized than mocking a horse), and ended his life in exile in a wild region where the rocks were a good shape.

Further down the valley we came on huge bushes of wild single roses of five or six varieties. The simplest and purest forms of roses which are the ancestors of all the European complications have a dignity of their own, even as you see them in English gardens, but these were as different from anything I had seen before as the luxuriant health of a country child is different from a child in hospital. They were better than the roses in Isfahan, but almost as complicated. The first bush was a white rose with a pink centre as it opened, and the next a deep pink darkening to crimson with a gold corolla in the centre; the flowers were small and extremely strong-scented, so that you smelt them before you saw them. They had an abundant habit of growth, with thin springing branches tensely interwoven in big bushes of fine leaves and little flowers. A rose that was two and a half inches across would be overblown. Where the roses grew we were sometimes under the shade of trees and by this time I was feeling sprightly and it was Bruce who was tired. But stage by stage we came down to the region of poplar woods and a wide river, and at last to a confluence where another ruined tower dominated the living trees and water like a dead finger. We met parties of men walking uphill, who wanted medicine and hopelessly retailed their symptoms. In one place or another in Afghanistan we were asked for medicines of nearly every kind, and this is the experience of most travellers. Wood in his day was asked for a love-charm by 'a handsome youth who had come many miles'. There was nothing we could do as by this time we were carrying nothing but water.

We stayed on in Bamiyan for a few days, taking ramshackle but passionate notes about the art of the grottoes and the Buddhas. It is the deep shadows of the Buddha niches which give some relief and meaning to the sandy texture of the rocks and the arid softness of the volcanic ash. When the niches and cliffs and grottoes are all shadow-sculptured in the evening they are very impressive indeed. The green agricultural valley floor makes the dead cliffs look unreal; one could not begin to imagine the world of the upper pastures. On the last afternoon I went alone to the Kakrak valley;[15] I had to run most of the way on fieldpaths through the crops and past the ruins, as my watch was broken and I was frightened about the time. Bamiyan is the meeting of two streams, each fast and voluminous enough to be a formidable obstacle, and the guidebook said that even the tributary I had to cross was impassable when the water was in spate. It was knee-deep, the pressure was heavy and the bottom pebbly, but having triumphantly crossed with the guidebook in mind I noticed a bridge further down.

In the grassy cliffs beyond the river was another colony of caves with a standing Buddha.* His heavy topknot and his peaceful face were worth running for. He seemed to embody a harmonious, heavy, motionless movement. The niche was dark. It was a wilder and a better place than the main site of Bamiyan, which as well as its many more important qualities has in the end a slightly ridiculous air, probably because the big Buddha figures are after all so surprising. The Kakrak valley is like the other upper pasture valleys, with a distant view of snowy peaks and the clear, voluminous water shouting over the pebbles. Buddha is naturally

* It was in these caves that a wall-painting was recovered with a strong Sassanian flavour. It had been deliberately hidden under mud; it has now been taken to the museum at Kabul. It shows a king on his throne wearing a pearl diadem with three crescents. He has a bow, a quiver and a dog and sits under a tree with stupas and flags in the background. He may have been painted as late as the eighth or ninth century. There are ruined fortifications on the cliff above the grottoes.

silent and the noises of this valley are also natural; it is the cliffs and the idea of dust that are frightening. Shahr-i-Golgola, City of Voices, which means hill of ghosts, is a ragged and frightening mound. But the bees were clamouring in the lucerne; I thought, no doubt stupidly, of Virgil, and it struck me as I rushed past that blue glaze pottery and lapis lazuli and turquoise come from Asia, although admittedly even the Romans had pillars encrusted in fragments of blue glass, and lucerne is one of the few reasons for associating the colour blue with Virgilian landscapes. The sea belongs to the heroic horrors of the *Aeneid*; it is not Virgil's element, and if you disallow smoke, the only other blue element is the sky.

The wind was louder than the bees. We were due to fly back to Kabul in the small De Havilland Otter that still called in those days at the tiniest Afghan aerodromes. In time we learnt to respect it highly as a machine, but we also learnt to avoid flying in the afternoon, when the heat creates peculiar wind and air conditions and flights are often cancelled. The plane came jittering in to land at Bamiyan more or less sideways, and out stepped the smartest-looking veteran pilot with the longest, curliest moustache I have ever seen, adjusting his dark glasses. He was a retired Pakistani pilot from the old Royal Indian Air Force, and an astounding example of the personal style once associated with flying which somehow survived the 1939 war in faraway places. He smoked cigarettes in a long holder and his uniform was a good deal whiter than the snow. 'We will go,' he said, 'if you don't mind in a few minutes; in a few minutes the disturbances may have died down; just now coming over the pass she was' (gesture) 'like a butterfly.' He flew his small aeroplane like a magic carpet; there were just enough bumps to reduce a party of American engineers in ten-gallon hats, whom we had taken against, to silence and airsickness, and we occasionally went up and down as if in a lift, but we had plenty of time to focus binoculars on the entire extent of country we had travelled over. Looked at from above, the inaccessible hills and ridges below Koh-i-Baba were reduced to a system of even swellings, criss-crossed by thin paths in every direction. What had seemed from below like a desert in the upper air was obviously an important grazing ground. We passed nomad tents very high up. This flight was an even sharper lesson about nomad movements than the drive from Kabul. To the north the crags and crests of the Akrobat route to Balkh and the Oxus appeared and vanished in a terrifying series, far worse-looking at a glance than the majestic peaks of Koh-i-Baba: an enormous rim of mountains. We saw a valley with dark green trees, probably mulberries; it should have been the Buddhist monastery of Fundukistan, where a princely society in the seventh century produced clay sculptures of authentic originality and almost epicene delicacy. Looking at those statues one has the sense of a vulnerable luxury, an oasis in history.

We did a tricky turn into the plain north of Kabul as we left the mountains; the cabin door was open for coolness and we saw a leisurely hand put down a coffee cup and reach for a pair of binoculars, which the hand put to one eye with a motion as if it had been Nero watching Rome burn through an emerald. We came down at Kabul with a most exciting but perfectly smooth fit of acrobatics. We balanced somehow on our nose and then went skittering sideways into the wind and landed perfectly at what felt like five miles an hour, skating along the runway like paper in a sudden gust. We turned out to have landed in a cross wind of twenty-one knots; the pilot had been flying seven and a half hours that day. He said, 'I am sorry, I am afraid the wind has been just too much for the little aeroplane.' We got into conversation with him later, and he spoke with reminiscent awe of a much worse route, the Gilgit flight. 'We used to do it from Peshawar and Rawalpindi, you know before India was divided.' I dared not ask in what kind of aeroplanes, but I have seen photographs of biplanes flying in those mountains.

We returned to the embassy garden to read and recoup. All but five per cent of the peace corps in Afghanistan get serious diseases, mostly jaundice; we were luckier. I had a lip-sore, a septic hand and a bruised toe, Bruce had mild heat exhaustion and a sunstroke temperature; we were both thinner. He sat dazed on his bed dressed in a long Arab gown, reading fearsome sentences from the Royal Geographical Society's *Travellers' Guide to Health*, such as 'after collapse, death soon ensues'. The half dozen turkeys stalked about the lawn in a slow procession, looking spectacular among the geraniums. They were fatter; the night of the tennis club dance was approaching. We put out Bruce's handful of eremurus seeds to dry and did our best to keep the turkeys off. It seemed to us that turkeys or a fine-looking ginger hound which used to visit us would fulfil the functions of an ambassador on almost all occasions better than any possible human being.[16] The hoopoes came every afternoon, usually in a little flight of three very young ones with fluttering black and white crests that they flirted like eyelashes. Once I saw a black-capped, pink-chested foreign finch whose flying was not as graceful as his markings. Every evening we heard a donkey screeching with unsatisfied desire.

Then came days in the countryside when the mountains were petrified elephant-hide, and mid-days when we collapsed in the balconies of teahouses, running sweat faster than we could drink tea. The sun's point struck through your shirt. But driving into Kabul in the mornings almost every day was like a birthday; the taxi-driver maybe singing and high on hash, bicycles with two or three passengers, some of them sidesaddle, carts of fruit, painted lorries with eloquent handshakes and sprays of flowers expressive of love, and peacocks depicted singing louder than nightingales against a big moon. Even the foreign community was strange. I am not thinking of the hippies, who constituted a club we had no interest in joining, and who looked like a deluded and unenterprising set of people. But we met a visiting church dignitary in petunia silk, come to do a currency deal in the Kabul money market. Stranger still, we heard of a foreign company, most of the staff of which were German, all of them having left Europe in 1945 and none of them having lived since that significant date anywhere but in South America and Afghanistan. A few years ago they had turned up *en masse* for a new year's ball at the International Club, in full SS uniform including boots and pistols. It was difficult to find these items in good condition in the Kabul bazaar, although you could certainly dress a musical comedy there for any date since 1900. There was a fight and all the ex-Nazis were thrown into the swimming bath.

PART THREE

The West and the South

CHAPTER
5

Just as in Greece there is a certain more or less circular tour of the Peloponnese which every good tourist makes, in Afghanistan there is the road from Herat on the Persian border through Kandahar and Ghazni to Kabul and the Khyber Pass, which is part of the main tourist road from Europe to India; for part of its length it covers the footprints of Alexander's army. After the excursion to Bamiyan, and a few days in the Kabul museum, we formed a plan to visit a remoter monument in wilder country, the minaret of Ghor, and then somehow to make our way to Herat and so back to Kabul by the main road. The order in which we took things was not dictated by historical order, but by geography and the limited possibilities of transport. Ghor is Islamic, Herat mostly later Islamic but also much older, and Kandahar and Ghazni are the same: Islamic cities with Kushan Buddhist relics on Greek and probably pre-Greek sites. All of these places once had early medieval Jewish colonies. But the way in which we set off happened by chance.

We heard at the last moment that a huge annual nomad fair was being held at Chagcheran in Ghor, a mountainous and barren district of desert grazing grounds towards the north-west of Afghanistan.

The population of Ghor is only eight to the square kilometre: just half what it is in Bamiyan, which is wild enough. It is roamed over by wolf and boar, and in autumn one can find flocks of forty and fifty of the huge partridges called *kaouk*. There is not one town in the province bigger than a small English village. Chagcheran is an artificial creation; it depends on the airfield and is hardly ten years old. On recent British maps it is not even named. Its establishment as provincial capital and compulsory fairground was probably designed to put tighter control on the meeting places of the nomadic herdsmen. Surprisingly, the map made by Lieutenant Macartney of the 5th Bengal Native Cavalry in 1809, and reprinted in Elphinstone's *Account of the Kingdom of Caubul* in 1839, does show Chingh Chiran as an important meeting-point of tracks, although the river is not shown.

This fair is the annual meeting of all those throngs of nomadic herdsmen who scatter into the north-western pastures for the summer grazing; it is the one occasion when a foreigner can easily study the many genuine elements of nomadic culture that have survived among these people from remote antiquity. Naturally, such an assembly is the subject of romantic rumours; no one we could find in Kabul even knew its correct date or how the date was calculated (probably by the state of the grazing grounds or the birth of young animals). Bruce is a specialist in the study of nomadic peoples, and their movements are crucial to the whole history of Afghanistan. So we took the first aeroplane we could get, the usual small two-engined plane which carried luggage in its nose; they were always piloted extremely well, though not always with the veteran brilliance of our friend from Bamiyan, whom we seldom met again.

Chagcheran is as remote from Kabul as the Welsh mountains are from London. There was a long delay in that special world of tedium and dust in which travellers' anxieties solidify, which is the atmosphere of provincial journeys since history began. We travelled with a large, cheerful Turk who had a black stick with a silver knob, and a worried Hazara who methodically plugged his ears and the ventilator with paper; there was someone's .22 rifle loose underfoot, banging our ankles.* Since we started late it was already hot, the wind was up and the mountains were glowing; it was a buckety flight, quite low over the whole cobweb of mossy valleys and upper pastures, between dun crests and red sandstone outcrops, with one big snowy crest or another never far away. As we came close to Chagcheran we could see travelling groups of nomads in the hills and small camps; the nomads were moving away, and you could see the main tracks as broad as highways snaking across a barren landscape of hilltops without losing height, showing more clearly than at any other time of year because they had been trodden by flocks. We circled down to a tiny village on the bend of a broad river;† the whole country tilted down towards it.

* The province contains leopards and bears, as well as many wild birds and some strange small desert animals I was unable to name.

† This river is the Hari Rud; it runs down to Herat and loses itself in the desert of Khorasan.

The water was ice-blue and very strong; we dropped onto a rough landing ground and into a thrilling emptiness in every direction. An atmosphere of leisure swallowed us up. We waited peacefully while a handful of grand officials slowly arrived; the military governor was leaving on a journey. We were processed and befriended and taken in a Russian jeep to the offices of the civil governor of the province, who was also a colonel. He worked in a big, cool, oriental parlour, up a flight of high brick stairs; outside it waited a sleepy crowd of servants and minor officials, some of them armed; inside there were slow, sweet courtesies and large gestures. The administrative building was like a somewhat battered *mairie* carried on a magic carpet from the French provinces; it dominated only an empty square used once a year for parades, and farther off one or two half-planted avenues and a small bazaar. Downstream well away from the village the last remnant of the nomad assembly was encamped like a medieval army, with lines of horses and camels behind the tents.

We were lucky in the friend we made at the landing, a strange young man well dressed in city clothes who was the son of an official. He stuck to us for the day, and took us about in a jeep which he drove like a motorcycle, gleefully terrifying children and drovers. He was friendly, riotously funny to talk to, and extremely lonely. He turned out to be an Olympic lightweight wrestler, which in Afghanistan is like being a bullfighter in Spain. He had been in trouble for a *crime passionelle* in which he had stolen a girl, and ended by shooting her, her parents, and her parents' lawyer.* It had cost him about £3,500 to get out of prison after a year. There remained a blood-feud which had not come to anything although it meant he never travelled unarmed; he was also taking Librium 10. In the evening he talked about who one is and the acceptance of life.

We went with this small, trim boy to visit the Kuchi tents. A week before, there had been over a thousand tents, now there were about forty. We arrived in a dust-storm like great whirls of low sand-coloured cloud, and we pulled up in a kind of shellburst of dust from the jeep. One of the most beautiful white stallions I have ever seen was rearing and plunging in the yellow light, and at the sight of the jeep he finally broke his tether-rope and went galloping away, but he was soon back, being calmed and re-tethered by three men. Most of the horses we met in the province

* We were able to check this story; it was confirmed.

of Ghor shied badly away from motor vehicles; they were not used to seeing them or to the diabolic noise they made. It was very common to see lonely armed horsemen, and even in the bazaar of Chagcheran, a place of metropolitan sophistication compared to anything we saw later, horsemen would sometimes come to do business at the shops with rifles on their backs and without dismounting. The bolts and triggers or the whole gun were usually wrapped in flower-patterned cloth against the dust and sand, so that the pistols in the holsters of the policemen looked like women's Christmas presents, and when in another part of Afghanistan we saw trophies of flowers and guns and knives together painted on the walls of mosques and teahouses, these decorations seemed recognizably a product of the same society. But the world of the Kuchi is even more remote from us; Kuchi means travellers and they are hard to know.* We found them stoical about disease and distrustful of the local doctors, and in their tents their behaviour was regal. I remember with regret that when I praised the white stallion they offered to saddle him and let me ride, but I was too embarrassed and too crippled by my poor Persian to accept; we never saw such a good horse again.

The Kuchi come up once a year from their own lands south of Gardez. They are the frontier tribes who used to move indifferently between Afghanistan and the north-west frontier province of the Indian Empire. They hate the Pakistanis, who are now attempting to control their movements by requiring passports. When they discovered we were English they looked at one another with a reminiscent glitter in their eyes, and then touched their guns and caught our eyes and roared with laughter. They asked why we ever left, and laughed even louder in their beards. They spend three or four months each way on the journey and about four months in the north-western grazing grounds, the big fair at Chagcheran is the climax of this time, and after it they head for home. There used to be several of these fairs in different places, but all the Kuchi we met said they were more satisfied with the general assembly of the last few years; there was a lot of thieving and murder at the old scattered sites. They had left their families in the hills north of Bamiyan. They bring clothes and guns to sell, and they buy sheep which they can sell for a good price at Kabul

* We heard rumours that some of them came from Arabia and spoke Arabic; but *Arabistan* means Pakistan. Certain tribes are accused of childstealing, and children definitely do disappear, but only in towns, I think.

on the way home. They also have big flocks at home. Nowadays the goods mostly arrive by lorry for the fair. The nomads use an interesting multiple tether for goats. It is a long rope with loops fixed to it at intervals; you catch the goat's horns in the loop, and one rope can hold thirty goats. Camels are sometimes roped for travelling nose to tail; so that one rider can lead the whole string.

We discovered to our amazement, by a number of bits of evidence, that the Kuchi were regularly crossing the Russian as well as the Pakistan frontier. Years later I heard in London that it was the Kuchi who took Gillette razor blades into southern Russia. How long ago that seems.

Their tents are big and military-looking, some of them in fact may be old British army tents. When we asked what they did with their profits they laughed again and said they bought cartridge-belts 'for the next time'. Among the rifles we saw there was a British army issue rifle of 1945, which we were told would sell here for about £80; it had been decorated with a fine gilt grip.* There was even a pistol disguised as a fountain-pen which they gleefully demonstrated. If I would not buy a rifle, if I worked at a desk, this would surely be useful to me in Oxford!

From inside the tents the dust-storm, which raged every afternoon punctually from one to six, looked like battle-smoke; the light during those hours was like a perpetual stormy dawn, with animals appearing and disappearing in the mist and light. Outside, life was hazardous; on one late afternoon we were charged by an enormous yellow-brown dog like a husky, and it was only by good luck that no one was seriously mangled.† The great tranquillity of the place, particularly in the mornings, consoled us for occasional emergencies with these ferocious and slavering animals, and we avoided the fate of Euripides. In the morning I used to climb the big dunes behind the settlement; the situation was memorably phrased by the chief of police: 'Desert is toilet, all Chagcheran is desert, all Chagcheran is toilet.' One could look down on the first stirrings of the oasis, the building of a house with mudbricks thrown from hand to hand, the camels

* But in Nuristan, which is far wilder and poorer, we were shown Victorian and Edwardian army rifles still in excellent order and common use.

† A few years ago two American travellers left their car at night, since it had broken down, and started walking. They were never seen again and it is believed they were torn to pieces by dogs. Most dogs operate by an instinct for private territory, but the Kuchi are travellers and their dogs are wilder and less predictable, particularly at night.

going out to graze, and the horses standing saddled at the edge of the desert. There were small patches of snow on the long, low line of hills to the south, and every hill was faintly and delicately tinged with green, as if with a faint discolouration; in the foreground stood the usual big, bony downs with their ribs showing. The most surprising characteristic of this almost desert landscape, at least in the morning and evening, was its variety of colours and tones: tawny ground, sandy highlights and ferruginous red smears, with many faint and some intense shades of blue.* Camels going out to graze were a tranquil, almost a formal image of motion, they were a dark fawn colour and as they walked their legs seemed like an inverted grove, swaying gently.

One evening we went fishing on a bend of the river upstream where there was a ruined clay castle on a rock at the edge of the water. I drew it while the others fished and the young wrestler, having failed to induce any of us to wrestle on the grass by the riverbank, threw rocks with one hand in competition with a man whose daughter he was engaged to marry. The rocks were heavy and he threw them formidable distances with either hand. Another night we found music in the bazaar. We sat in a teahouse after dark, while three or four little boys of twelve or thirteen sat in absolute sobriety eating much the same dinner on the other end of the carpet. We saw an instrument like a long-necked, bulbous guitar, and asked if anyone could play it, but what was produced was an accordion and a drum with a hollow booming note and sudden thunderous bangs and claps. Someone was induced to dance to a drum-piece many times repeated and expressive of ecstasy; it was called Shishkebab. Later at night we found two young men singing the endlessly repeated words of a popular song, which they sang with constantly varied harmonies, laying their heads on each other's shoulders and sometimes breaking down into giggles; the music was a twelve-stringed guitar like the dropping of a hammer into cold water.† The words of the song meant 'the camel needs dates and the earth needs flowers'. The musician had the quality Lorca calls *duende*.

We wanted to reach that mountain unicorn among Islamic

---

* I find in my diary an attempt to give an exact number of colours; it says three or four greys, seventeen greens, seven or eight reds and blacks, and the infinity of tawny yellows, with fortresses and fungi of red stone on the horizon.

† The musician was called Mulajan, the instrument was the *rabab*, the music was an *awaz*, the climax is called a *tiz*.

monuments, the minaret of Jam, a twelfth-century royal commemorative tower the existence of which in its ravine was quite unknown to historians and archaeologists until almost yesterday.[1] It was first visited in 1957, and it may well be the clue to the lost capital of the kingdom of Ghor, an early and amazingly powerful mountain Islamic kingdom which was strong enough before the Mongol invasions to mount annual expeditions against India. In the reign of Ghiyathuddin in the late twelfth century, the public prayer of Islam was proclaimed, so it is asserted, in the name of the king of Ghor from northern India to the limits of Babylonia and from the Oxus to the straits of Ormuz at the mouth of the Persian Gulf, and it was Ghiyathuddin who built and inscribed the Jam minaret between 1193 and 1202.[2] Two of its inscriptions come from the Koran, but two longer ones glorify Ghiyathuddin. About a hundred years earlier, Ghor had been scarcely penetrated by Arab geographers; on a map of Khorasan of about 976 it was simply a circle inside a ring-fence of mountains, but it was already known to be rich, and the people were noted down as unbelievers and therefore potential slaves.[2] They were probably in fact Turkish-speaking Aimani tribesmen, many of whom are still to be found in these mountains.

They were protected by huge natural obstacles and by the force and purity of the seasons. Even at Chagcheran, the snow lies three or four feet deep for five months of the year. Signs exist of a later city of some grandeur at Taiwara, which has been little explored and which we failed to visit, although it is not far from Chagcheran in similar country, but the minaret of Jam is a magnificent monument: somewhere close by in those ravines must surely have been a city as well as a stronghold. A number of Jewish graves with Hebrew inscriptions have been found there.[3] They were discovered in 1962 and can be dated to the late twelfth and early thirteenth centuries. Many of the inscriptions end with the formula, May his soul be bound with the bond of life, or May his rest be in Eden. They include quite long quotations from the prophecy of Isaiah, with the ending 'and they shall say Amen, and Amen'. 'Thy light shall break forth as the dawn, and thy health shall be suddenly in bud, thy justice shall go before thee, the glory of God shall follow thee.' 'Let peace come; may they rest in their beds who walk in the right way.' The inscriptions are finely incised, most of them on the natural smooth surface of big water-smoothed stones from the riverbed. The craftsmanship was skilled, but the only instrument used was a chisel, so it seems likely that no stone-cutting saw could be found, and this in fact fits what we know of the brick architecture of Ghor and of the whole of eastern Iran. It suggests a substantial colony of Persian Jews living here among primitive conditions with no loss of cultural identity. Whether the Jewish community came with the Islamic religion or had been in these wild valleys a long time, we have no way of knowing, but its presence is another indication that at least in the eleventh century this must have been a city of consequence; if so, it was surely the capital of Ghor.

Getting there was a problem. The minaret stands on the same river as Chagcheran, and at first we prospected the possibility of hiring horses and if necessary servants, and simply following the river downstream. The map[4] shows the river at this point as a dotted line across a featureless landscape, which means that it has not been surveyed. We were told that a path existed, that it passed through wild woods where deer and goats wandered, and that it would take us two days' riding; the local police corrected the two to four, and introduced us to the horse serai. It contained about a dozen horses and twice as many foals and donkeys, some of the horses lame and every single one terribly afflicted with untreated sores. A sick child was sleeping in a niche with several hundred flies crawling all over him, and I thought for some reason of the buzzing of the flies around the elephant-pits of the Greek and Islamic kings. We hung about for nearly a day in the hope that some fresh horses which were expected might arrive, but it was no use, and we decided to try to reach Jam from Shahrak,* which is not in the same direction but is at least nearer to Jam and can be reached by road from Chagcheran. In several ways I was sorry to leave. With a mixture of Persian and even more broken Russian it was becoming possible to carry on conversations, the bazaar bread, which was cooked on fires of a kind of scrubby marjoram, was delicious, and I had discovered the word for an egg. More seriously, I had the beginnings of a vicious attack of what turned out to be bacillary dysentery.

We set out in the early morning and among early morning noises. A boy of nine rode past us on a black hump-necked bullock, singing loudly and tunefully with pauses to hawk and spit. There were skylarks above the beginning of the desert, one could hear hoarse voices calling across distances and the last

* Qala Shaharak on the British map.

woofing of the night-dogs. We travelled in the back of a small
lorry fitted with side-benches, crammed in among half a dozen
old men, what looked like a pair of bandits, three little boys, and
an old lady dressed in a kind of tent with eyeslits. On the way we
picked up a magnificent figure in white silk, with a watch-chain
and a polished stick, who was travelling as a witness in a murder
trial. The journey was indescribable; the dust, the inclines, the
jolts, the dry and the wet riverbeds that we crossed, the swerves,
the wooden wheel-chocks for the many emergencies, and the sheer
continuous battering, will be familiar to all travellers on Afghan
tracks, but no one else can imagine them to be as bad as they
were. By this time I had bought a turban with a long and elegant
tail, so I was able to keep the worst of the dust out of my mouth
and nose, but the journey was slow, gruelling and very long. We
drove through quiet valleys where nomads were grazing their
flocks, and where the women seemed far freer than any village
women. Some of them were at work weaving the black tentcloth
they use for their small travelling tents. The children wore long
rich frocks and Persian caps.

We passed below many bluffs and up and down some vast
hillsides like the dreary flanks of Ben Nevis. High overhanging
outcrops of rock are believed to be haunted by djinns. The
whirling columns of dust or sand that move here and there across
plains are said to be dust-devils. These superstitions are universal
in Afghanistan, but in Ghor a peasant who found an ancient coin
would often be afraid to touch it because it was magical, and
belonged to the ancient unbelievers and black magicians. At one
point, not more than an hour or so above Shahrak, we saw a
valley with a whole cluster of forts and quite an important castle
guarding its entrance; more than once we saw big ruined
caravanserais, square, substantial encastled buildings of mudbrick, with fine gate-towers; we stopped close to one at the modern
teahouse that has replaced it. It is impossible to know the date of
these ruins without exploring them thoroughly; perhaps nothing
that we saw was pre-Islamic, although at a certain moment I
thought I observed squared stones. There is a broad valley above
Shahrak, dotted with mounds; nothing found here has ever been
earlier than about the eleventh century. Some of the mounds are
the remains of settlements, with the ruins of clay castles sticking
up on them like broken teeth, some seem to be tombs. They all
appear to yield the same characteristic Islamic red pottery laced

with black paint. It has a misleading neolithic look but is also found at Ghazni. There is no record or memory of any Greek or Kushan coin ever being found. We saw a newly robbed mound, and it seems that in the last ten years the local antiquities of this region have started to fetch big prices in Herat.* When archaeology arrives, it will be too late in this territory, as it has been elsewhere.

Shahrak seemed an odious place only redeemed by its smallness. Bruce was in a battered condition and I was by this time hardly able to walk. In the teahouse some young men deliberately tortured a quail; at first we tried to buy it but the more we protested the worse the torture became. We found a friend at last at the meteorological station, a grossly ugly building in a pleasant, ragged flower-garden, and this became our headquarters. I was feverish and dazed and took little interest in the world, except to tell my fortune for tomorrow by opening a page of Horace at random; what I found was 'But now if I want I can go as far as Tarentum on a croptailed mule, with bag-sores on his flanks and saddle-sores on his shoulders.'[5] In the morning we were called at five by three horses, a boy and a soldier. In a groggy and unshaven condition, but fortified by Horace and by being told Jam was only eight hours away, I mounted a skewbald pony called Avlach, and the boy was lifted on behind. With very few and very short stops, the ride took fourteen hours. Fever in my case intensified the qualities of the landscape and apart from being sick at midday and arriving stupefied with fatigue at night, so that I remember wanting to weep at the last tiny stream we had to cross, I enjoyed that day very much. It was a perfect ride for a petromaniac.

We turned north up a stream from the Shahrak valley and soon came into an idyllic world; we were facing a composition of rock, waterfall and tree like a Chinese drawing, and when we climbed above it we saw a series of fine, fresh-looking goat drawings on the rock-face. No one knows who makes or made these drawings; the villagers say the nomads, and this is probable enough. They occur in many parts of Afghanistan where nomadic herdsmen pass, and there is no need to suppose they are extremely old. Whoever was responsible, these were crisp, formal, observant drawings and there is no age of history or of prehistory they would

* The antiquities sold in Herat in summer of 1969 included a fine Achaemenid bronze jug with a goat handle and a quantity of prehistoric material. The prices in the best supplied shops were those of the international art market.

have disgraced. It was soon after this that my girth broke as we were climbing rocks, the saddle slipped backwards and the boy slipped right off. Fortunately he was not much hurt, but what with lameness in one horse and a strange pecking habit in another, and the agonizing shortness of the longest possible Afghan stirrups, we found it better and quicker to ride and walk alternately; I found I was too weak to walk uphill so I mostly rode, and fortunately for me my pony behaved better than the others. We came to one place where all the horses had to plunge through fifty yards of water three feet deep between rock walls, walking on slippery pebbles. Avlach went into this adventure with rather too much enthusiasm, but I was thankful it was Bruce and not I who had the pecking horse.

We rode several times through the middle of what we took to be nomad camps; most of them were simply summer grazing camps only a few miles from their home villages, but sometimes the people turned out to be true nomads. At one camp we were entertained with bread and *mast* and green tea, at another the horses waded steadily through a sea of angry and savage dogs, but it seems that the superiority of rider to dog is a presupposition of Afghan life, and not one of the dogs attacked a horse, nor did the horses ever shy, except once from camels and once or twice from the abysses below their feet on high mountain paths. They did show signs of unhappiness very high up, but since the main pass was at 9,500 feet that is hardly surprising. We climbed up and up through immensely long valleys into a region of vaster mountain solitudes than I had ever seen before, and then down again past heavy bluffs of rock the size of Acrocorinth, marked with every kind of massive weathering and scoriation. In the early afternoon we were crossing a grassy plain between bluffs and later we climbed again into John Buchan or Rider Haggard country, up a steep cleft between purple and deep pink rocks. It had been cloudy and the distant mountains had been black and grey, but when the sun broke out they played like a school of whales, light silver and lightly gilt. The flowers were awe-inspiring, particularly the thistles very high in the mountains. It was on this day that Bruce collected the seeds of wild tulips.

Night fell as we came down from the hills past the last stones and prayer-flags into the Jam valley. Everyone was tired and I was on my last legs; just as the light went we saw water pouring deliciously in small streams through the apricot groves, and fires blazing in the courtyards. We lay down at once on a rug and pillows outside a house where we seemed to be expected. I remember smoking a pipe of tobacco in a haze of content, a blanket was put over us. I had difficulty in speaking, but cursed vehemently when I was woken and shifted indoors. The next morning apart from stiff legs I was practically well. The walls of the valley are very tall and we woke to a square of window full of blue sky and mountainside fretted with apricot leaves. The soldier leapt in through this window like a large dog to explain that the sun was up. We breakfasted on tea we carried ourselves, and on apricots fresh from the tree, washed and presented by our soldier on a silver tray. A grove of big apricot trees full of fruit is lighter and airier than an orange grove, and in its own landscape an apricot tree is as fine as an overgrown lemon tree. There were yellow heaps of drying apricots on the roofs of the houses, and piles of fruit where it had just been harvested under the trees. We walked downstream two or three miles to where the Jam river discharges into the deep waters of the Hari Rud; the point where the rivers meet is the Jam minaret.

The stream of the Hari Rud is thirty yards across, very fast and chalky green: the mountains are like cool clinkers; the minaret is a tall, elegant, shadow-cut, biscuit-coloured pencil magnificently inlaid with turquoise inscriptions, built where its muezzin could best fill the valleys with echoes. Seen from below, the obsessional strength of its detail and the depth of its shadows have a mind-blowing power; seen from above it is a miracle of simplicity and proportion with the rocks. It stands on a spur of gravel where the Hari Rud emerges for a few hundred yards from a labyrinth of ravines. There are the ruins of a bridge beside it, and the river can be forded a short way upstream, although we saw a man and horse nearly carried away from the ford, and I know by having swum in it that the river near the minaret is dangerously strong and deep.[6] There are the ruins of a castle on the opposite bank, high up in the rocks and very badly eroded. The paradox of the existence of a royal minaret among these appalling cliffs and desolate rock-refuges cannot be resolved unless the stronghold of the high valleys was the centre of the kingdom of Ghor. It was a defensive position and it protected nothing but itself. When we saw it later from the air on the flight from Chagcheran to Herat, it was obvious that the mountains to the north of the minaret are extremely rough and there is no easy pass through them, nor would it be at all easy to follow the Hari Rud either upstream or downstream.

The mountain where the minaret is has the local name of Free mountain. We were told in the village of Jam of another site, with some castles and a ruined town where seven towers are still standing, as far away again as Shahrak, but across the river and downstream. Even more interesting but even less reliable, we heard of a place three or four days away called *Malminj* on the Murghab river, which lies between Maimana and Chagcheran; the story is that close by the river there are men and lions carved in relief or in outline on two stones, one on each side of the water. This report, which we heard from the headman and mullah of Jam, might refer to anything or nothing; it was not an eye-witness account. But if the carvings really exist it is possible, among many other possibilities, that they are the monumental boundary stones of the Persian Empire. If this were more than a tenuous conjecture, it would be worth mounting a special expedition to find out. But we were also told on the same occasion that the temple of King Solomon used to stand on the mountain next to the minaret, and that it had a platform where the king's guests used to go to admire the view of the minaret. In the same way I was once told at Kardamyli in southern Greece that some rock cuttings on the edge of the ancient fortress there were the site of a kiosk, a pavilion of pleasure, where the King of Kardamyli used to invite King Menelaos of Sparta to take coffee and admire the view of the village.

We spent the evening resting, in the farm at Jam where we had first arrived; Bruce gave out medicines and cooked an elaborate meal of rice and chicken stewed in apricots. There were three or four kinds of apricots which at that time we could distinguish, though I have now forgotten the difference. At sunset the pater familias went up on to his rooftop to face the dying sun for the time of evening prayer; even the Kuchi in their tents observed the moment of sunset and even the porters on a frosted mountainside at thirteen thousand feet observed the moment of dawn; midday was less regular, but buses and lorries always stopped somewhere around noon for the passengers to pray. We were called the next morning at four; already an old lady was smoking a pipe over the tea-fire. The business of departure, of which all the Afghans make more than they do of arrival, took some longish time; we were sorry to leave our smooth clay room, with its nobly proportioned niches and wooden roof, but I was more flea-bitten, probably from an old carpet, on the first night than I have ever been before or since. It is interesting that Horace and Basho, perhaps except for Homer the two best travel-writers in the whole of history,[7] both write well about sleepless nights, diseases of the stomach, the howling of dogs, and the monotonous aggressiveness of fleas and mosquitoes. The horses were in worse, but we in rather better condition. We wound upwards among waterfalls and balsam poplars to the whispering prayer-flags and the stony track.

The soldier took us by a new route, which took exactly fourteen and a half hours. We saw vultures, buzzards and hawks of every kind, a yellow, red-headed bird, swarms of blue dragonflies over a reed-bed, and once, I think, a pair of marsh harriers. Blue had swallowed the whaleschools of thunder-stricken mountains of a few days ago; herds were moving on the Shakespearean downs like birds or flies; it was a long, hot ride. We came down in the end a few miles higher up the Shahrak valley than the place where we left it, and reached the meteorological station at dusk. It was strange to move back through the same sober pre-road and pre-railway landscape without any touch of fever in oneself. It was like revisiting a dream by daylight and seeing that it really existed. People had no European sense of the measurement of time or of distance. The soldier had no exact idea where we were or how long the journey would take, and the people who had told us Jam was eight hours from Shahrak turned out to be very surprised to see us back so quickly; they had never supposed we would get there inside a day. It is said to be possible to arrive by jeep or Land-Rover in four hours, but the road, which we saw several times, is extremely demanding and dangerous and excessively lonely. The long ride or walk is the best method, but it should be remembered that a traveller on foot is less safe from dogs, and whatever difficulties we had with the horses I at least was sorry to be back in a lorry to Chagcheran. We bought seats in the front cabin, which as usual in Asia was a home-made wooden construction that creaked and quivered like a galleon in a storm.

Chagcheran was waiting for us with its inspiriting desert horizon and its swarm of stars. The river above the gorges reassembles its voice and speaks more fully at night. Next day from the air it was a chalk-green angry snake locked among wild bends and pathless ravines. The minaret looked tiny, but perfectly proportioned to the mountains around it, just as it is from the ground. We flew on between high cliffs towards Herat.

CHAPTER
6

Herat is almost as far west as you can get and still remain inside
Afghanistan. Its fine buildings are closely related to Iranian
buildings; some of the finest of Persian miniatures were made for
the library of a prince of Herat,[1] and Babur was very well
entertained here by some luxurious and hard-drinking cousins in
the same generation; later alas they lost their kingdoms. Some of
the best of the great architecture of Herat was destroyed by British
engineers in the refortification of 1885, when the Shah of Iran was
believed to have his eye on eastern Afghanistan; the city's
defences had not been put in order since the great siege of 1837–8,
when Herat had been saved by a stray Anglo-Irish lieutenant.
British policy was to exclude Russian trade, and keeping out the
Persians would help to keep out their Russian friends; Afghanistan
was to be the bastion of India.

It is a sign of the crazy disorganization of the British that in
1837–8 when the Indian Army lieutenant was defending Herat
there was an Indian Army lieutenant-colonel fighting for the
Persians on the other side.[2] The history of Herat in the nineteenth
century is fascinating, but it is no part of this book.[3] Lieutenant
Pottinger is important only because of the Victorian degree of his
personal courage and confidence; to have pulled down a great
complex of buildings which were among the masterpieces of
Islamic art in order to make a city defensible is another matter.
Perhaps that is the difference between 1837 and 1885. Colonel Sir
Thomas Holdich, who sounds like an eye-witness, describes the
demolition with ruthless professionalism.[4] About such an appalling devastation there is nothing one can say so many years
afterwards. What was destroyed was a vast college and place of
worship; nine minarets were left standing, but three of them have
fallen in earthquakes in 1931 and 1951.

What interested me in prospect about Herat was that it existed
in the ninth century B.C., before the flowering of Persia, when the

Iranian tribes were pushed eastwards by the Assyrian Empire, and a tribe called the Hairava settled in what was already called the oasis of Hara or Hera.[5] After three centuries this territory became a frontier province of the Persian Empire; we know that Herat was taken by Alexander the Great from Bessos, satrap of Aria, and that Alexander rebuilt and refortified it.[6] The castle of Herat as it now stands is a Timurid building on Seljuk Turkish foundations, standing on a mound which certainly contains Alexander's fortress, and in all probability a Persian fortress and the satrap's palace. The modern ground level of the mound seems from the rather passing inspection which is all one dared to make to represent a late classical occupation; heaven alone knows what treasures of archaeological evidence lie underneath it; we must hope that the future may reveal them. At present the ragged walls and towers of the castle are a military area, and they have an important national significance for modern Afghanistan; Herat castle is represented on the national flag. The castle has never been excavated or scientifically described. It carries some magnificent Timurid decoration in turquoise and cobalt on its walls, the remnant of a panegyric on Shah Rukh, who was Tamburlaine's youngest son, written by his court historian;[7] I have seen a small pot which a friend bought in a Herat antique shop; it is of no particular value or beauty, but it was made not much after the first century A.D., and it is almost certain to have come from the Herat mound.

We flew down to Herat at about mid-morning and put up at the Park Hotel. The best thing about this hotel is the arrival. One clatters along a dusty road in a smart little pony-trap, its harness heavily decorated with sprays of red and blue pompoms; one passes a small, lonely policeman in the centre of a vast, deserted square, directing two donkeys and a bicycle with a majesty and ferocity more appropriate to the Champs Elysées, and a baroque fountain with cast iron horseheads and no water; one proceeds down a huge avenue lined with conifers dominated by a new Russian art nouveau or Hollywood Moorish official building conceived in a spirit of abandon, and one turns into a quiet, Persian garden containing a substantial Victorian hotel. The connoisseur of Paghman and of Balkh and of the vanished railway by the Kabul Museum with trees growing out of its carriages will recognize in these streets the endearing grandiosity of Amanullah, and the hotel still holds reserves of comic relief untapped even by

Robert Byron, who stayed here when he was writing the *Road to Oxiana*.

The atmosphere is one of tubercular green marble and comfortable chairs, one can buy beer and fruit-juice and Russian bottled peas from a glass case in the hall, and one of the refrigerators works, although the other by some fault of wiring makes things hotter instead of colder. The bath had better not be described, but the staff were numerous and charming, and I highly recommend this hotel to travellers of decent sensibility. I personally liked it so much that I almost refused to go out, and stayed there reading and writing, so that I missed an expedition on which Bruce visited and photographed an important and most beautiful fifteenth-century building near the frontier that no European scholar has ever reached before. Sedentary habits die hard, and I was drinking tomato-juice and trying to finish a poem; we were both satisfied with the day.

The fifteenth-century ruins that do survive in Herat[8] suggest it must once have rivalled Meshed, which I have never seen, and even the sophisticated glories of Isfahan. There are four tall minarets dotted around a dusty pine grove which have the pure and surprising beauty of lighthouses. One of them has scalloped hanging niches high up under its collar, of a dark, brilliant indigo outlined in turquoise and speckled with formalized white and yellow flowers. They all have decorations of kufic script and floriated lozenges something like the Indian motifs familiar in England from their persistence in Paisley textile patterns.[9]

The greatest monument in this pine grove is a flamboyant mausoleum, which has unfortunately been very badly restored. It has a ribbed dome which is now bald-headed but was once turquoise picked out with delicate geometric patterns in cobalt. Like the minarets it was part of the religious college founded here by Queen Gawhar-Shad in 1417, and it used to be believed to be her own and her son's tomb. But the queen's own mausoleum, a building very like this one only in comparatively fine condition, is almost certainly the one that Bruce visited and photographed near the frontier. This queen was the wife of Shah Rukh; she reigned for over fifty years, survived the death of her husband in 1447, and was in the end murdered in 1457 when she was over eighty years old. Shah Rukh was the typical youngest son of an overwhelming father: his and his queen's importance as lovers of peace and patrons of art can hardly be exaggerated, but alas, the qualities of sweetness and light pay diminishing returns to great dynasties. The next generation saw one of the greatest princely libraries there has ever been, and the construction of a splendid observatory at Samarkand. The library was collected by the queen's favourite son, Prince Baisunghur, a poet and a fine calligrapher who died of drink at the age of thirty-seven; the observatory was built by Ulugh Bey, her eldest son, who was defeated and killed after a reign of three years. Within a lifetime, Herat had fallen to the Uzbeks.

Inside the mausoleum substantial fragments remain of a white marble balustrade carved in relief with an intricate and deeply cut pattern of interlacing stems of leaves, and some thin slabs of a darker stone with sharp inscriptions. The gravestones of the princes are made of a dark green marble; I am not sure where this stone comes from. The dome is stuccoed and painted in elaborate detail, lapis lazuli blue, gold, brick-red and white; it has a cool, speckled effect and we sat there a long time. By the time we had come out the minarets seemed even stranger. Two of the six that survive stand a little farther out of the city; it was incredible that all these glittering pillars and the mausoleum were part of one complex of buildings. One of the minarets showed no bare brick at all; it was decorated in a series of drums outlined with white bands, with turquoise and cobalt stars; it wore a complete decorative sheath like the scales of an Inigo Jones mermaid. The strange and brilliant towers made the sky look pale. From a distance, the four minarets in the grove look like big brick cigarettes stormed by swarms of cobalt and turquoise butterflies. I believe they can be seen for forty or fifty miles across the desert.

The covered bazaars of Herat are an Edwardian provincial version of an ancient *agora*, and there is no better way of understanding what a Hellenistic shopping centre was like, the division of trades, the social visits from shop to shop, the bargaining, the crowding and the foreign riches. The commonplaces of Herat become exotic in London, and the reverse is also true. Bruce once spent hours of inquiry in this town following the rumour of an ancient gilt or golden crown for sale in the jewellery bazaar; it turned out to be a British hussar's brass helmet. In the dark shops near the castle you can watch silk-weavers working in the corners of a room the whole centre of which is filled up by an enormous rotating, rattling wooden shuttle; I longed to ask who they were, was it a Herat trade now, or were they Jews or

Armenians, but the work was so concentrated one hardly dared to interrupt with what might have been an offensive question. A few doors away the inside of a shop had been turned over to a dusty, blindfolded camel walking round and round for ever to turn a huge stone oil-grinder full of sesame seed. At dusk we had wandered a long way, there was a sudden, light noise of drumming in a back street, and a procession of veiled women swept through the alleys about some unexplained religious business, I think a birth or a marriage. On that day I bought a bowl made in the Gardner porcelain factory in Moscow, painted with Chinese peonies and chrysanthemums, and inscribed with a Turkish or Persian poem in light blue lettering round the inner rim. It must have been made about 1820 for the Turkestan market, and had obviously been in use ever since.* I gave it to Maurice Bowra, and I believe it is still in his memorial library at Wadham.

We began to hear disturbing rumours: first a bus of Pakistanis who asked us about a report of the border being closed and nine hour delays even if one got across, then when I asked in the hotel for cold water the manager talking evasively, 'the well only twelve metre, is better drinking tea and drinking from clean thing'. With tea that morning they brought an empty water glass. It was cholera, but no one would mention the word. At lunch in another hotel, the waiter said inconsequently 'this is good water'. Finally at half past four in the afternoon in a less respectable café I heard there had been eighteen deaths that day in the bazaar. At the Park Hotel they said no, not so many, only six, but that had been the number at one o'clock. It is extremely hard to find out the truth about cholera epidemics; every country says it is the fault of another, but the disease would not in fact spread if the same filthy conditions were not more or less universal. Some years ago when there was a really terrible outbreak in Loghar, I have heard that the government sealed off the province and refused entrance to a United Nations medical mission, simply denying that any outbreak had taken place. I wish I could say that I found such a story hard to believe, or that it was the only story of its kind we came across.

We decided to leave Herat almost at once to escape from the epidemic, but we went first through the roaring, bewildered wind to

* In 1969 Gardner porcelain was not yet uncommon or expensive in Herat, where it was evidently still in common use, but it was beginning to command big prices in Kabul. Five years ago only one antique shop existed in Kabul; there are now at least a hundred.

Gazurgah, a holy place with the right of sanctuary on a hillside in the desert above Herat. There was a blue and white haze over the desert and the Herat oasis showed up as very dark green. Even in the inner court at Gazurgah, the most sacred and peaceful place, the wind made wild gusts and wails. Outside this court stands a luminescent, wind-startled pine tree of knotty age and great size, like a pine tree in a Chinese drawing. It streamed light and energy, and roared very loudly. The centre of the shrine is the tomb of an eleventh-century poet and philosopher, but it was rebuilt and its fine brick-roofed well was first built by Shah Rukh. The saint's tomb stands in a shabby green-painted wooden kiosk with an old hollow tree sprouting out of it, peppered all over with nails. A blind old man was chanting the Koran in a corner of the courtyard.

Everywhere in Afghanistan and Persia there are these old, blind singers. There was one at Isfahan with the thinness and fragility of a very old cat, being led into the sun by a boy, and at Istalif, near Kabul, we saw a boy leading a blind old man through the paths of a dense garden to what was obviously his favourite rose tree; the boy picked a thick cabbage rose and held it for the old man to sniff. At Gazurgah there was a boy asleep in the giant stone basin Shah Rukh had used for giving away sherbet; probably he belonged to one of the old men. We ventured into disused side-chapels full of tombs and chaff, with coloured drawings of naive flowering trees peeling off the domes. A bald, white-bearded man who looked like a scholar was poring over a book in his cell; the scholarship of mystical religions is not a tradition into which one can easily intrude, since even more than other kinds of learning it includes a certain deliberate ignorance and darkness; but the thought of such an old man is not to be dismissed.

The most striking single thing I saw in the few days we were at Herat was a small garden of a few ragged sunflowers in the haze and dust of a big square near the fullers' market; we passed that way on a last long ride to see the strings of camels and small groups of donkeys and cattle that pass over the ancient bridge called the Pul-i Malan. Babur visited this bridge in 1506, and the date of its construction was already obscure in the fifteenth century; to English eyes it has a Henrician or an Elizabethan look. At any rate, such a long, graceful mass of heavy brickwork piers could scarcely be much earlier than the fourteenth century, and since it is supposed to have been built by a woman, it is probably Mongol work.[10] The bridge is several miles out of Herat; at this point the river is clear, but scanty and divided, and punctuated by gravel wastes and dragonflies. It marks the ancient route from western central Asia to India and to the sea; there was no direct route south through the deserts of Seistan and Baluchistan, but by Kandahar and Quetta it was possible for caravans to reach the Indus.

We left that night for Kandahar in a long black taxi by the modern bridge, along the asphalt road that travels eastwards through Kandahar and Ghazni to Kabul and down to Jellalabad and the Khyber Pass. A police road-block had just been set up to check cholera vaccinations; it was soon going to be difficult to leave Herat in any direction; the border stayed closed for several weeks and a quarantine camp had opened on the Iranian side. A German boy who became hysterical and tried to crash the border was shot by the guards; an American who took photographs of this incident was beaten up with rifle-butts.

We drove all night through the desert under more and clearer stars than even above Chagcheran, one in particular like a distant rag of paper on fire. We slept in our seats, more or less, and woke to a loud bang and a skidding motion at about two in the morning, when we blew a tyre. Bruce saw small desert animals, racoon-like creatures and foxes and some hares, but I saw nothing until dawn, which was a long thin lemon line, and then suddenly mountainous rocks swimming into view here and there on both sides of the road. A deep blush came and went in the sky, and the sun came up through a thick yellow haze; at first it was a pale circle but it soon hardened to the usual blazing gilt rivet. Outside Kandahar, where the mountains close in on the road, we passed the site of a big fortress, with older ruined clay walls and a number of mounds.

Near here in the summer of 1880 a British general with three thousand or so men fought the battle of Maiwand against an Afghan army of 25,000 men advancing on Kandahar from Herat. The British were badly cut to pieces and a thousand men were killed outright; Kandahar was saved by General Roberts, who marched a British army from Kabul, 313 miles in three weeks, the first 225 of them in eight days.* It may well be asked what on

---

* Not without casualties from exhaustion and dysentery. As usual it was the Indian 'followers' who suffered worst. Roberts himself was so fevered and exhausted by this march that on the last days he could scarcely walk and was quite unable to ride. After the victory, which was won by charges of Highland Ghurka infantry, he became Lord Roberts of Kandahar; Kandahar was abandoned in 1881 after a violent debate in the House of Lords which reads like something invented by Brecht

earth the British Army were up to in Afghanistan at this time; the naked truth is that they wanted to push British India to the Hindu Kush: the result of this policy was succinctly analysed at the time by Lord Hartington, who wrote in a despatch that 'as a result of two successful campaigns, of the employment of an enormous force, and of the expenditure of large sums of money, all that has yet been accomplished has been the disintegration of the State which it was desired to see strong, friendly and independent'.[11]

At Kandahar it was ferociously hot; the year was moving on and this was the first time we had met temperatures of around a hundred and ten or upwards. Modern Kandahar stands at the mid-point of a fertile and abundantly watered plain, between the mountains and the river Arghestan; the ancient city[12] and the fortress lay on the eastern slopes of a long spine of rock to the south of the road at the western approaches to the modern settlement. It commands the passage between Kabul and Herat and the road south by Quetta to Pakistan and India. The name Kandahar is probably the only genuine relic of a Greek place-name to have survived in Afghanistan; it comes from the Arabic form of Alexander's name, Iskander: the Greek name of this city was Arachosian Alexandria. As a Greek site, it has the important distinction that two of the long Buddhist inscriptions of King Asoka were found here, the first only in the early sixties, by a young Afghan schoolmaster; there seems to have been an attempt by a German doctor to smuggle one of these important documents out of the country; fortunately he was stopped at the frontier and induced to present it to the Kabul Museum.[13]

It consists of fourteen lines in Greek and eight in Aramaic; the Greek is perfect, with a strong Hellenistic philosophic resonance, and the lettering, which is scratchy but more or less regular, belongs to the third century B.C.[14] The mixture of Aramaic and Greek is not surprising, since double language inscriptions occur even on the coinage of Demetrios II who reigned as his father's viceroy at Kapisa not long afterwards, but the penetration of Buddhism so early into a Greek society has astonishing implications. It means that the Greeks in Afghanistan may some of them have become Buddhists and have affected the development of Buddhism. By the end of the second century, the Greek ambassador of a Greek king was inscribing a column at Besnagar in Brahmi and quoting an Indian epic, but about the same time a Buddhist Greek governor in Swat inscribed a vase in the Kharosthi script with the details of the foundation of a Buddhist stupa.[15] Gandaros, according to Hesychios, was the Greek name of an Indian bull-god.[16] In the Greek levels at Sirkap (Taxila) there was no Buddhist sculpture, although it was found in the later levels, and the Bhir mound at Taxila, which was abandoned in 189 B.C., produced none at all; but this was bound to be so, because Buddhist sculpture, as opposed to the religious cult of relics embodied in the great stupas, had not started in the Greek period.[17] We have no easy archaeological method of measuring the first influence of Buddhism on the Greeks or of the Greeks on Buddhism;[18] two of the few pieces of evidence are the Kandahar Asoka decrees, written only two centuries after the death of Buddha.[19]

At the north end of the long spine of rock which shelters the ancient site and where the Buddhist inscription was found, there is a strange place called the Chelzina, where forty-nine steps have been cut in a very steep and irregular flight up the mountainside to a platform levelled in the rock-face, with a recessed and inscribed arched niche cut from the cliff; it carries a list of the victories of Babur, and another of the victories of Akbar. The strange thing about it is the fine workmanship of the niche, the great size of the platform, and by comparison with these the crudity and irregularity of the steps. They recall rather strongly the rock-cut steps leading to the altar on the peak of the Areopagos hill at Athens, and it seems perfectly possible they may originally have led not to a fine renaissance arch in the rock-face, which seems peculiar and out of place up so many steps and is certainly a unique monument, but to an altar. The niche in fact shows markings in the rock that go deeper inwards than the architectural carving of Babur's time, and once again suggest some different, earlier, perhaps cave-like niche that he destroyed. It is possible that the steps and the platform were made to be the setting of a Kushan royal statue like the platform on top of the terraced and stepped hillside at Surkh Kotal,[20] but Kushan workmanship, at least at such a site as Surkh Kotal, was as fine as Babur's, and perhaps nothing corresponds so well to the contradictions of the Chelzina as the cult-altar of a provincial Greek community.

In blazing heat we walked round the ancient city. It was almost too hot to record anything and far too hot to think consecutively. I noticed little more than the classic form and extent of the city, the wanness and the strength of the walls,* and the enormous height and mass of the central mound, which is a solid detritus of mudbrick about sixty feet high; also the birdnotes and the cabbage-patches. We saw a rich abundance of fragmentary pottery, some of which was certainly early Islamic† but none earlier, and a child came up from the fields to show us two bronze coins of the same period. It was interesting to see how few genuine Greek coins were for sale in almost any Afghan city, and in spite of all that has been said and can be inferred about Roman trade, the number of Roman coins found so far in the whole country is very small indeed.[21] We retired from the hot weight of the sun to drink a local Coca-Cola, which tasted like effervescent hair-tonic. Donkeys were rolling in the dust or leaning weakly against walls. The British excavations of the seventies in Kandahar were still in the future.

Apart from its classical ruins we both found Kandahar more or less disagreeable. For one thing, it is the centre of the drug trade, and everywhere we went we were pestered to buy hash. We had seen enough of this at the Behzad café in Herat; at Kandahar it was a big industry and even small children tried to sell us hash in its various forms. In liquid form it looks and smells worse than methylated spirits. Every kind of smuggling device was for sale, strings of hash beads, hash belts, hash-heeled shoes and for all I know hash codpieces. We were told as if it were a funny story about an Australian boy who was taken to a garden in Kandahar where they grow different varieties of hash in different patches: he was kept continuously high for eight or nine days and then found himself in the street with no money.

The sun had been streaming into the hotel bedroom. That afternoon the water in the water-bottle by my bed was as hot as tea, and the metal of the bedframe was too hot to touch. I did my best to think about the frosty Caucasus, and about the *gelidi Scythae*, icicles tinkling like metal in their beards. In the evening there was a faint, foggy coolness in the air and we tried the effect of going for a walk. We went to the fields below the town past fetid ditches of black water in which children were swimming, and met a small boy of eight with a hawk on his wrist. He pointed

---

* Roberts found the walls of Kandahar thirty feet high and fifteen feet thick and was infuriated that the garrison had considered the possibility of its being taken.

† Some red pottery with white bars, and a very early white with dashes of blue glaze.

at a row of black and white pigeons shifting their feet uneasily on a balcony above his head and proudly and gleefully explained that his hawk lived on them; he waved his hand in love and magic in front of the hawk's eyes. In another street we saw a wolfcub on a string. In the gardens, which smelt abominably of human ordure, stood a tiny reed hut entirely overgrown with a mass of intertwining flowers like convolvulus, inside it a dark-faced wisp of a gardener was putting the last touches to a gigantic formal bouquet of tightly packed marigolds. I believe the track we were on then was the ancient road, and if so Alexander must have used it. The sky above old Kandahar was lime-yellow; the sun disappeared with a hiss, like red-hot iron into water; we went to bed with much the same sound.

From Kandahar to Ghazni is not a long way by car, but by coach it takes a long time. The bus we travelled in was a Little Ease, and the lurching, the spitting and the smell of crude petrol made it worse. I have long legs and there was no room for them, and when I observed angrily to Bruce that the Afghan next to me was smothering me in spittle all he said was, 'Well, why don't you spit back?' The only thing to be said about that journey is never again. The road was more or less level, through long scrubby plains lined with low mountains. We passed a number of breakdowns and a recently crashed petrol lorry; sometimes I saw moving groves of camels and butter-yellow crops. At night, camels wander onto the road and get run down by lorries.

Ghazni was wrapped in the deep dreams of provincial peace. It clings to the skirts of an enormous mound below big castle walls with houses peering over and through them; a mile or so to the east on the edge of a desert plain is the site of the medieval palace of the Ghaznevid kings with the remains of two great triumphal minarets of decorated brick, and about two miles farther east again is a village with the enshrined tomb of Sultan Mahmoud of Ghazni, and the Italian excavation museum containing the material from the palace.[22] The whole area between the small palace and the enormous fortress of Ghazni itself is of great archaeological interest, but even the part of it quite close beside the palace excavation is now used as a military and tank training area, the dumps and undulations of the surface which are characteristic of an ancient site being peculiarly suitable to this purpose. Even worse, there is a huge barracks with tanksheds and gunsheds which extends the military area three-quarters of a mile eastwards from Ghazni castle, the whole of which of course it includes.

Ghazni may have been and probably was a Greek city; perhaps it was the Gazaka or Gauzaka listed by Ptolemy among the cities and villages of the Paropamisadai.[22] It was certainly a great Buddhist city; its monastery and castle were recorded by Chinese pilgrims in the seventh century and by the end of the tenth it was a very important Islamic trading centre for Indian caravans;[23] it had become Islamic by conquest before the end of the ninth century. On the plain south of Ghazni, Mahmoud, who became king in 997, mustered his elephants and his armies for seventeen annual raids into India. We shall never know much about the early history of the settlement unless the army moves out of the castle; there if anywhere we might find the same kind of story as lies buried under the mound of Herat, which is no mightier. The arrival of the Russians has not added to the arguments for optimism.

The Buddhist stupa and monastery stand on a low, isolated rocky hill in the desert or plain about a mile south of the main road and due south of the palace; this site was being excavated by Italian archaeologists. The clarity of the reports, the importance of the results, and the scientific and practical skill of the excavation could hardly be bettered.[24] But on this first visit to Ghazni we were mesmerized by the fineness of the Islamic palace, with its small scale, its nudes and its richly cut marble, and by the tomb of Mahmoud; his shrine stands in a ragged garden where we were discovered by an official.[25] 'Good afternoon,' he said, 'how are you, I think you are very fine. I think' (looking at me, half asleep among the rose bushes) 'he is very tired. Will you have tea?' In the village a stream was running through an ancient lion spout, with the other dismembered pieces of what was once a square monumental fountain lying not far away.

In the museum we saw a relief carving of the Sultan's long-skirted guard, who looked like Turks, and a number of signs of the closeness of Persia: a lion with two bodies and only one head, and a big relief slab with winged queen-faced lions and dog-faced dolphins, winged tigers chasing winged deer, a griffin, a peacock and an elephant. The animals were in octagons and the whole design suggested a Byzantine or Sassanian textile pattern copied in stone. The antiquities of Ghazni are as rich in quality as they are in variety, and they too deserve a book of their own. The colossal wealth of the ancient indigo trade passed through Ghazni and Kabul; it is almost possible to forgive the Sultans their wanton luxury, their religious imbalance, their depredations and their slave-trading, for the sake of the contents of the Ghazni Museum, but perhaps it would be just to suppose kings were no more related to the essentials of art and commerce than bad weather to the harvest; the positive elements in the movement of civilization in that time were more closely connected to the indigo trade than they were to the slave trade or to the rise and fall of these disgusting dynasties.[26]

The two minarets near the palace, once thought to commemorate Indian victories, in their present state appear as lesser predecessors of the minaret at Jam; the mosques they belonged to have perished, and their upper storeys; they were supplied with somewhat ridiculous roofs by Abdur Rahman, in order to prevent their falling down altogether; they still have a fine, honeycombed and biscuit-coloured brick texture, but there is now a plan to fence them round to keep out children, which will be the final indignity. Fortunately, one at least was photographed when it was taller, apparently by P. V. Luke, a field telegraph officer at Kabul under Roberts in 1879. I do not know whether he took part in the march on Kandahar.* If I am to be truthful I must confess it was with expectant pleasure that I turned my back on the military chaos surrounding the palace and the two towers, which are impressive monuments after all, to walk across the plain to Tepe Sardar,[27] the Buddhist site on the isolated hill.

It was a hot afternoon walk which later I took many times, but the first time seemed the longest, and at the end we found a notice prohibiting admission, which since the place was in full view of the soldiery we thought it prudent to obey. Weeks afterwards, when Bruce had gone home, I was lucky enough to spend a few days with the Italian archaeologists at work there at the beginning of the season's dig; eventually I was ferreted out by an Afghan policeman as an unauthorized foreigner and sent back to Kabul; he explained that only important persons could visit the dig, and to show what an important person was, he produced some visiting cards, including one of my own which I gave him when he was being difficult during our first visit. We also went through a strange interrogation in which I thought he was asking if I arrived in a bullock cart, but he turned

* Communication on that campaign was by heliograph. Mrs Luke presented her husband's photographs to the Embassy library at Kabul in 1933.

out to be saying black car, meaning blue. I only lost a day or two by being turned out, and since the agonies of negotiating with the cultural department of the Afghan foreign office are to be avoided whenever possible, I made no attempt to get reinstated, but meanwhile I had been lyrically happy for nearly a week, which is something in this world.

The site was a stupa on a hilltop surrounded by smaller monuments and by a monastery. Its importance lies in the high quality of what has been found there and the success with which the unbaked clay sculptures, lying in hundreds of fragments face downwards among a mass of ruined, unbaked claybrick walls, have been disengaged from their chaos. The central stupa which crowned the hill had been despoiled of its dedications at an early period, so there exist no coins or inscriptions to date it by, but the lines of the monument itself are magnificently crisp, and the row of smaller stupas beside it is very richly decorated. Some of them float above the ground on ornamental lotus leaves, and this kind of stupa has in fact been found full-sized in Tibet. They look like small multi-storeyed castles of Buddha-covered cornices, serrated in a complicated irregular geometry, mounted by tall flights of terraced steps and resting on a flowering lotus. A Buddha on an elephant throne was certainly modelled by someone who knew elephants; they have round button eyes and waving trunks and huge ears wrinkled like big leaves. The modelling of the relief figure belongs to the final and most mobile style of Buddhist figurative art; I thought I saw some analogy with the aristocratic Buddhist figures from Fundukistan, with their thin waists and fine ornament and their pretty princely faces and beautiful hair, but these figures are stronger, and the same Sassanian wild geese occur here, at once very formal and very natural, as occur at Bamiyan. Later in the season, a big clay figure of an Indian goddess riding on an elephant came to light among the wreckage sealed in with everything else below the destruction level, so we can be certain that in its last stages the Buddhist sanctuary was already penetrated by pagan cults. The sources of the red clay for the clay sculptures are local, one in the mountainside behind the museum and another six or seven miles towards Kabul. The date must be the seventh or eighth century A.D.

The stupa was built first, in two stages with a distinct difference of technique which remains unexplained; when the stupa was complete and its flanks and mouldings and cornices received their stucco the terrace was still unfinished. The destruction was gradual; at a time when the place was already in decay and the Buddhas were half buried in earth, a fire broke out which involved the collapse of the wooden roof which had protected the clay statues from simply washing away, but the fire was not an immediate devastation and most of the small finds are unmarked by it. It even had the good effect of baking one or two clay figures into terracotta. The throne and feet of one colossal Buddha have been found, and one hand of another. Work was going on that year to discover how far down the hillside the terracing and its substructures extended.

The craftsmen of Buddhist Ghazni knew how to build up a richly textured design from simple elements. The reddish clay was applied to a core of greyer clay, even in the case of the most massive-looking ornamental elements, and even in the case of heads, so that below the traces of paint on elegantly formed statues there is always a thin skin of reddish clay on a grey core. The baroque whirls of some of the reliefs were therefore easily possible, and a certain formal repetition many times over in Buddhist iconography suits this technique: it is hard to say which created the other, and the same problem goes back to Hellenistic art. The proportions of the usual trefoil niche for example are a given formula, which occurs even on the coins of Huvishka, but the proportions of the figures are given only in so far as they are determined by the niche; pose and treatment however often repeated are an impromptu application of given formal elements. The most sophisticated facial sculpture has the same degree of formality, and the marvellous coiffures were built up by the same repetition of easily manageable formal elements as an entire decorative scheme. The faces are not moulded, and the head and body sculpture in general rather reflects a known form and way of working than a copied drawing. The flat conception of most of the decorative aspirant Buddhas does suggest an original drawing, but they are freely and often three-dimensionally modelled. There is an important difference between stone and clay sculpture; you can cut a stone relief according to a drawing on the stone, but because the clay is built up by the application and handling of parts, copying becomes a more distant and more personal process.

Some of the most interesting small sculptures are the heads and one body of some soldiers, who are quite clearly Mongol. They are certainly modelled from life, and they are unique. It is astonishing to see that the army of so southern a fortress as Buddhist Ghazni, which was fortified against the Persians and one must assume against Islam, and culturally linked with pagan India, was at this time drawing on nomads from the steppes, and it is wonderful to have a representation of Mongol soldiers of the seventh or eighth century. They have slanting eyes, round, fierce faces, flat noses, pursed lips and angry silken eyebrows. Their armour is almost more interesting than their faces; they wear a round pointed cap with a curious crescent and circle device on the front of it, and some kind of scale-armour fitting tightly like a balaclava helmet, and ending in a wide-flapped leather collar. Below this they are naked to the waist and they seem to wear breeches. The scales might be leather but since each of them has a dot in the centre it seems likelier they are the traditional horsehoof scale-armour which Pausanias saw at Athens and says the Sarmatians wore.[28] The cap seems to be metal. There are three of these heads and one of them wears an alternative helmet of the same general form but evidently meant to represent leather strengthened with a line of metal studs running over the crest and a line above the brow. The habit of fighting stripped to the waist persisted to the time of Babur.[29]

Babur was fond of Ghazni and says somewhere that there was no other place where the white deer were so fat. There is also no other place where I have ever heard a pack of wolves. It was about dawn, and I was standing outside the hotel looking at the desert; they were howling somewhere towards Gardez.* There are two other vignettes of Ghazni which I would like to record, the first during the dig, a picture of one squatted ancient workman gently lifting the trailing shirt-tail of another to brush away the dust from beneath it, and the other of my absently smiling at a man on the road who was holding a nasturtium between his teeth, and his taking it out, saying 'Salaam', and putting it back in.

When we left the Americans were on the moon.† Meanwhile

* I have heard a wolf before, but not a whole pack. These were not dogs, not even Afghan dogs, but they woke every dog for miles.
† Where they declared that all men were brothers and that it was a great privilege to be there. The event caused a great stir in Kabul, and the bank manager explained to us several times how true it was that all men were brothers. A few weeks later in Nuristan when an aeroplane passed overhead, the porters asked us, Is it true those are made by humans in places like America and Russia, or it is true they come from heaven? When we said they were manufactured on earth they nodded their heads. Yes, they said, that was what we suspected.

we found a clear-water spring on the way to Kabul with bats and tiny frogs. I dreamed that night about the Jam minaret and the next morning Kabul looked like a huge metropolis. In the evenings the city bathed in the cool, lucid light with a faintly lime-green tinge that you get in certain nineteenth-century prints. In the centre of Kabul as soon as it was cool there were always little boys wrestling on the patches of grass. We visited Buddhist Hadda and Jellalabad, and I went on my own to Gardez.

The most exciting part of the journey from Kabul to Hadda was the road dropping through the ravines like a waterfall, the huge cliffs and the extensive lakes.[30] The lakes are artificial; they were built with foreign help for development schemes; one of them was a gift from the Chinese and has a fishery and a boatyard where they make Chinese boats. The road shoots down, overtaking the horsetails of water and submerging itself in plum-purple shadows; the lakes have an estuarine look. From the Kabul plain down to Jellalabad, which is near the top of the Khyber Pass, is a drop of three thousand feet. There are deep blue cloudy distances which recede as you descend into them. The site of the Hadda monasteries[31] is still desert though it will soon be irrigated. We walked across sandhills among the craters of mined stupas, a hawk flew up from under my feet, the wind whined and hummed. The latest excavations are sheltered under a roof; one of the first figures you come to is a Buddha on a throne with spotted cobras tying themselves in a reefknot for good luck: classical and Indian elements are as interfused as ever. The Buddha wears light, swirling draperies and someone anoints his head from a Greek scent-bottle. A woman with a Romano-Egyptian hairstyle has a child in baggy trousers and Kushan boots but the same hairstyle.[32] Men wear their hair like Henry V. A gladiator gestures in a cornice. One of the small stupas has a sacred canopy of seven discs on a taller scale than its entire dome. Red Ionic or Corinthian capitals hold up the arches that frame a niche of statues like an Italian side-chapel or a compartment in Madame Tussaud's waxworks. Time and weather have reduced elaborate figures to the purely classic shapes that underlie them. There is a kind of peepshow of a full-sized Buddha in a lotus-tank, with fierce, squirming devil-headed fish and its clay walls modelled into curling water. This whole strange scene has an air of metamorphosis and richness about it more appropriate to the world of a late Greek poet like Nonnos than to the surrounding desert and the broken stupas.[33]

Gardez is not a well-known tourist site. A road of some kind still leads there from Ghazni, and Mountstuart Elphinstone mentions Gardez as an important village in the early nineteenth century. To judge from the routes shown on his map,[34] it had been completely overshadowed by Ghazni and Kabul in the early Islamic period, but it lies almost due south of Kabul and therefore also due south of the ancient capital, Kapisa; this route is without obstacles of any kind except for one fordable river and one ridge of mountain, which maintains its vultures and eagles and loneliness, but which is not at all difficult to cross. The road from Kabul crosses a connected series of wide grazing plains; in the higher plains the road lies between crops of maize and tattered sunflowers, but as the plains extend southwards they approach closer to desert; you see tumuli and votive rags and ruined caravanserais. At Pul-i Alam, the bridge over the Alam, you pass an undatable Islamic fort and an impressive hilltop stupa site with massive stone walls about ten feet thick still standing to a height of thirty or forty feet. The diameter of these vast rock towers, which in Greece one would certainly mistake for the remnants of a Mycenean fortress, is from twenty-five to thirty feet. The associated pottery suggests that there may in fact have been an Islamic conversion of this hilltop to secular uses, since I found a fragment of a blue-glazed bowl and several pieces of Ghaznevid pottery.

Gardez itself is a small town with a big rectangular mound and a castle, which the army still uses. The mound is about seventy yards by a hundred and fifty, and the quantity, variety and condition of Bactrian Greek coins which are found in it and are for sale in the bazaar is unparalleled in Afghanistan; there are also Kushan and Ephthalite Hunnish coins. No road runs from Gardez into Pakistan, but a frontier officer I met in a teahouse told me it was an easy three hour ride on horseback, and the frontier valleys go straight down to the Indus. The province called Paktya, which lies between Gardez and Pakistan, was even then difficult for foreigners to visit. It is the home territory of the frontier Pathans; a lot of smuggling went on, particularly of wood from the coniferous forests, and in early summer of 1969 there seems to have been a pitched battle between smugglers and the foresters and police, which left three hundred dead. The head foresters were German; conservation in Afghanistan is a difficult undertaking; even in Kabul forty years ago the bare hill behind the Spinzar hotel was covered with flowering trees, but every one has been chopped for firewood since that time.

PART FOUR

❁

The North and the North-east

CHAPTER
7

The greatest archaeological wealth of Afghanistan lies north of the Hindu Kush, towards the Russian border, and when we left Kabul again for another long expedition it was northwards along the Russian asphalt road past the site of Kapisa, which as usual we strained without success to see beyond the thick trees in the plain, past the turning for Bamiyan, and up over the Salang Pass to Surkh Kotal and Balkh, and then eastwards by Kunduz into Badakhshan, south up the Kokcha river past Faizabad to the lapis lazuli mines. We hoped to ride over the Anjuman Pass and come home to Kabul by the Panjshir river. It was a formidable but not at all an impossible journey, and it was only bad luck in the end that stopped us at the last part of it. I have not bothered to record all the travellers' troubles, negotiations, frustrations, crazy soldiers and sullen officials we encountered here and there; they were numerous and ought to be foreseen by anyone planning an ambitious journey. Equally I have not recorded all the gestures of kindness.

The plain was a green and yellow haze of wealth, with the mountains crouching over it. At Charikar we saw metal workers making knives of every kind, including swords: the crude matter of Afghan knives and of most other metal instruments is pieces of broken motor-cars. Still, we were travelling in a new *Volga* taxi and felt confident. The only time in fact that either of us had bad motor trouble in Afghanistan, apart from the blow-out on the Kandahar road, was in a Land-Rover I hired at colossal expense from the official tourist organization; its gear-lever broke right off as we were coming down a precipitous road, and its multitudinous broken springs tore away most of the seat of my trousers. We now faced the Salang Pass, crusted wings of mountain and flying rock-curtains opening and shutting behind us, and just under the snowline one of the highest tunnels in the world. The snow came down to just above ten thousand feet, but it was hot enough for open windows; the top of the pass, inside the long tunnel, was at almost exactly eleven thousand feet. The tunnel had the sinister and strong look of a ferroconcrete bunker in a spy film. The road is asphalt but in the tunnel we passed horses and donkeys, and one day a month later, at the beginning of winter, I saw a long line of hundreds of cavalry horses led by Hazara soldiers under a mounted Afghan officer, moving up into the pass.

The north face of the Salang is wilder and more abrupt than the south; the valleys are narrower, there are deep patches of snow, pure strong streams, and hillsides spiked with juniper. Clouds drifted among the supreme crests. We stopped for a while, far above the highest village, at a river of terrific water with boulders of speckled black and white granite, at the level of the junipers. It was a peaceful spot, dippers patrolled the river, and inaccessible white hollyhocks grew on the other side of it; on our side there was a sizeable bush of wild roses almost but not quite extinguished by the season. As I write these words on a catarrhal November morning, my nostrils are suddenly full of that smell of air, water, snow and roses, and I can see the texture of the rocks and of the foaming pools and the clear falls. The journal I kept records butterflies and a gold-honey-yellow bee in some purple flower and ragged yellow flowers, but those I no longer remember.

We descended to the territory of goats, of moon-ignited lichen, of cattle and cherry orchards and balsam poplars. A string of thirty camels was moving up towards the Salang Pass. From now on we followed deep, muddy rivers running purposefully away northwards towards the Oxus, into the distance across a series of interlocking plains. Already above Pul-i Khumri, which is a mining and quarrying town with an important bridge and a hydro-electric scheme, the river was a hundred yards across. Pul-i Khumri has a remote likeness to any small industrial town in the Yorkshire fells; from here the straight asphalt road north leads to sleepy Baghlan and to Kunduz, and finally to the river-port of Qizilqala, which is the Russian frontier, but another road goes north-west and through the deep gorges of another river to Tashkurghan and Mazar-i-Sharif and the enormous, unplumbed ruins of Balkh.

At that time we had no expectation of travelling the road between Pul-i Khumri and Kunduz ever again, although in fact we came to know it well, but I wanted to see as many Kushan and maybe Greek sites as possible, and we knew that the road north was rich in them; it turned out to be even richer than we had imagined. We went first to Baghlan,[1] where the governor's house is built on top of a mound; the evidence that this mound, which has been trimmed and overlooks a park of roses and conifers, was a Kushan settlement with a palace or a big public building, is a round Roman-Ionic column base, standing on a block and supporting a flower-urn, on the terrace on top of the mound outside the house; it was dug up when the house was built. These are very rich plains and it would be very easy to reach them by following the Kunduz river, which splits and dies out in the desert region less than a day's ride south of the Oxus. Not far to the east lies Fallul, an unexplored village where only in the early seventies a farmer turned up a golden treasure of the late third millennium B.C., which reproduces in gold of a fine execution motifs already known in terms of pottery from Maurizio Tosi's excavations in the Seistan desert, and from similar material found in Russian Turkestan. The treasure consists chiefly of gold cups; it is in the Kabul Museum but has not yet been published or exhibited. My information comes from the museum, from Mr Chatwin and from Dr Tosi, both of whom have seen the Fallul treasure. The treasure seems to have come from a pit like a shaft-grave, but that may represent the shape of the excavation rather than any archaeological context; so far as I could ascertain, there appeared to be no context, in which case this was simply buried treasure.

The Seistan site is an extensive town, where fragments of lapis lazuli seem to have been used for foreign exchange, just as obsidian from Melos was used in Greece: the only ancient sources of lapis lazuli were high up in the valley of the river Kokcha, so the northern slopes of the Hindu Kush must have played an important part in this almost unknown civilization. Probably every generation of nomads that entered Afghanistan penetrated the mountains by the same routes, the plains of the Kunduz river are generous and the tumuli are so frequent as to be a feature of the landscape; little by little they are being flattened, but almost none of them have been investigated. To know the history of this territory we would need the graves as well as the small settlements properly excavated; the cities and a magnificent shrine like Surkh Kotal[2] are not enough. As for my own journey, all it enables me to do is to ask myself interesting questions I cannot answer.[3]

We visited an important Kushan site at Cham Kala, south-east of Baghlan, but while we were looking for it we came on another settlement mound quite close to the road, with a farm nestling around its base, and an old threshing-floor on top. There was characteristic but undatable Kushan pottery sticking out of it and the dark line that represents a destruction by fire showed up almost everywhere about ten feet from the top; below the line one could make out the ruins of mudbrick. It was about fifty yards across at the top, about the same as the governor's palace mound, and we saw another mound like it in the fields closer to Baghlan, more or less on a line between the two. Near the farm there were some sizeable stones of which one could hardly say if they were roughly cut, or more probably badly weathered rectangular blocks. At some stage before its destruction, this mound seems to have been a farm as it is now, since below the dark layers of ash there was the leg-bone of an ox. The site of Cham Kala[4] itself lies at the south-east edge of the plain, separated from the road by broken ground, and by a series of one-pole and two-pole bridges over deep canals. The canals intersect the ruined earthworks, swallows wheel above the mounds, and in the distance we could see nomad tents. The principal mound has others to the east of it, and the heavings and hump of a ruined town disturb the ground in a semi-circle to the east and south. Walking over the site we came across a pair of crested skylarks, the birds that sleep at noon on Theokritos' walk to the threshing-floor, and a green Persian bee-eater, a chip of brilliant feathers and a needle beak. We also hopefully explored a massive rectangular fort near the mounds, which seems to have been built to withstand artillery, and with some use of baked brick, probably by Abdur Rahman or by Dost Mohammed during the unification of Afghanistan. It was about a hundred yards square with massive corner towers sixteen paces across and an elaborate gate. Abdur Rahman built a chain of fortresses like this in the late nineteenth century; as late as 1890 he was accustomed to travel with ten thousand horses, three thousand camels and four elephants; the queen travelled two days ahead with a guard of two hundred women slaves riding astride, dressed in veils and solar topees.[5]

We returned to Pul-i Khumri for the night, crossed the river, and dined in a hotel garden under the full moon. The next morning we set out for Surkh Kotal,[6] an almost isolated spur of hill facing eastwards across the plain on the western side of the river. In its way it is one of the most surprising and impressive of all archaeological sites. In sheer height it rises about two hundred feet, and so steeply that one can hardly scramble up the sides without occasionally using one's hands. The entire hill has been cut into eastward-facing terraces, with a series of fine marble steps which would be no disgrace to Hellenistic Athens; the top was devoted to a big platform for dynastic statuary, set round with heavy pillars and three sides of a hollow claybrick square of smaller rooms, originally stuccoed and roofed, and around them again at some distance three of the four sides of a big Hellenistic agora, lavishly marbled and pillared, so that the east face must have been visible from a great distance as glittering white steps sweeping up to a central statue with a canopy or temple roof, and lesser pediments with pillars on either side.

The outer colonnades of the agora faced inwards to a balustrade with engraved pilasters and a raised walk with a double row of twelve-foot columns surrounding the central dynastic shrine open only to the east. The most astonishing thing about this ruined hillside must have been its full-blooded use, with some local difference, not only of the elements but of the substance and mainstream of Hellenistic monumental architecture, and its considerable scale. The royal dimension of height belongs to Asian and not to classical conceptions; the origins of this style were certainly Iranian, and analogies exist for the building.[7] The central statue was Kanishka, the most famous and surely the greatest of Kushan emperors, so that the date must have been around the twenties or thirties of the second century A.D.[8] Well to one side, behind the vast colonnades on the north or north-east, lay a less monumental complex of dwelling-houses, in scale not unlike the priests' houses at the sanctuary of Amphiaraos at Oropos in mainland Greece, but more of a jumble. On the other side stood the small claybrick sanctuary of a sun-god with an altar of perpetual fire. We know that the entire conception of the monumental shrine was over-ambitious, since an inscription has been recovered from the ruins, recording that it was abandoned for lack of water and rebuilt with a new source of water.

When this akropolis, sanctuary of Kanishka the Victorious, to which the lord Kanishka gave his name, was finished . . . water failed . . . the gods were taken away . . . the akropolis was abandoned. Then Nokonzoko lord of the marches . . . came in the month Nisan . . . (rampart) and dug the well . . . inscribed by Mihraman.*

* This inscription is now shown in the entrance hall to the Kabul Museum.

There are twenty-five lines of this inscription, written with incised guidelines on a smooth-sided, rough-backed slab of white limestone. The script is based on Greek with some special Kushan characteristics, the language is the eastern Iranian language of the Kushan Empire, of which this inscription is the longest example; Surkh Kotal is not a local but a conventional name dating from 1952; its ancient name was Bagolango. The site was first discovered through inscriptions, not so long or important, but strongly and freely written, which came to light during the making of a road at the end of the summer of 1951.* Excavation revealed three stages in the history of the hillside; first, a series of three terraces, each with its classic flight of steps in the centre, one above the other, with the sanctuary ending at a monumental gateway on the lowest terrace, and a final flight of steps to ground level outside the sanctuary, then Nokonzoko's restoration with a new lowest terrace below the lowest flight, and a canal for water, and finally later again a well beyond the canal, with a stairway leading down into it, built of the re-used inscribed stones from Nokonzoko's lowest terrace; at this last period the canal was moved back and narrowed and it was walled in and bridged so that the well could be part of the sanctuary. Each of the terraces is about a hundred yards wide and fifty deep. There must also have been three stages of building on the top of the hill; almost everything was complete at the first stage, when the entire sanctuary was commissioned by Kanishka in his lifetime, then came a second period of minor changes which may possibly correspond to Nokonzoko's restoration, that is to the building of the canal and the lowest terrace at the foot of the hill, and finally a thorough destruction by fire followed by a modest rebuilding. Nothing except guesswork connects this last period with the digging of the well, and neither the reconstruction nor the well has been exactly dated.

Fragments of three stone statues have been found, all representing men in full Kushan dress with breeches and the swell-toed boots which were probably used for riding with thong stirrups. The statues are as flat as kippers and have a hieratic but secular appearance; they are very like the small limestone relief figures of Kushan chiefs in the Kunduz Museum.† But the fragments of some clay sculpture found at Surkh Kotal at the same time show

* Now in the Kunduz Museum.
† These small reliefs are in a 'Gandaran' style but in a harder medium than schist or stucco; the local limestone in which they are carved makes them a very exceptional case.

the full swirls of classic drapery which one may suppose Kushan artists knew and imitated from Hellenistic stucco. It is easier to model elaborately in clay than in stone, and a similar disproportion of development between clay and stone figure techniques can be seen in Chinese animal figures under the T'ang dynasty not long afterwards; but at the time of Kanishka all the resources of Gandaran Buddhist art both in schist and in clay were available for a great Kushan sanctuary, and there existed a contemporary Buddhist sanctuary with big clay statues within easy walking distance of Surkh Kotal,[9] so it is possible that both the style and the material of the dynastic limestone[10] figures at Surkh Kotal were deliberately chosen simply because they were thought proper for dynastic art. The obvious analogies are in Parthian and Iranian princely art, and at one corner of the classical colonnade we found the almost obliterated ruins of a lion throne like one that was found at Hatra. This is an important piece of stone sculpture in a terribly battered condition; I do not believe we were wrong about its being a lion throne, since Bruce and I had separated for a time and each of us noticed what it was independently. There is no way of knowing what prince it represented; even the lions are very hard to make out.

Today the plain below Surkh Kotal is well irrigated and very rich, but the hills behind it are bare. In the plain we could hear the cries of brightly coloured birds; I counted sand-coloured hoopoes, two varieties of bee-eaters and some big blue rollers, and above the monumental hillside and the drovers' track behind it the white vultures, with their curious combination of grace and ungainliness, which are so common in Afghanistan that they seem part of the desert or of the sky. From the top we saw an eagle below us flighting down to perch on one of the terraces; later, wandering over the edges of the excavation we put up a pair of partridges; they disappeared again with a rattle and a squawk. The hilltop was idyllic and the ruins were plentiful, the fire-altar was roofed over and locked up behind a claybrick building ornamented with deep arrow-shaped marks on the clay. The hill beyond the drovers' track to the west was an Islamic cemetery, and further away on the upper plain we could see camels grazing on some blazing yellow scrub, the colour of stubble and brighter than sand. We wandered about Surkh Kotal for three or four hours. In a way it was like an eastward-facing theatre, and in a way like a ziggarat, but it was the top of the hill I found hard to leave; the remoteness, the silence and intensity which increased as the heat increased, and the monumentality of the spaces, a piece of wild nature transformed into classic architecture, then the same image in reverse, architecture transformed into nature, the strong, broken pieces of these elaborately balancing and counterbalancing colonnades devastated by time and abandoned to partridges and hoopoes. Surkh Kotal is a unique site, but the sharp impression it makes even after its excavation is perhaps not unlike what the unrestored and unvisited sites of Greece made on the first travellers who saw them.

The country north-west from Surkh Kotal is not unlike a Greek landscape, in everything, that is, except its history. Sir John Marshall, the excavator of Taxila in Pakistan, first fell in love with it because it looks so Greek, and Henry Miller records that when he and Lawrence Durrell first visited Mycenae, Durrell kept saying how like the countryside was to north-west India. But history does determine landscape, and neither in modern nor perhaps in ancient times could a Greek have quite deluded himself he was at home here. The plains extend too far, the undertone of sand and thistles is too insistent, the yellow and blue mixture at the horizon is too rich, the mountains are too formidable. There is something equally not Greek about the Buddhist settlement at Samanghan,* to the north of Surkh Kotal. In the seventh century A.D. Samanghan was an important and fertile place, and its grandeur seems to have lasted to the time of Genghis Khan;[11] today it looks like any forgotten, scattered village rather off the road, and even the modern route to Mazar which passes close by is less important than the road to Kunduz.

The Buddhist site[12] is called Takht-i-Rustam, which means Rustam's Seat; this is a common name in northern Afghanistan for any high place associated with antiquities; it comes from the epic of Rustam which in principle is Sassanian, but it is only the name of Rustam that comes from the poem: the local story is that Rustam used to sit and drink in a kiosk built on top of a stupa which is the shape of an enormous igloo carved downwards into solid rock, standing in a deep quarry-like pit. The kiosk on top is a square folly once supporting a sacred canopy, probably of about the fourth century A.D. From a distance nothing else is visible, and the huge rock dome below it, which is about forty feet high, is

* Its medieval name was Haibak, but it was renamed in March 1964 with its original name.

as unexpected as the lower masses of an iceberg. The texture of the rock is a mottled grey with black lichen. You approach the foot of the stupa from below through two natural rock-tunnels made regular by cutting. The inside of the dome is probably deeply hollowed, but the entrance has been blocked with white ashlar masonry. I found a crack with birds nesting in it and a tree growing up, and we saw a few handholds and footholds cut in the side of the stupa that make it possible to climb to the top.

Not far away from the stupa a series of cells and galleries and cave-sanctuaries has been cut back into the rock and hollowed out to an astonishing depth and height. Compared to the hive-like cliff-colonies at Bamiyan this one is very tiny, but its ambitious conception on a small scale and the precision of the rock-carving demonstrate an impressive degree of wealth and talent. One of the caves is a double gallery parallel with the cliff-face, that is a long inner cave which is lighted from an equally long formal gallery in front of it, which in its turn has lights giving on to the cliff-face. This is a *vihara*, a place of religious retreat and private meditation. Another of the caves has a tall dome hollowed upwards into the mass of the cliff, and perfectly carved into the spreading petals and central sunburst of a huge flowering lotus.* All the rooms are tall: the inner part of the double gallery runs about ninety feet, with a height of fifteen feet and a width of about six; one of the domed shrines is twenty-five or thirty feet high. It housed an elderly donkey who coughed with fearful effect in the darkness.

In the main street of the village most of the shops were devoted to guns, leather and stringed instruments. Water was being poured on the wheels of carts. Not far to the north we came to tractor-drawn heavy road-rollers with spikes (which were Russian) and to the roadworks that marked the end of asphalt and of luxury. The road ended just above the mountain gorge which leads down to the Oxus plain, at the beginning of Uzbek country, frescoed walls, domed mudbrick cottages like beehives, and occasional pointed cloth hats shaped like the helmets of London policemen. The Uzbeks are a Turkish people who occupied the Oxus valley in the time of the Mongols; they took Bokhara, Herat and Samarkand and it was Uzbek pressure that drove Babur

* This astonishing lotus dome must certainly have been painted. The petals overlap like fish-scales or dragon-scales, a technique of carving found also in the decoration of Hellenistic marble roof-tiles.

southwards to Kabul and the conquest of India. The only people who could stop them at that time were the ferocious confederate tribes of what was then Kafiristan, the eastern Afghan mountains and the Pamirs. The northern Uzbeks now live in Russian Uzbekistan;[13] resentment at the unification of Afghanistan survives in local stories; for instance that Abdur Rahman sold his soul for power to a hairy monster in a lake in the mountains. The final plain was drowsing in a haze of dust and a light like fire in which horses waded and grazed. We started to pass huge herds and domed embroidered tents. We caught a glimpse of a trophy of yellow and blue flowers and guns painted on the walls of a mosque. The cliffs spread enormous rocky wings over our heads, colours and textures roughened and darkened and the gorge swallowed us. It was a thousand feet deep and nearly as narrow as the Corinth canal. High above flood level two Buddhist caves faced across the chasm on to a wrinkled wall of absolute rock.

We swung out of the mountains to look down on Tashkurghan* and the blaze of desert light; Tashkurghan was dark, dark foliage and a towering abandoned mudbrick castle that commands the entrance to the gorge. This castle is comparatively modern and we had no time to do more than gape at it and to strain for a glimpse of the Oxus thirty miles away to the north[14] in forbidden territory. The Oxus plain is a huge dream-like desert field; we drove westwards across it for two or three hours with our noses out of the window of the car like dogs on a hot day. The desert pasture glittered; it was tawny with distant bars of green and blue where the water from the mountains died out; it was not quite featureless but more like the sea, with occasional events or visions like lines from the *Odyssey*, big scattered herds and at one moment a herd of donkeys. Twice we passed by fortified Uzbek villages, and finally and suddenly we came to Mazar-i-Sharif, an unattractive town with a restored mosque something like a poor relation of Brighton Pavilion built in porcelain under Queen Victoria. It had some gothic windows and a clock tower like a present from Blackpool which might have contained bathsalts; the interior was full of a bee-humming music, the outer court was a squatting-place for sacred singers and reciters, all with hands to their faces and weaving backwards and forwards on their hams as they chanted, none of them without his circle of listeners.

It darkened, the clock tower lighted up, bulbs glittered on the

* Also called Khulm, discussed in a later chapter.

domes, avenues of green and pink neon lights blossomed around the mosque. In the hotel it was impossible to get clean water, so we gave ourselves long, doleful drinks of Kabul whisky. The manager offered to buy what was left of the bottle for literally ten times what the whole bottle had cost. I remember the room we slept in as dirty, but by this time I was probably prejudiced.[15] If so I suffered for it, since I neglected to see the Mazar mound, which is Kushan at the latest and has classical column-bases like the one at Baghlan sticking out of it. Later on in the bazaar at Ghazni I saw a red-painted terracotta relief figurine of a Kushan woman which was said to have come from the mound at Mazar; it was of an almost purely Greek type except for some details of dress and the features of the face.[16] I bought her, and later gave her to the Ashmolean Museum, where, alas, no one is very fond of her, and she has never been exhibited. There were several mounds near Mazar; a few weeks later we saw them from the air. But on the first morning I was only anxious to see the desert again, and to see Balkh. In early morning light the tawny colours in the desert were brighter and the dark ones fresher, and the mountains glittered, but the plain was still dreamlike. We drove through the inward-looking ruins of a royal fortress with grandiose, half-melted mudbrick houses. Often we passed small ruins like haycocks, and haycocks like small mudbrick ruins. We were soon at the enormous village of Balkh. It lies among the long wide avenues and spacious coniferous groves laid out forty years ago by Amanullah,[17] but the size and scale of the ruins are greater still.

CHAPTER

8

Balkh was a great city long before the time of Alexander, and before the time of the Persian Empire.[1] Already in the earliest literary sources it was flag-crowned Bakhdhi,[2] and when the Greeks followed the Persians up the Oxus valley it became the name city of the entire Bactrian territory under Alexander and his successors. Balkh fell to Alexander without resistance in the spring of 329 B.C., and it appears to have fallen as easily to the Kushans. Its religious shrines were very rich at every period; Alexander found a statue of Anahita the water-goddess wearing a crown of gold sunrays and stars and a cloak of thirty otterskins,[3] and at some time, probably under the Kushans, there was a great fire-altar at the biggest temple in the city,[4] and there were very rich Buddhist relics.[5]

All this is the index of a rich and complex mercantile culture. Balkh surrendered to the Arabs very early in history in A.D. 645 only three years after the collapse of the Sassanian Empire, but in the ninth century it could still produce a strong Persian literary flowering under the kingdom of Bokhara.[6] From at least the seventh until the thirteenth century, it was a metropolitan see of the Nestorian Christian Church, and it was from Balkh and Bokhara that the Nestorians and the Jews reached China.

In 1220 Genghis Khan crossed the Oxus at Balkh with a hundred thousand horsemen; a massacre followed too terrifying to write about, and the devastation was as nearly complete as a hundred thousand Mongol horsemen could make it.[7] Balkh was still a ruin fifty-five years afterwards, when Marco Polo passed it on his way to China, though he was able to make out the remnants of 'palaces of marble and spacious squares', and as late as 1333 it was 'a ruin without society',[8] but people, perhaps the grand-children of the dead, were already coming back; in 1359 Tambur-laine was proclaimed king there and he and his son Shah Rukh rebuilt it; its last age of greatness, and its only glittering ornaments today, belong to the same Timurid renaissance as Herat and Samarkand. Building was in progress as late as the seventeenth century, and the final decline, which went hand in hand with cholera, malaria and the rise of Mazar, occurred only in the second half of the nineteenth.

A story like that is bound to awaken romantic expectations; the crucial point is that Balkh was not so much a fortress as a merchant city, and because of its situation, its watercourses and fertility and the routes that meet there, it was a unique meeting-place of peoples and cultures. Alas, it is also the despair of archaeologists. No excavation of Balkh has ever uncovered the Greek city. Pits have to be dug very deep, they fill up with water at once and need to be pumped and drained. The late Islamic detritus is massive and the disentangling of levels in the ruins of mudbrick architecture is not easy under any circumstances. A prolonged, specialized study of the measurements and brickmakers' marks on the bricks from a properly stratified excavation demonstrated that almost any measurement of brick and almost any brickmaker's mark can occur in almost any period.[9] An attempt to reduce the pottery to a coherent series was hardly more hopeful.[10] Almost everything has been tried at Balkh, even down to a kind of archaeological acupuncture, with the exception of the one certain method,[11] a thorough, complete excavation carried out with rigorous accuracy on a huge scale. Neither the money nor perhaps the talent for such an enormous undertaking has ever been available; it would have to be an enterprise on the scale of the American excavation of the Athenian agora, which has already taken nearly fifty years. All that Balkh reveals to a day-visitor is the scale of a metropolis, the immense, wan walls extending far away into the fields, and the brilliant shell of a seventeenth-century mosque[12] in the centre of Amanullah's star-shaped and abortive city plan.

The central circle of Amanullah's Balkh consists of old men asleep under mighty oriental plane trees. The only sound is cooroo. The mosque has a ribbed turquoise dome where the doves congregate like white flakes. The niches and balconies in the walls are white, picked out in green; all that survives of the mosque is this western dome framed between two twisted dark blue pillars that coil straight upwards like a ropetrick and break off in mid-air. The dome once had white lettering on a turquoise ground. Inside, the dome has cobalt ribs and yellow and green flowers, with fine stucco and a cobalt and turquoise *mihrab*. But some of the painting is late and popular, the clock is an English schoolroom clock vamped up in turquoise and gold, the light is one poor oil lamp from a dome fifty feet high. At the far end of the square, that is the eastern end, the empty gateway to a theological school has survived like a ruined triumphal arch. This gate had a star-vaulted roof, and cobalt lettering on a yellow ground. It was built in the late seventeenth century* and the walls carry geometric decoration in a style that seems to be copied from Herat. It was deliberately stripped of decorated tiles in the eighteen sixties for the building of Mazar-i-Sharif. I found both these monuments moving perhaps because of an inbuilt preference for ruins and a particular sympathy with the ruins of religious architecture, which when intact so often tries to say too much and to improve too much on its patterns, but seems in a way to become more articulate when desolated.

Southwards towards the mountains the earliest outer city already extended far beyond the centre of Amanullah's square and the limits of its walls are visible from the main city walls, with the dome of the mosque glistening among the nearer treetops like a blue fruit. After the destruction by Genghis Khan the city of Tamburlaine grew out from the original square stronghold westwards towards Herat, and its slighter walls are relatively well preserved, but no part of these outworks at any period extends as far north, towards the invisible Oxus, as the original central fortification with its river-facing gateway. You can see from the battlements for many miles into the hazes of the Oxus plain, though not as far as the river. The bulkiest and probably the highest early Islamic tower stood at the south-east point, above the eastward extent of what was then the new city.

We walked together round the walls reducing ourselves to a deepening silence. The inner city must be a mile across, there are stony heaps underfoot, and of course a chaotic abundance of fragmentary pottery. The earliest fragment we noticed was a jug-handle of the second or third century A.D. The ragged lines of dark and light clay battlements trailed into the distance, and outside on the west we could see mounds and several big Islamic ruins rearing up among the trees and cottages. Bright greenery laps the walls, and you could hear orchard birds. But inside the

* By Sayid Subhan Kuli Khan. The Chinese motifs come from the famous shrine at Gazurgah in Herat.

big ramparts death takes over. We saw thirty silent men carrying sickles walking home in single file through this dead, shrubby ground. On one of the humps lay a scatter of big clinkers from a metal foundry. The gate in the south wall looked from a distance as if the sky had simply bent down and bitten off a piece of the ramparts, though when you reach it you can make out the ruined towers of the last refortification. Beyond it lie reeds and marshes full of water birds; we saw a hoopoe in the reeds. We walked back outside, under Timurid towers with their roots eaten away, on a path above the moat, and in again through a west gate with pointed arches, still standing almost complete. Inside this gate is a spring of water with a tiny garden full of deep purple hollyhocks, and a very small ramshackle shrine with votive rags. The well-bucket was made of old motor-tyres. We made our way back to the village and drank green tea out of celadon bowls under a café awning of dried bushes strung together; we had to answer a lot of questions and someone played the flute for us.

In that café we made an unexpected breakthrough. We knew of a report by a lady archaeologist, in a Russian publication that Bruce had come across, of the ruins of a very early, probably ninth-century mosque, like the oldest buildings at Merv,[13] somewhere close to Balkh. It offered no photograph, the building had never been described or noticed elsewhere, and no western archaeologists gave any sign of having seen it at all. Naturally we were anxious to see and photograph it, but it was only on the tenth or eleventh time of asking that someone in the café suddenly understood what we meant; we were taken straight there. We headed south to a point beyond the walls and beyond the ruins of two stupas, where we crossed the asphalt and forked south-west. We passed a man riding for shade in a net under the axle of his cart while his horse ambled along with no driver. The place was known locally as Kob el Akhbar, or alternatively Nouh Gumbad or Hajji Piyade, and the site lies a hundred yards to the right of the road, by a grove of ten plane trees standing round a pool. The mosque was stronger and more harmonious than is easy to describe. Three walls with engaged columns and four free-standing stucco-covered pillars of an almost Norman height and girth had survived. The texture of these pillars is a fine, deep wickerwork ornamentation, with sharp flowered and foliated bands at the bases and capitals, and on the underside of the arches between columns. Big Roman-looking rosettes decorate the sides of the arches, and among the recurring circles of foliation there are still traces of dark sky-blue paint and thin white plaster. The decorative effect is one of immense richness and vigour. The diameter of the pillars is about four feet; the lower bands are all partly buried, but the wickerworked bodies of the pillars are about six feet six inches high; they support square blocks a foot thick and the arches spring from these blocks. From the top of the blocks to the top of the band above the point of an arch is about seven feet. There are two fallen pillars at the north-east end which have disintegrated and show the substance of each column to be baked brick with applied stucco decoration.

We drank in every detail of this fresh and interesting monument; its solemnity and sobriety of conception and the tension and fullness of the decoration would give it a high position in the history of architecture by any standard of comparison. The fact that it represents a lost meeting-point of Sassanian and Islamic art makes it even more valuable. I have seldom felt so strongly about a building, not just about its strength and beauty but in the same way that I was electrified by the first sight of San Marco at Venice when I was an undergraduate and had never seen a Byzantine church. This is a poorer though not an intellectually simpler style, and at any rate a humbler place, at least today. The miracle is that this mosque stands ankle-deep in earth, quite unexcavated, virtually unknown, and beautifully preserved except for being roofless. After Madame Pugachenkova had described it, the Afghan archaeological service put metal guards on top of the pillars to prevent erosion; the only damage it has suffered from hooligans of any nationality is two sets of initials in the European alphabet, freshly cut into a decorated pillar. We sat down in a happy daze under the plane trees by the pool. It was hot and the plane leaves dropped their shadows straight down into the water. We shared the shade with two or three small groups resting from their work in the fields, and also with two or three cows, a donkey and a black goat. By the time we were back on the road to Mazar, it was so hot that a vulture would hardly bestir himself to flap away from the road in front of the car.

We drove east again in headache heat, glutting our eyes with distance as far as Tashkurghan,[14] where the road snakes up southwards into the gorges. From Tashkurghan a rough track continues east along the north skirt of the mountains and the south skirt of the desert as far as Kunduz; it was marked on maps and we intended to take it, but our driver refused to face it; he was a smooth, unpleasant man, but everything I heard and saw of that track afterwards confirmed that he was right. At Tashkurghan, Bruce and I separated for a time. He went to see the covered bazaar, which is probably the best in Afghanistan, and to sit in a garden, where he was offered slices of four different kinds of melon and spent a happy hour reading a book in a summerhouse. I was driven northwards through the graveyards and suburban gardens to see the mound called Shul Tepe,* which is the ancient city of Khulm. What is more, it would have been easier to have ridden or walked, but horses take time to come by and walking in the heat of the day also takes time.

The main mound was enormous; like Balkh it stood well out in the plain, with some Islamic walls and a small fort to the south, but it was all mound, not ramparts, all the solid detritus of human settlement, city piled on city to a height of forty feet, half a mile across and three-quarters wide. The surface and flanks consisted almost entirely of pottery, like a huge rubbish-dump; it was much like the surface pottery at Balkh, with a predominance of incised unpainted ware and some fine Persian glazed wares going back to the last period before Genghis Khan, and one or two much earlier pieces of cobalt and white low-fired tin-glazed bowls. The walled fortress of modern Tashkurghan which hangs above the road and commands the gorges is a castle built by Ahmed Shah Durrani in the eighteenth century. Marco Polo mentions no place of any kind between Balkh and Taliqan, which lies east of Kunduz, a journey of two days on which he had to carry all his food.[15] The mound is said to have been abandoned when it was destroyed by Ahmed Shah, but I saw nothing to suggest it had ever been effectively occupied since Genghis Khan. Further out in the desert to the north or north-west there are two other small mounds one at least of which was a Kushan settlement; it has been investigated by Japanese archaeologists.[16] I was unwilling to venture there alone, since the whole territory between the main road and the Oxus is forbidden to foreigners, and I was already technically out of bounds. The Oxus is the Russian frontier.

In Tashkurghan I had arranged to meet Bruce at a teahouse. It was a room as dark as a forge, and the conversation was naturally

* It is not clear which of the mounds is really Shul Tepe; there are three in the same area.

in Persian, so while the driver was explaining I sat crosslegged, shoeless and inarticulate on the carpet, communing with a furious *kaouk*, a big cock-partridge with a bustard-shaped body, red legs and black and white striped feathers. His eyelids and beak were as red as his legs, and he chuckled and danced with anger until I was allowed to feed him. Finally someone put a cloth cover over his cage and he went to sleep. These birds are bred for fighting and gambling, and a champion can change hands for thirty or forty pounds; Afghans will watch and bet on fighting of any kind, and the same stadium at Kabul shows human wrestling, partridge-fights, camel-fights and dog-fights on different evenings. Male camels are intractable creatures and their only social functions are sex and fighting, a situation not without its human resonance. In the teahouse an old man started to play a two-stringed instrument, and from some other teahouse I could hear a sweet and liquid flute. A young man danced with a knife in his hand, sweeping it round in lazy gestures, but the knife was just something he happened to be carrying and with his other hand he was smoking a cigarette. Bruce arrived and we wanted to stay the night, but the driver was beginning to pine for Kabul and pretended there was no resthouse of any kind, so it was only from the car that I caught glimpses of early nineteenth-century gazebos and kiosks lost in the gardens; and I never saw the bazaar at all. In the whole summer that is the mistake I regret most.

We must have been hot and thirsty, since the handwriting in my journal deteriorates and there are notes which must have reflected conversation about possible types of ice and water-ice, including horseradish ice made with cream and served with boiled duck, lime water-ice, melon water-ice, and an obscure note about blackcurrants and lemon-scented geranium leaves. Somewhere on the road there was a diversion from the asphalt on to a desert track; the soldier directing the traffic had been asleep and the traffic was out of hand, with lorries shooting off in all directions. The soldier went berserk; he was a tall, muscular boy with mad eyes and a gaunt face; he flung his stick at a windscreen, battered a radiator, and finally leapt into our car and sat beside the driver, shaking and shouting and threatening to strangle the driver. There was a nasty moment when a crowd of soldiers doing road work pressed close up to the car, but fortunately our soldier leapt out to explain something, so we locked the doors and rolled up the windows, and the driver accelerated. It was all over as quickly as it began. We passed the hill of Surkh Kotal with the blue animal shapes of mountains behind it, and had dinner again in the hotel garden at Pul-i Khumri, under two or three electric lights hanging in cypress trees and a nearly full moon that seemed to belong among them.

From Pul-i Khumri next day we turned north, through Baghlan with its avenue of catalpa trees, and followed the Kunduz stream down through its hills towards Kunduz. Just beyond Aliabad we noticed small mounds in the fields on the left of the road, and behind them, to our extreme amazement, a huge hill-fort at least a quarter of a mile long, commanding a bend on the river.* We made our way to it, terrified by an angry mastiff and comforted by a hoopoe, and climbed up. It was early in the day but the crested larks were already silent on the ramparts. The hilltop is about a hundred feet high, there are still two or three houses and the ruins of others, mostly on the east end. Its defences are like those of any Welsh or British bronze age hill settlement, a descending triple series of ditches and ramparts dug out of the hillside. There was not much pottery, but not all of what we saw was modern. The hill stands close to a pass and dominates wide plains and has its priestlike resident vulture, who came to inspect us. There is another long, lower mound to the south on the bank of the river, and a suspiciously humpy area to the south-east on the opposite bank. Among the bits and pieces of pottery in the ditches half-way down the hill we found pieces of baked tilebrick. It is a bit foolish not to be able to say more about this fortress, but archaeologically it is virgin land. One would guess it was a fortified village from the time of the nomadic invasions, but there is no way of knowing it was not a pre-Greek stronghold like the Swat river site at Birkot and Raja Gira's castle above Udegram, which were both probably taken by Alexander himself.[17]

The river broadened into a wide, hazy valley, the asphalt sang under the car, we passed advertisements for the Spinzar cotton company on which the whole economy of the one rich province in Afghanistan depended, posters for Spinzar soap and the Spinzar hospital; the road swung round under pine trees between gardens, suddenly pony-carriages were everywhere and the bicycles had multi-coloured powderpuffs inside their wheels; we were in Kunduz, where we stopped at the Spinzar hotel. Kunduz has

* The site is called Aliabad Qala. It is not unknown; so close to an asphalt road it could hardly go unnoticed, but it has not been excavated.

been created by an enlightened private despotism based on marked industrial and social enterprise; for Afghanistan this is unique; it is entirely the creation of the Nashir family, and of the head of the family, who founded the Spinzar company thirty or forty years ago. The Spinzar company is an enterprise with a nineteenth-century tint, but in Afghanistan that is already an advance; the society of Kunduz is already post-feudal, the beginnings of a local intellectual life are just forlornly sprouting.

When the company was founded, modern Kunduz was over-grown land, and 'go to Kunduz if you want to die' was a proverb.[18] In the nineteenth century, Badakhshan was several times depopulated to recolonize this area and every time the settlements died out from malaria;[19] the malarial mosquitoes were annihilated by an American mission after 1945. They are said to be coming back, but in thirty years Kunduz has become the most alive town in Afghanistan. It has two theatres with a change of programme every night, more than can be said for Kabul, it has a museum and a strange small unused library. At the same time it is very much of a country town, camels loaded with blue-grey artemisia pass the painted lorries and the pony carriages; the asphalt to the east dies out almost in sight of the central traffic policeman; you can buy for sixpence the best melons that exist in the whole world, sometimes Uzbek boys ride through the street bareback on tall horses. There exists a certain distillation of dust, shade and peace which is the atmosphere of the provinces everywhere in the world, and Kunduz has this atmosphere very purely. I am speaking of the past, of course, before the Russians came.

The main street was full of pleasures; on the first morning we found a watch for sale in working order dated 1748. Then we found a conjuror and snake-charmer who spat a series of pebbles the size of oranges, swallowed a bundle of needles, and whipped the audience with a handful of cream-bellied fawn snakes; to everyone's delight a few of them wriggled free whenever he shut them up. The conjuror filled in time with wholehearted obscene gestures and jokes that seemed to depend on magical practices; meanwhile a teahouse was playing an old record of *Bye-bye Blackbird* through an amplifier. We wandered into a meat market like the chamber of horrors and a vegetable market that smelt of sacks; it had tomatoes, long aubergines, carrots, onions, potatoes and green peppers. I declared loftily but truthfully that all this was nothing to the fishmarket in Venice. Bruce turned out to be another enthusiast for that labyrinth of experiences, but infuriated me by saying, Aha, it was nothing to the fungus season in the market at Brno. We spent a long time among some magnificent Uzbek chelim carpets. On another day at the back of one of these carpet shops, Bruce suddenly caught sight of his personal grail, the complete trappings of a Kazak nomad's tent. He gave a cry, and the shopkeeper another; he was an old man who had settled here thirty years ago as a refugee from Russian Kazakstan, the tent had been his own and it seemed to him a kind of magic that a foreigner after so many years could recognize the fabric and admire it and say Kazak. In the afternoon, Bruce took a seat in a taxi for Kabul to fetch his wife,* who was flying out from England, and I was left alone for a few days of reading and writing and mound-spotting at Kunduz.

I walked for a mile or two through a tangle of dusty lanes and mudwalled gardens in the blaze of clear sunlight, to find the river. There was a site called Chardara on the other bank I wanted to look at. In the end I emerged on a low mud cliff above a lush plain with the river winding through it. The plain was steaming, the river ran through mud-flats, the opposite cliffs were indistinct in the haze. A boy was standing in ankle-deep mud on the bank, catching coarse fish a yard long. The water was too powerful, too fast and too filthy to swim in or to wash in without extreme need, so I climbed back into the lanes and bought a melon. It is curious that the Afghan watermelons are tarbuz and the true melons kharbuz, a Turkish word used for watermelons in Greece, karpousi; the Greek word *peponi* is an ancient Greek word for any ripe fruit, especially a kind of melon that could only be eaten really ripe. Was the watermelon introduced to Greece by the Turks? Was the true melon earlier? The best Kunduz melons come from Ashkalon, a village to the north.

From the hour of this walk, all my time in Kunduz was a mounting excitement embroidered on perfect provincial calm and vacuity. First I heard from a friendly American water engineer of an ancient canal high up on a hillside further east near Khanabad,

---

* A front seat to Kabul cost 250 afghanis, about a pound. The reader had better be told here, since this is not a book about people, that Bruce's wife comes from New England and is called Elizabeth. She had never been to Asia before. Anyone who thinks of bringing his wife on a journey like this should be warned that Elizabeth has unusual qualities.

which might well be Kushan. It was an ambitious irrigation project, and must have been hard to build and in the end ineffective, since the soil was terribly porous and scored with gullies.[20] Probably it was one of those schemes dear to the heart of administrators which are superimposed on the countryside by slave labour to solve longstanding problems at a single stroke. At the same time I saw some more interesting pottery from the same general area washed out of a Kushan mound by vertical erosion, including some baked bricktile three inches deep, and the base of a formidable urn.[21]

The next move was obviously to get into the Kunduz Museum, but no one I met knew where it was. I spent a happy morning in some Chekhovian government offices where a rough-chinned elderly clerk with his hat on bowed and beamed at more sophisticated officials in silk robes. Long personal calls across the town succeeded each other on their shared telephone. Outside, the horsetraps jangled their bells like trams, and there was a continuous susurration in the branches of a plane tree. The carpet was too big for the room and was rolled up at one end. Finally an inspector of schools and a local intellectual arrived, as diffident as young children. I never saw the inspector again because he had a bicycle and was busy, but the intellectual turned out to be a writer and later I was to meet him again.

The museum is a long reading-room or schoolroom;* it houses material from Pul-i Khumri and from Kunduz and the original Corinthian capital and votive base from Ay Khanoum found by H.M. the King on a shooting expedition, which led to the identification of the site as a Greek city.[22] Even more interesting, the material from Chardara was very rich, and there were small figures from a site called Momokhil which I had never heard of; both these places appeared to be close to Kunduz west of the Kunduz river. Taken together with the known concentration of Kushan and possibly Greek sites south of Kunduz, the mounds and the canal to the east, the comparative closeness of Ay Khanoum on the Oxus and the Russian Kushan sites around Termez, they became trebly important.[23] Ay Khanoum was still as much forbidden territory to us as Russia, but I was anxious to see whatever was possible. I drew a blank in the horse bazaar and

* On your right beyond the central circus with the traffic policeman as you arrive on the asphalt road from Kabul; labelled 'Nasher and Co.; open by private arrangement so far as I could see. Write to Mr Nashir at the Spinzar Co.

went on to the taxi bazaar; this is a crumbled courtyard behind a broken down *hamam* where the taxis wait and the drivers sit talking. In the middle of the yard I thought I saw a Greco-Roman column base, but by this time, just having seen the Chardara material, I may have had column bases on the brain, so I ignored it and argued resolutely about taxis.

We drove to Chardara over a bridge I had failed to find walking; the village stands on the cliffs just across the river, and the ancient site is three long, low mounds in the fields to the south of the track just as you enter the village.[24] I never got close to them because of a misunderstanding about Momokhil. The taximan had explained it was much further, much more expensive, and lay towards the Oxus. I said that was no good because I was a foreigner, and I knew there was a police post on the road to the Oxus, where I would have to show my *firman*, which expressly ruled out the Oxus. In fact Momokhil lies directly west on a bad road and we could have gone there, but when we arrived at Chardara I was handed over politely to the chief of police, who was told I wanted him to look at my passport. He was delighted with this courtesy, but since he had no stamp to stamp it with he most politely sent me back to Kunduz with an officer and a private soldier to have it stamped there.

Chardara police headquarters was a large potting-shed in an unkempt, huge and extremely beautiful walled garden with a strong gate and hollyhocks and tall planes. Inside the potting-shed a small court was squatting on rugs in a circle, there were almost more rugs than people. The chief man, of whom I was later told, 'Oh, he is a villain, he was exiled there', got to his feet with a broad smile and shook hands. He said, 'I am the governor of this small place Chardara, my English also is wicked.'

The mounds flitted past, the bridge rumbled, and we were home in Kunduz at the same offices where I started the day. The officer rapidly made himself scarce, and the soldier and I tramped round from office to office and down a street to a house and back round the offices and back to the house and so on until nine people had seen my passport and four had refused to look at it, and not one of them wanted to stamp it. We sat in the shade and shared a melon and agreed to forget about the whole business.

I went back to the taxi bazaar and looked more closely. It was quite certainly a Kushan site. The column base was unmistakable,[25] standing on its own in the sun so fresh-looking it must recently have been dug up. Behind it there was a heap of stones from the dismemberment of what the taxi-drivers called 'an old *serai*'. Everyone assured me my base had not been brought in by van, but it was found there. Among the steps to the offices there were two others, one upside down, one buried and showing only as a block. No one knew what they were until I explained, but they soon caught on. Among the pile of broken stones there were at least three pieces which showed unmistakable traces of their origin as architectural elements in a classical building, although they were so broken it was impossible to see whether they belonged to the upper or the lower part of it. At the back of the taxi bazaar there were several holes in the ground a few feet deep; they contained baked tilebricks. The drivers, the authorities at the Kabul Museum and common sense agreed that this mass of material had not strayed into the bazaar from a site excavated elsewhere.

Naturally I went straight to the museum full of news, and naturally my Persian was so bad and the news so improbable that everyone assumed I must mean something else. Eventually a tall, courteous young man with whom I conversed in garbled Russian and a cheerful-looking fat man with a huge moustache carried me off to a rehearsal of Afghan music in the Nashir theatre. It had an elaborate, sweet, bee-like sound. The tall man was Mr Tawab Nashir, the patron of the theatre, and through him I met one of the actors, who spoke English; it was the same intellectual I had met before. He was a poet who worked as an accountant with the Spinzar company, Wazir Mohammed Nakhat (which means perfume). We became close friends almost immediately. They were far more anxious to show me anything I asked to see and take me anywhere I wanted to go than to come and inspect the taxi bazaar, but we did inspect it in the end, although when I left Afghanistan the owner was still refusing to let his antiquities be taken along the street to the museum. Almost the first thing Wazir Mohammed said was in answer to a question about Afghan poetry, 'We have five or six poets in our institute; Mr Aswat, very humorous, all poets are humorous persons.' Then he said, 'I am statistician, and electrotechnic; also I am actor but not professional.' We went together by trap at a Victorian pace to inspect the Kunduz Bala Hisar, the huge fortified mound south of the town. Seeing how utterly ruined it is, it seems strange that only a hundred and forty years ago, scarcely two lifetimes, Lieutenant

Wood was received in this fortress by Murad Bey, 'the head of an organized banditti, a nation of plunderers'.[26]

It is not a fortress but a bulky fortified town, some four hundred by two hundred yards, defended by a fifteen-foot ditch below a thirty- or forty-foot mud rampart. The pottery is Islamic, with pink baked tiles and a later yellow tile; on the north-east corner separated by a bridge is a massive mound sixty feet high which evidently represents Murad Bey's castle. The lowest level of this mound contains pieces of a thin, finely made ware of a vivid red colour and pieces of big grey storage vessels which I believe to be Greek or early Buddhist; but the surface scatter was the usual late Islamic and timeless mixture and there were glazed wares almost everywhere; a fine turquoise glaze which I imagine to be fourteenth or fifteenth century starts fifteen or twenty feet from ground level, but of course it is hard to distinguish the genuine substance of the mound as it was laid down from outer layers which may have been washed down from the top or disturbed at any period. The Japanese dug a hole and are believed to have found gold coins that were taken to Kabul; Greek coins of Hermaios from the southern kingdom[27] were for sale in the bazaar and I was told they were found in the mound. Murad Bey's keep is called Rustam's Seat. These ruins have a distinctly Victorian personality; it was Friday and people were walking in them to see the view; they were haunted by bee-eaters and blue rollers, and swallows flitted and screamed over the water. It was somewhere in these fields I saw a strange and beautiful small bird I had never seen before, called *Chloris chloris Turkmanicus*, and some pink and purple-breasted finches. A small rebuilt sixteenth-century mosque called the mosque of Momin shelters in the trees and roses to the south of the walled town. It has the simple purity and authenticity of small country shrines anywhere in the world, and the reused tiles on the minarets, which you can see best by climbing the narrow stairs on to the roof, still keep the deep stains of blue and ochre colour from their dead century.

We clip-clopped home to Kunduz among the melon lorries; at that time, at the beginning of August, eighty or a hundred big lorries a day travelled southwards from Kunduz by the Salang Pass to Kabul and Peshawar, all riotously painted and heavily loaded with melons. We talked about drugs. This is a country where hashish is the opium of the people, but the Uzbeks take opium as well. The Afghans smiled about it but not without reserves of cold disapproval, and they told appalling stories about the results of addiction. 'Hashish,' said Wazir Mohammed, 'is for sleeping, wine is for waking. It is the opposite of wine.' We ate lunch and in fact most meals during those days with Mr Tawab. There were tables of magnificent dovegrey and charcoal Kandahar marble, but we generally ate on the carpet. Lunch consisted of rice cooked with a little meat, a *ratatouille* of aubergines, green peppers and mutton, served separately but eaten with the rice, delicious Uzbek bread, which no one used if forks or spoons were provided, and a salad of tomato and onion with spices, pepper and fragments of green pepper. The meal began with a sharp, cool drink of sour milk and mint sauce, and ended with an enormous dish of melon and grapes. This menu was Afghan food at its best, and it was seldom much varied. In a teahouse the only thing to eat was usually bread and kebab; the one great cooking discovery I made that summer was the use of apricots in rice and in stew.

At night we went to the theatre. It was a performance like a school concert, with special cheers for local jokes. All the plays I ever saw at Kunduz were farces, simply constructed, half improvised and acted with amazing verve. It was comic acting at the same concrete and visual point that Chaplin reached in his silent films, and I ought not to have been surprised when Wazir Mohammed asked, 'Who is the first and greatest comic genius?' and then supplied the answer, Chaplin. He told me that sometimes visiting Russian companies played at Kunduz; he admired their powers of tragedy, particularly in Chekhov, but scorned them as comedians. He was extremely serious about the theatre and one day he showed me his books, which included a theoretical work by Michael Chekhov and an American textbook on theatrical production. I would like to have seen the Kunduz production of Wazir Mohammed's local adaptation of Molière; Molière seems to fit Kunduz and a number of the improvised farces were based on his plots.

On this night I was befuddled by sweet music and lack of Persian, but delighted by the liveliness of everything. Most of my friends in Kunduz went to the theatre most nights, either as performers or to watch. There was a riot after the first half hour, when the shilling seats at the back rushed the emptier half-crown seats and half a dozen policemen lashing out with their belts failed to hold them. The performance went on uninterrupted and the police withdrew with no hard feelings. The concert started and ended with music, individual singing and dance acts by three glamorous girls with made-up faces and ample proportions, giggling like schoolgirls, and the actors played in a three-act farce about a mad professor (Wazir Mohammed) in a clothes shop. Wazir Mohammed told me there was a fight behind scenes, 'blood flowed, but we played . . . No, it was bad, bad for art, and art is important. They are children, you know, but they will become stronger.' We dispersed in galloping carriages with their small lamps lighted. The dogs were asleep in the road and the moon was dripping with coolness.

CHAPTER
9

Every day at Kunduz something new happened. One day I went to Shakh Tapa, the mound site above the airfield where four nomadic graves were opened by the French. The graves had been robbed, but they must once have been rich; they seemed to date from the invasion of the Huns, and one of them contained a Byzantine coin.[1] The airfield is a tiny area in a vast plain; the prevailing impression is the fineness and density and extent of the toasted grass and skeletons of thistles. In Kunduz the sun strikes downward like a piston, but up on the plateau you feel breaths of wind. I saw birds I never found the names of. The mounds hang on a higher shelf of hill, at the near edge of a higher plain; they dominate the ground below and stretch in a long line of bronze humps and swellings as far as a human eye can penetrate the distance. Like long barrows in England, they have almost but not quite the air of natural features.

> And such the Roman Camps do rise
> In hills for Soldiers Obsequies.[2]

I counted thirty-four grave-mounds on the same long edge of hillside to the south, and there were others on the edge of the huge plateau where the airfield is. A few weeks later when we flew in to Kunduz from Faizabad we saw a whole range of tumuli further to the east and south-east, out of sight of the airfield, in a long continuous series like an encampment.[3]

Several sites were too difficult to visit or I was too absorbed in life at Kunduz to visit them. I bitterly regret not having seen Hazar Sum, nine miles north of Haibak, where there are 'crude nomadic type drawings and sundry geometric designs' which it might be possible to relate to other examples, perhaps to the designs on pottery.[4] It was found by Moorcroft in 1824 and visited by Major Yate in 1886.[5] The settlement consists of cave houses, with front and back rooms and plastered walls, some free-standing

stone buildings and the ruins of a canal. I did manage to see Momokhil. We drove out in a trap westwards through Chardara, but halfway a taxi passed us and we transferred into it. This time I saw four or five tumuli at Chardara, but when we climbed on to the plateau on the west corresponding to the airfield on the east of the river, at first we saw almost nothing; nothing that is, but desert and camels and a bare-looking distant mudbrick village. We passed a small Uzbek shrine with faded votive banners and caught a glimpse of two or three big settlement mounds in the green plain below us stretching away towards the Oxus. After an hour or two we came to a willow wood bounded by a small canal, with three more mounds standing in the fields to the north. A scarecrow stood close to the road. It was a standard of red and white flags dressed in a child's red vest and topped with corn-dollies. Near here we left the road, such as it was, and plunged into deepening thin woods and darkening narrow rides. They led to a farmyard, with hens and children and dogs flying and baying in all directions. The village was called Churok and the farm was Tawab's and the background of his childhood.

From Churok we took horses to the place called the Tomb of Afandi.* Afandi is an Islamic saint; his small open shrine is about fifty years old and it stands above a graveyard on the lower disturbed ground at the foot of a mound about fifty feet high with another not so high fifty yards away. Tawab gave a whoop and galloped his stallion up the perpendicular sides, Wazir Mohammed trotted quietly after him, and I dismounted and looked at the pottery. The finds at Kunduz already proved it was Kushan, and my only motive was curiosity. There was a lot of plain red and coarse grey ware and the cheek of a big red jar with faint incised lines. Several lip fragments had moulded or applied raised bands about an inch below an outward turned lip with casually incised ornamental waves or leaning loops below that again. The farmer told us about another mound further west called Kushtapa which leaks baked brick. Just as we were leaving I found the simple base of a column, a square block with a raised drum like the two Parthian bases in the garden at Teheran. It was not much of a work of art but it filled everyone except the horses with excitement and raised my stock to a new height. Tawab and Wazir Mohammed decided that it must be taken back to the museum. Only the old farmer protested, because it had been

* Tepe Afandi, Afandi's mound. Momokhil is a more general name.

found a few yards from the grave of the saint, whose possession he considered it to be. 'No,' he said, 'it is a hidden thing, it is secret, it belongs to the grave. Bad will come in your life if you touch it. You will dream tonight because of it.' Tawab loaded it on to a horse, which shied away, making matters worse. When we did take the stone, the argument was that I as a non-Moslem could carry the curse far away; weeks later the old man sent a charmingly worded inquiry whether the saint had troubled my dreams.

We sat or rather lay endlessly in a garden of purple flowers, over lunch and over green tea. 'When we become old,' said Wazir Mohammed, 'it trembles our fingers and our neck.' Tawab unwrapped his Czechoslovak rifle and we shot at sixpences on a wall without moving from our places. Tawab told me about the authentic version of *buzkashi*, a horseman's game with few rules in which a dead, water-soaked, stone-stuffed goat has been half-buried in the ground and from two to three thousand mounted men race and jostle to carry it to one or other of two marked circles. At Kunduz this game is played on the plateau where the airfield is and the great plains of Turkestan are its birthplace.* The man who scores the goal takes a collection which may amount to above a hundred pounds, and becomes a hero; he is famous for life. 'He is a hero,' said Wazir Mohammed, 'in a true sense; it is really a heroic game, it is meant for that.' Tawab said the game is a matter of strength more than it is of danger. Few people have ever played it, and children never play it among themselves. A good *buzkashi* horse can cost four hundred guineas. The game played at Kabul has limited teams, umpires and rules. Tawab had not only seen the original much wilder version, but played in it. It does have gentleman's rules, for example to use your whip on a horse but not a man. When riders meet they hook their legs up closely so that they almost kneel in the saddle. Thesiger in his *Arabian Sands* describes the Bedouin as riding camels in the same way. Riders are sometimes injured or killed but only as they would be at hunting or polo. The importance of horses on the Oxus and the quality of its traditional breeds can hardly be overstated, but now these horses are extremely rare. The first Chinese ambassadors under the Han came to Fergana looking for horses, and a curious piece of mythological geography recorded by Hiuen Tsiang in the seventh century A.D. explains that the

* Or the great plains of Siberia? The riders are not numbered in thousands except for example at a big Turkestan wedding.

Ganges flows from the mouth of a silver ox, the Indus from the mouth of a golden elephant, the Yarkand from that of a rock-crystal lion, and the Oxus from that of a lapis lazuli horse.[6] It was an afternoon for such thoughts.

The only pony trap was away for the day, so in order to hire a car to get back to Kunduz we negotiated and sent messages to neighbours for two horses; we then had to rescue a lorry which was stuck across the only road with one wheel jutting through a broken bridge. At the Spinzar hotel in Kunduz I found Bruce and Elizabeth, with a new *firman* including her name for the Anjuman Pass, and some new information Bruce had collected about the route. He had found a record from 1967 that the local Hakim had at last exterminated banditry in the pass, most of the bandits forced into retirement being his close relations. Kunduz is a hot, muzzy place and we were hungry for snow and height. We had hoped to explore the old trade routes to China through the Wakan corridor, but that was forbidden; so we looked forward at least to the southern link over the Anjuman and down to Kabul. Bruce had seen in an embassy logbook that a military attaché who crossed this pass in the twenties had taken a fourteen pound trout out of a lake where we planned a day or two. There was much preparation of gear for fishing.

That night I went back to the theatre and once again when we came out the drivers were asleep in their carriages; they woke and cantered away over asphalt into the coolness. It was the last asphalt we were going to see for a long time. We set out for Faizabad rather late next day in the back of a Russian jeep, and the last sight I remember in Kunduz was a young budhorned gazelle tied to a tree; he was standing on a Bokhara carpet eating a pile of grass.

The beginning of the journey east was marked by the mounds of ancient settlements which started after about four miles; we saw one in the fields to the south the size of Aliabad Qala. Several of the smaller ones had been cut like eggs and used as threshing floors, some were almost demolished. The mounds thinned out and the road battered us into semi-consciousness. We moved through a dust haze superimposed on a damp haze, but the rice crop was a sharp green beside the road and the dappled, scallop-sided hills which were insubstantial at first drew together and closed in.

Khanabad was horses padding through the dust, dark aubergines and boxes of chives, a teahouse on the river by a seventeenth-century brick bridge, the silence of horses on dust. Then back into the jeep, which we already hated and feared, and a stony river-bed with the old Khanabad fortress high up above it. The hills came close up and solidified, the sun slanted level and deepened and lengthened the trees and the hollows. We passed up a flat valley, the hills were fawn and red, and a river of green, muddy water flashed below the road. We stopped at Bagh-i mir, some huts made of packing-cases with caged birds hanging in the branches of trees. A policeman came past hand in hand with a soldier who carried a folded umbrella in his other hand. We moved on up the valley and the road began to climb more seriously. We crossed a broad forceful river and saw it a little further up being forded by two heavily loaded men. The cliffs in that valley were a flowerpot pink and the fields were rich. There were tumuli on the hills on the left bank and the hills themselves had bald domes accented by the decline of the sun. At the head of this valley we came suddenly out on to a plain of a fabulous greenness where horses were grazing between two rivers; we followed the left-hand river upstream and at once came on a village built among a great mass of mounds, and soon afterwards the single mound of a small fortified town at a place where we crossed a watersplash. The two or three miles in darkening light from here to Taliqan were among very rich, mound-studded country, culminating in a vast Islamic graveyard full of strange tombs. It would take a long time to count and to chart all these interesting disturbances of the ground, let alone to sort them out in a semi-scientific way. There must once have been a dense occupation of the whole plain, and the remains are at first sight so rich as to be dizzying. Taliqan stands at the head of the plain, and we spent the night there. We could see a big range of snowy mountains, very high up to the south-east and topped with clouds.[7]

It was the moment of dusk and someone was singing prayers in the hotel garden. When he stopped, the crickets chirred on a curiously high note. Elizabeth and Bruce went to look at the river and I waited with an oil lamp under the masses of foliage while a police officer came to look at our passports and permissions; I tried hard to persuade him to let us go to Ay Khanoum* and almost got away with this, but not quite. So the next morning we

* Not far away and a road exists. It seemed at this time we should never see Ay Khanoum, and Bruce in fact never did.

were up before dawn and back into the jeep when the sky was still streaked with yellow. We travelled for thirteen hours that day along drovers' tracks and river-roads of big pebbles remade every year when they were washed away, and up dry river-beds, sometimes through axle-deep water for twenty yards at a time, and up and down switchback cliff-roads.

This road is extremely dangerous in bad weather and sometimes in good. No one should use it without very recent news about its condition. A fortnight before us, the British ambassador had tried it in a Land-Rover and failed to get through, and Tawab warned us it would be hair-raising even if it was practicable. If the river had been a foot higher we should have failed to get through. On the other hand a French mountaineering expedition got through with an enormous supply lorry. It hardly needs to be said that a guide is much more use than a map.

It was a journey I should hate to have missed, but once seemed at the time to be enough. We started up the river and bore east up a tributary until it thinned to a stream; here we left it and climbed across a stony neck of land and down to another thicker-wristed stream. We followed this water down its valley past some bun-shaped Uzbeck tents and then of all things an English sheep-dip, apparently operated in season by English volunteers, installed where it would catch the big flocks on the main droving track in and out of Badakhshan.[8] The water we were following swirled into the Kokcha, slate-coloured water into brown; the road turned south-east and from now on it followed the Kokcha upstream to Faizabad. The Kokcha valley impressed its character at once; huge slabs of limestone hung above the water, sometimes in tall pillars holed like a dovecote by the action of floodwater, sometimes in deep gorges. The only sources of lapis lazuli in antiquity were in this valley; and it has its own variety of ruby;[9] its visible qualities are loneliness, wild rocks delicately coloured, and dashing, powerful water.

The road went through Kishm and its grave-mounds, where Marco Polo spent the night and where a police barrier marks the entry to Badakhshan. We found that Badakhshan is still locally used not only as the name of the province but as if it were the proper name for the town of Faizabad; if this tradition is old then Marco Polo must have followed our route.[10] It took him three days and they must have been difficult. The most interesting part of the road was its passage through a mountain gorge above drowned woods and river-islands with pink flowers visited only by a fine-looking eagle with a huge wingspan. The river was so wide that villages built on opposite sides must have been unable even to shout to each other for many months of the year. We drove several times over the only telephone line to Faizabad which was down in many places. Vulture-shadows flitted across the cliff-faces. The river boiled along two or three hundred feet below the jeep wheels. All day as we became less conscious of it the country became more and more exciting; the discomfort of the journey, the quietness and remoteness of the valley, and its virginal resources of romantic beauty increased together. More or less every village had its ancient mound. At long last the valley opened into a plain; it closed again, and we descended a zigzag cliff-road to the new bridge into Faizabad. The old unfenced stone bridge was intact beside it, but drowning; during the five or six days we were in Badakhshan we saw it awash under a foot of water. The river rises whenever a lot of snow melts on the peaks, first in spring and then again in early August, and sometimes three times a year. The town was silent except for the river; we left the jeep at the entrance, and the only other car we saw that day was parked in the central square with no wheels, resting on four piles of bricks. After dark the only lights in Faizabad were oil lights carried in the hand.

We slept at a barrack-like resthouse with a swallows' nest in the main corridor, on a rock above the river and the drowned bridge. I sat outside watching the stars come out in handfuls, and thinking that the same stars I could see shone over Russia sixty miles to the north and over China ten days' walking away to the east. Elizabeth was having difficulty getting to bed; word spread as if by telephone that there was a young western woman undressing, and as the process advanced more and more Afghans flocked to the room to appeal to Bruce about a less and less likely series of medical emergencies. The worst was a man with a filthy foot covered in festering bee-stings, but after him the ailments became lighter and patients began to reappear in new roles, like the chorus in *Aida*. Suddenly I heard a beating of drums like the booming of a water-ram and a flute like a bird-whistle. It was a wedding procession: first a single dancer twirling a thick red candle alight on a square tray, then two other dancers and four men beating and cross-beating each other's batons in a fast double rhythm, all of them enclosed in a cheering, whistling, moving crowd. They came across the old bridge and disappeared into the town.

In the morning we woke to clouds and a light watermist, but then the sun emerged blazing. We were guarded day and night and followed everywhere by a sweetly smiling Hazara soldier called Sholtan,* with a face like a russet apple. In the bazaar he shooed away children and told us the best place to eat, and when we went to explore the country upstream on the opposite bank he robbed ten kinds of fruit-trees and kept politely bringing us the spoils in his military hat. We had trouble with the *firman* for the Anjuman Pass. Our plan was to go south by any transport we could find, up the Kokcha to Jurm, and from there take horses or donkeys up into the mountains. But the complications mounted with the slow self-regulating pace of a disease. We found ourselves waiting in a police office with windows full of leaves and market chatter, and then in a bigger, gloomier room with a notice saying 'Pas Pot'; finally we came to the insuperable obstacle, a tough, grey-haired officer who made us dramatic maps with inkwells while a boy soldier waiting outside fiddled with the bright metal bullets in his bullet-belt. When the *firman* was copied in Kabul to include Elizabeth's name, Bruce's name and mine had been run together as one word, and my passport number left out; this caused endless trouble but it was possible to iron it out by pointing to other parts of the document which did refer to me. The new catastrophe was worse; in copying a list of names of villages from one document to the other the clerk had left out Anjuman. We were therefore refused permission to cross the pass named after the village. We were allowed to go up to Jurm and to see the pass as far as the lapis mines. We were also told that the Anjuman Pass was impossible from our direction, which was demonstrably rubbish; Dasht-i Rewat, the village nearest the pass on the north side, is very little higher than Jurm, and the path over the top is negotiable in both directions; the police officer had certainly never gone further than the village above Jurm where the motor-track ends.†

* He came from near Bamiyan and was near the end of his military service; he already had a wife in Kabul living with relatives and wanted to become a Kabul policeman. I once saw the name Sholtan cut on a rock at Bamiyan in the Russian alphabet.

† The miscopying of the documents was a genuine mistake. The best maps for the journey must be got from the Kabul Cartographic Institute with a letter from one's embassy.

This was a blow, and much worse for Bruce than it was for me. We were also in difficulties about changing money; we had been told at Kunduz that travellers' cheques could be changed in Faizabad; this was untrue, and there was only one bank that took them even at Kunduz. The last chance to change money was a dash to the Faizabad airport to change it with the air company officials. Bruce made the dash in time so we did solve that problem, but he came back rather pale, having ridden into Faizabad in a battered lorry with a broken birdcage in it. The driver, who was high on hash, said his lorry (taking one hand off the wheel) had just (gesturing with both hands) somersaulted into the river; 'bird smashed up, also lorry smashed up'.* It was a morning of disasters; in the afternoon to cheer ourselves up we wandered up the river.

The Kokcha at Faizabad is a torrent of ice-cold snow-water of an unexpected force and rage. Herdboys can call across to each other only by whistling. It makes the most wonderful river-pebbles of any river in the world, as good as the best marble beach-pebbles from Monemvasia in south-east Greece, or from Patmos than which there are none better. I was apologizing to Bruce and Elizabeth for hanging about a particular fringe of stones for so long, swimming in an eddy, washing fleas out of my trousers and groping for pebbles, but he answered, 'But you are about to be dragged up one of the remotest valleys in the world just to see a stone I have a passion for.' Above the river we climbed up through a fringe of blue-green sea-holly to see green walnut trees and tall white poplars trailing vines of green grapes, and white and purple mulberries and huge straggling rose trees full of dead roses like coloured paper. A grey stallion was grazing in a level evening light in a soft-coloured field below high, steep hills, like a picture half by Stubbs and half a Welsh landscape by Richard Wilson. Fortune began to alter. Some children in the lanes were persecuting a quail and Elizabeth bought it for a shilling; we carried it home in a hat.

We came to love Faizabad and understood why Lieutenant Wood and Marco Polo had both been happy here. We liked the small town shops and the small town jokers, the big herds and the tiny herdboys and the sense of being at the end of a long road, like being in the last village at the end of a railway. No doubt the chief

* *Kharob* is the word. It means ruined, broken or useless. One of our drivers said 'this road is *kharob*, all Afghanistan is *kharob*'.

ingredient in all this was the snow-river and the mountains, the silence and total absence of news which imposed a new timescale, and the simplicity and lightness of the architecture. We saw some fragments of a local marble. In the morning the same black and fawn herd streamed slowly out across the bridge at dawn that came in the night before in a mist of shadows. Men wore puttees or leggings, although most of them and all the boys were barefoot and the horses unshod; the bazaar had thick grubby-looking fairisle winter socks made of oiled wool.

We travelled up to Jurm in the back of a lorry. We were asked about 500 afghanis but the right price is 30 or 40. There are American shooting parties that pay $6,000 a head to be taken up to Wakan for the heads of Marco Polo sheep. It is just as well this is a rather prohibitive price, but it does inflate the expectations of poverty-stricken villages and of lorry-drivers. We found that 3,000 afghanis would buy two donkeys, which we could sell again for 1,500 (for £6).

The quail had spent a good night; it ate breakfast and appropriated a corner where it hid and watched us with bright eyes. It was very tame but its wings had suffered from being pinioned and at first it would eat only the tiniest crumbs. We bought a cage and took tea, before leaving, in one of the teahouses with huge pre-revolutionary Russian samovars, like pieces of a railway engine of the eighteen forties. An old grey horse wandered by with two baskets of late apricots. The back of the lorry was ten feet by five; by the time we set off it held twenty-two people, perching on and among baggage, a tin trunk, sacks of grain and loaded saddle-bags, with a heavy ballast of rocksalt and a bicycle inscribed 'Hercules, aristocrat of bicycles'; we carried one or two guns, one of which I had to hold because its owner, a boy of fifteen, needed both hands to hold on to the cool place on top of the driver's cab. We were full of forebodings but the motion was far quieter and gentler than the journey in the jeep, and even the quail took it tranquilly; it drank water and ate bugs in its cage, and made itself a nest out of grass.

The journey was four hours, maybe sixty kilometres. We stopped twice, once at a place where a man was selling smoked trout and cannabis was growing wild by the roadside, and once near a shrine with sunstruck flags of pink and yellow and red. We saw Vitruvian-looking cantilever bridges and climbed through a long gorge with lichened rocks beside the track and water-carved, shattered and scalloped rocks standing out of the water. At the top of this gorge where the plain starts stood an abandoned cottage with a lonely garden containing nothing but enormous sunflowers. The main road branched away to Bahrak and we could see a mass of snow hanging on the crests of the Pamirs. Once or twice after that everyone had to get off and walk, but it was not much longer before we trundled down into Jurm.

We stopped at Jurm in a dusty resthouse in a garden of petunias and spring onions. On the hillside below this building, which stood on its own and was made of cement, we explored a deep orchard of alfalfa and mulberry and apricot trees; they were very late apricots, red-cheeked and scarred by birds and very sweet. Two small, light-footed old men worked in the orchard and invited us into their headquarters, which was a rug spread under an arbour of giant vine. We discussed grapes and they were very proud of the infinite number of local varieties. An obsession with local varieties of fruits is at least as old as Babur and this is the mother-country of the vine. The varieties are all produced from seed. All seed-grown grapes are 'new' species; it takes grafting to prolong a species. There is no end to the natural process; advanced viniculture is selective. The vine is native in Afghanistan and eastern Iran; it was domesticated in Mesopotamia probably before the end of the fourth millennium B.C. Wine is no longer made in Afghanistan for religious reasons, except by an Italian company at Kabul, which produces a good, brisk tablewine and is improving every year. The eating grapes at their best are the best I have ever eaten. The native stock of Afghan vines was used for the foundation of the Californian wine industry.

The village was a little further away wrapped round in tall walnut groves and small water-falling streams. I offered one of the old men a pinch of English snuff; he took a huge pinch like a charge of gunpowder, sneezed and wept and beamed with happiness and came later to ask for more, because he said his eyes were bad and the doctors despaired of them, and none of the medicines had such an excellent effect on them as this powerful snuff.* We became fast friends and he introduced me to his friend

---

* Afghan snuff is for chewing. It is a coarse green and has the same smell of herbs and donkey-dung as a hillpath on a hot day. Everyone in the remote countryside carries a snuff-box with a mirror ornamented with coloured glass, made in Peshawar I believe.

who asked me with a speculative eye where I came from. A country called England, I said. Oh yes, he said, England; would that country not be near Kabul?

As we sat in the arbour, a boy came running through the trees to tell us that there were foreigners coming up from the village. I went down to the wall to see whether they looked as if we might want to talk to them. In a few minutes they filed up the field-path like persons on a long march, with tired faces and a winning air of gaiety and purpose. It was obviously an American family, father, mother and three daughters, youngest last and aged ten. Good morning, I said from my apricot trees. They looked at me, looked at one another, looked very startled, smiled at me, and started to walk on. I said it again, and added, 'Have you come far?' 'Hey,' said one of the daughters, 'it's an *Englishman*!' I had forgotten that only my head appeared and I was wearing a turban. They were an American doctor and his family, and they had just come across the Anjuman Pass. We got to know each other of course, but everything about them, their courage and style, the doctor's cool enterprise and his wife's tranquil ability to create a family hearth wherever she was without any fuss of any kind, their confidence in the children and the children's in them, and perhaps more than anything the clean dresses kept at the bottom of their baggage not to be worn until Faizabad, fills me with admiration whenever I think about it.[11]

They had taken ten days to cross the pass, travelling with two donkeys, with time off to climb a peak, and exactly exhausted the last crumb of their provisions on the last day. They were able to tell us of the existence of the kind of ruins we hoped for on the near side of the pass, a big formal building close to a cliff, which looked as they approached it like the entry to a cave. Not far away on an eminence above the gorge or valley they had just left, there seemed to be the ruins of a castle. This possibly was all that is left of the last post on the ancient road to India: the famous gate of the Arabs from which the caravans set out.[12] The building Dr Frantz and his family saw was a mosque with decorative brickwork and with half its dome standing; it stood at 8,500 or 9,000 feet in a very wide valley.

The mosque was beyond our reach, and worse still, we now found that even our visit to the lapis lazuli sources was foredoomed. A soldier was now stationed at the approach, and the

Frantz family had been rather fiercely moved on* and told not to linger in the area, even though their *firman* was impeccable. It seemed quite likely that even if with some loss of time we reached the area of the mines we should be turned away. We had heard that the mines were now being operated by Chinese technicians under one of the foreign aid schemes, and later we heard from Indians working in the same general area that the numbers of the Chinese had greatly increased and that they now numbered hundreds; perhaps this sentry had something to do with their presence? It entailed yet another change of plan for us.

We decided to rest, look at flowers and explore the local antiquities of the area we were already in, and to try a day's walk upstream along what we already suspected and now believe with some certainty was Marco Polo's route and the natural route into Wakan. That evening we all dined together in the garden of a local official, around a long and extremely beautiful Yarkand carpet. A roan horse with delicate nostrils nuzzled at some windfall apples scattered under a walnut tree. The people of Jurm lamented the closing of the Chinese frontier five years ago; in the old days, Afghanistan exported opium and received carpets and silk, but now most of the Chinese goods come up through Pakistan, and it is not clear who buys the opium crop, which incidentally is certainly of no great size; recent writers have exaggerated. On that night the stars seemed more numerous and exactly constellated and smaller than ever. A month or two earlier there would have been bulbuls, night-singing birds like the rich relations of an Oxfordshire nightingale. As we walked home to sleep the night was full of a continuous high chirring and the pipe of a cuckoo-voiced night-bird in the woods.

Next day the river was still rising and we were told the road might soon be cut off. We went to inspect the ruins of a fortified caravanserai in the plain below the village. It had a stone base of big river-pebbles, with broken mudbrick walls and corner-towers rising gracefully out of a sea of opium poppies, some purple, some white and some striped red and white, some of them in flower and some in seed; cannabis in seed grew like nettles among the ruins. Some of the inner walls were made of brick, and we had to thread our way over big mounds of stone. There seemed to be three

* The Afghans were probably sensitive about Russian suspicions of the huge number of Chinese 'technicians' encamped nearby. They were right to be frightened.

distinct building periods but we could date none of them. There
was one mudbrick wall decorated with carefully chosen coloured
pebbles from the Kokcha, set obliquely in the wall in alternately
leaning lines in a technique which is still alive in Badakhshan and
which we often saw. The stones were black, grey, a cheese-white
with black veins, a speckled granite, pink stones, purple stones
and gull's egg stones. The natural root feeling for the texture and
solidity and true qualities of stones in that wall was like the feeling
at Strata Florida in central Wales, only with even richer materials.
Another wall had re-used rectangular cut stones set into mudbrick.
As we strayed about the ruins we saw two donkey-loads of ripe
seedheads carrying away the latest-ripening poppy-crop.

That evening we travelled a few miles to a big garden on the
way to Bahrak; we disliked the insistent protective soldiers at the
Jurm resthouse, where it was forbidden to sleep in the orchard for
fear of robbers and where people were brought to stare at us
under police protection, and there was nothing else to see within
walking distance but the Anjuman track, which we felt bad about,
and a few gigantic sunflowers. We were invited to the garden by
a friendly official, whose brother was its manager. It turned out
to be an experimental tree nursery which supplies all Badakhshan
with young fruit-trees. The garden was about fifteen years old,
and its centre was a labyrinth of roses and hollyhocks and of
hibiscus, called the flower-mulberry perhaps because of its smell
and its small spike. Vines wreathed through the apple trees. The
garden sold eight or ten thousand trees a year at threepence a
small shoot and a shilling for a five-year-old grafted mulberry.
The stock was mulberry, apricot, walnut, almond, apple and
pistachio, which last grows wild on these mountains, perhaps as
a garden escape since Marco Polo already mentions the nuts of
Badakhshan. It cost the government fifty or sixty thousand
afghanis (£200 or £250) a year and its income was about half that
sum. It employed a dozen men at five hundred a month,* and a
manager at a thousand (increasing to fifteen hundred) on which
he could hardly live.

After a night in the open in the garden, which to my regret was
not disturbed by nightingales or bulbuls, for which I at least was
still forlornly hoping, we travelled in the back of a more than
usually dangerous lorry to Bahrak. We were hoping for big,

* £2. A labourer on an excavation in the south gets about 235 afghanis a week,
35 a day of which is his basic wage.

fortified mounds, and we did see some huge swellings in the plain, but what we found was even more valuable, at least to us and at that time. The 'club', or to be exact '*k'loob*', as the usual concrete resthouse was called, was the pleasantest shelter we had seen for some time. The quail seemed to like it as much as we did, and expressed its growing confidence by taking a dust bath, and later by running up and down on us all during the night, perching on our shoulders and considering our faces. The room, which was admirably bare except for a carpet, looked in one direction at a hillside strewn with lichened rocks, and in another downhill at willows and white poplars with their roots in rushing streams and their leaves in rushing wind. The village architecture was a set of variations on a formula of mudbrick walls and light poplar frames. We were very tired, and fell asleep early to the noise of wind and water, talking about the origin of flags, and about Elizabeth's pet chicken when she was a child.

Every morning at Bahrak the noise of the water was louder. Every day the whole landscape seemed quieter except for this voice. Some of the boulders in the fields had been split for building stone to make roads, and they showed one face of a fresh texture and the others lichened black and orange. Night-black and charcoal-winged butterflies of great size and supreme elegance flew among them. Eagles with dense feathers like soft brown fire hunted over the plain, we sometimes saw them close. Elizabeth and Bruce saw a golden oriole while I was writing or reading; perhaps I should say that I was writing some poetry at this time, but all the poems seemed to be the same poem, and I had no strong motive to break up the truth I thought I was writing in order to move away from it, indeed I doubted if that was possible until I had written a long book in plain prose. The truth about something always seems nearly clear until you settle down to write it.

There was always the light, dense noise of the trees and the heavy rush of the water, and these noises coloured the valley with light and heavy colours. The hills appeared like green piles of fine dust with imprecise rock outcrops and a gilt light. Morning and evening were as simple as they are in words; every morning the trees took back their fresh colour from the water and their noise from the wind. The only motor transport we saw from one day to another was a lorry crammed with a party of mountaineers in red jerseys, shouting and cheering and calling, back in the world of

men from an expedition in the Wakan. The only flowers we saw
at all were the native white hollyhocks among the boulders.

Sunset would be a clear statement of yellow on blue, then
apricot to the colour of a piece of lime in green tea, fainting into
a duckegg blue and then darkness. At night sometimes the weather
changed and when we woke the sky would be a cloudy floor with
blue holes like the gaps in a bridge, then it would clear from the
centre, like the circle of sky in the dome of the Pantheon of
Agrippa. One night Elizabeth read us to sleep with Dante, and
the next morning I woke in a dream of writing Latin verse, but
when I woke the words were a non-language and some of them
were English words. The morning aspect of the village was very
sober; we fetched water from a cold, clear spring, hardly a trickle,
under a boulder near the bridge, and there was a dusty yellow
tansy growing in the fields; I remember thinking we were as
remote from the world then as we should ever be in our lives. This
village was at five thousand feet, and the mountains enclosing it
another thousand higher. It was perched on a shelf above the
plain where rivers met, and its own river, the Warduj, ran down
into the Kokcha. We walked a long way up the Warduj, and it
was then we discovered from the people higher up that it was the
natural route for men on foot[13] or for horses into Wakan and to
Sinkiang and to China. The river Warduj runs down to Bahrak
from Zebak.

The Warduj at Bahrak runs through a narrow rock passage
about sixty feet wide with the power of floodwater from a broken
dam. The banks are a shady slope strewn with old-looking
boulders and planted with fruit-trees and with vines coiling
upwards into forty foot poplars. We were on the left bank and the
track on the right bank, so at a certain point we had to leave
water-level and climb a hundred or two hundred feet to the level
of a high canal that carries water to the upper fields above Bahrak.
It was overshadowed by a huge and tall plane tree and looked
down on a gorge in which the river seemed very distant; it was
breaking in its course over massive sunny boulders like immovable
beasts, with the same shaggy wetness of shadow and dry backs in
the sun. Above the gorge we came into a wider valley with crops
and groves of trees, and here we passed close by many extra-
ordinary boulders. They were speckled granite smashed by the
weather into smooth planes and edges. They carried a withered
grey and a deep black lichen and a light green and a startling

ochre. The stone was very hard under a knifepoint but its surface flaked where it was green-lichened. They were the finest rocks I have ever seen, small rocks lost in hay and thistles and brocaded with lichens, and one big cracked boulder half in the stream and three-quarters in shadow, with herb robert* and thistles growing out of its cracks, and the colder-shadowed, fresher-fractured rocks in the gorge. In spring this valley must be a mass of meadow flowers; they were withered now but there was a residual sweetness in the air which must have been pressed out of the last few flowers and herbs by powerful sunlight. It was a light, heady smell, partly of hay which stood here and there in haycocks.

I went a mile or so upstream to explore a ford while Bruce and Elizabeth slept under a tree beside the river. The ford led to a low-built, mudbrick village called Nabahar on a low hill above the right bank; the riverwater was a hundred yards across, extremely strong and icy cold and waist-deep, and the footing was not good.[14] I sat and watched there for some time. A crowd of boys crossed it arm in arm in file, a man with a donkey that he first unloaded and carried the load himself, tugging the little beast. Last a small boy of eight came hurrying along the near bank and called to a bigger boy of about seventeen who was herding cattle. They crossed the river together, the little boy holding on to the big boy's arm and with only his head above water. They crossed slowly and with some difficulty and danger, but when the big boy came back he started well upstream and swam like a piece of straw from one gravel spit to the next.

We sat on the bank together to dry ourselves and he spoke about the track upstream. He knew it went to Lake Siva and to Wakan, but he had no idea where China was, only that it was a very big country. The Nabahar people are Tajik, so early travellers are probably right when they suggest that Badakhshan was populated from the region of Balkh. From the ford at Nabahar you can see snowy mountains to the north-east, and higher, blacker crests behind them.

Evening had a stormy, ominous appearance and the Warduj roared and shouldered like a Pennine river in its worst winter spate. It heaved in hills and waves of water over the drowned boulders under the bridge. I went down to watch it at dusk, and stayed until nothing remained in my mind and senses but the rocks and water and the voice of some bird in the near dark from

* Herb robert is probably a wrong identification.

a wall of poplars. On the day we left I stood for twenty minutes talking in the village street and came away with hands full of presents: two apples, three eggs and an autumn damask rose. Sacks of grain were waiting in a pile for the next lorry to Khanabad.* The people in the street spoke proudly of having been to Faizabad and seen electricity; in the teahouses there were pictures of China, which they knew only as 'very distant', and a picture of a house from an old page of *Country Life*, but no one we met had been to Kabul.

In the morning the quail flew for the first time as high as a low window sill where he poked around among the hats and apples and then returned to the floor. Soon after dawn young men appeared on the roofs of the shops and flung bucket after bucket of water down into the street to lay the dust. A lorry set out with a long dramatic shouting of the names of distant places. Bahrak is at least a late medieval village; some of the mulberry trees close to the river are ancient and there are ruins of heavy stone walls with no trace of mudbrick high up above the defile of the Warduj above the bridge, but the Bahrak mounds wherever quarrying has cut them open seemed to be natural hills. It would be interesting to know the date of the elaborate, high canal system on which the wealth of the village depends. One or two enormous and I suppose very old walnut trees were growing on the level of the highest canals, so the system was not built yesterday, but it need not necessarily be older than the early seventeenth century at the earliest. I spent most of the morning sitting in a teahouse talking bad Persian, eating apples and drinking green tea. These were the best apples we found anywhere, something like a Worcester Pearmain. By ten it was hot. A donkey disappeared up the steps into the teahouse lavatory, no doubt in search of shade. No one really knew whether the lorry would come that day. We ate an early lunch of fried eggs and rocksalt and started walking.

We had twenty hours to reach Faizabad in time for the next aeroplane; we planned to walk down through the gorges until night fell and then take shelter in one of the few farms or an encampment; we should have preferred to walk through the night but the danger from mastiffs is a real one, and there were big groups of nomads moving down from their summer pastures with dogs and flocks, so we intended to walk into Faizabad in the dawn

* Six or seven hundred afghanis (less than three pounds) a sack, depending on quality, one sack being as much as one man can lift.

light. While we ate lunch and prepared the quail's cage with a canopy, someone brought us a very bellicose grey fighting partridge which Elizabeth reduced in minutes to cheerful domestic chuckles with fresh water and kind words. A small boy wanted desperately to buy Elizabeth's quail, and I admit to being dubious about anyone carrying it, but by this time there was no question of her letting it go. When I suggested she might to Bruce, he said that sooner or later they were going to India. 'It would have been parrakeets and a monkey: better a quail now than a lion-cub later.' This seemed a forceful argument. So, festooned with water-bottles, kettle, sleeping-bags, a bird-eating vetch in a large cage, bags of books and a grill for grilling fish we never caught, we set out. We did see a boy taking a fourteen-inch fish out of the Warduj, fishing with a pole and a bait of mulberries.

We walked into a warm, dusty wind, down a track lined with little willows like sprays of green paint. Near the head of the Kokcha gorge, at the moment when serious walking was beginning to be a serious proposition, a lorry overtook us and picked us up. Suddenly the world was gilt and green, and the huge faces of wrinkled rock above the Kokcha, the mother-rock of the boulders, receded gradually from articulate evening light into mist, darker trees, and the curious sleep which overcomes these mountains before sunset and which they seldom shake off before mid-morning. We saw grain carried in from harvest on a wooden sledge drawn by oxen. The nomad camps were smoking in the last light, and long processions of camels and horses were still trailing down towards Faizabad with young animals born in the highest pastures. I saw or thought I saw a two-humped Bactrian camel: there are few of those in Afghanistan and still more curiously there are practically no mules at all.

That day the level of the river had begun to fall; we came into the town through encampments as the first lights were lit; I preferred to sleep out and lay watching unreadable constellations and chewing a piece of *panforte* for supper.[15]

The river mouthed its pebbles and the air grew colder. I woke five times in the night and every time there were always dogs howling up and down cavernous valleys. The last time I woke under the morning star, a sparkling white in a pale blue sky, annihilating all other stars. For several hours before and after dawn huge herds of sheep and goats and files of camels and horses crossed the bridge and climbed the cliff-paths opposite the rock where I slept, going north out of the mountains. The river was up again and the old bridge was covered. As the light increased I could pick out horses and foals we had passed high up the gorge the night before, moving away into a continuous smoke of dust along the ravine road. Produce began to come in to the Faizabad market, mostly across the old bridge through ankle-deep water; aubergines, peppers, trays of mulberries and donkey-loads of green fodder.

Our own departure was the usual melodrama,[16] but after an hour or two of ineffective raging we managed to outwit a conspiracy to delay and overcharge us and arrived well satisfied at the airstrip. The airport office was a tiny building in a large garden of young sunflowers and dense petunias. We were lucky to get on the aeroplane, which was small and overbooked, but it was late arriving and the wind was getting up, so the crew were persuaded to miss out their final call further north and the last three reserved places fell free. This last village in the north is of some interest, it is a military post at a village on the upper Oxus, so isolated that to reach it on foot apparently takes twenty-nine days with full mountaineering techniques. It would be much easier to reach from Russia, but it was included in Afghanistan by Anglo-Russian agreement and Afghan it remained.

At Kunduz we stopped overnight and transferred into a four-engined plane. My only new observation of Kunduz was that the more luxurious bedrooms in the Spinzar hotel had Murano glass ashtrays with glass dolphins on them like a faint echo of the twenty-four-inch glass dolphins of the Begram treasure.[17] It seemed strange for a few minutes that dolphins should so appeal to people who have never seen the sea, but after all, how many Europeans have ever seen a dolphin? A dolphin to Yeats was maybe as exotic as a gong.[18] The aeroplane was to go to Kabul, but it was rerouted by Maimana, Mazar and Herat, so that we travelled with hungry eyes as near as possible from end to end along the whole northern border, and then back to Kabul via Kandahar. Bruce and Elizabeth stopped for a few days in Herat, but I went straight on as I needed to work in the French archaeological library and badly wanted a proper bath. How tired and how much thinner we all were did not hit us until later.

The flight was full of incident: one engine streamed thick rivers of oil. We at last saw the nomads running up and down and the Oxus snaking through a desert of sand to exonerate itself in the

Aral Sea, and Elizabeth acquired the crew's dinner and a female quail from the co-pilot, who turned out to be a quail fancier and breeder from Kabul. Since the quail disappears at this point, readers should know in advance that the cock and hen quail liked each other and after some weeks in the Asia Society's garden at Kabul travelled to Pakistan, and finally to France and to Gloucestershire, where they are living together.

After Herat the river of oil had increased to a majestic estuarine wash. At a certain moment we looked down on a level oceanic disc of desert like the circular horizon from a ship out of sight of land.

PART FIVE

Nuristan

CHAPTER

10

The first impression of Kabul was heat, dust and uniforms. I took a hot bath, but even after a cold one I was continually drenched in sweat. I dressed in cool, clean, stiff European clothes and issued for dinner; the truth that arises in the heart withers to its rest in the heart, but I was the self which says I, which comprehends and analyses.

From this point my travel journal becomes obsessively technical and archaeological for several pages. The first sign of relaxed life is a note from Rabelais, quoted by Peacock in a novel, 'continuant nostre route, navigasmes par trois jours sans rien descouvrir', and then a note from Peacock, 'I am for truth and simplicity. Let him who loves them read Greek, Greek, Greek.'

Kabul was catching the edges of the Indian monsoon; it was curdled, cloudy weather, a sharp morning heat and ripe fruit and intense light, and some rain in the afternoons. At this time I went to the Kabul zoo. It has big parrots and a grove of flamingoes as clean as snow, white waterbirds and a small colony of rhesus monkeys. The tough old daddy monkey was making amorous advances to the female, who repelled him with a jet of pee and then came close to pick fleas out of his coat. I found a bird called *lophophorus imperialis* (monal), halfway between a guineafowl and a peacock, which I believe is the bird represented in a Sassanian-looking painting at Bamiyan, and which is native to Afghanistan. In the bird museum, I recognized many nameless friends: the fugitive *ammoperdix* from Surkh Kotal, the fighting partridge, *alectoris graeca*, I was pleased to see, and a small bird like a sandpiper I had seen somewhere, called *alaemon alaudipes doriae*. The grandest animal in the Kabul zoo is the Persian leopard, *Panthera saxicolor*; he has a honey back and a white belly, with black-rimmed tan spots, the colour of some unknown rock or uncollected lichen, and he has gentle, intelligent eyes and a dangerous build. There is a handsome young lion sent here from a German zoo, looking very much like a Hitler youth, and an enormous stag exuding an atmosphere of Victorian British calm.

One day on the way back from swimming in the freezing embassy swimming bath at five in the evening when the sun was off it, I saw a great dispersed flock of ten or twelve hoopoes flighting from tree branch to tree branch, through the garden, crests up, black and white bars flashing in every direction and ripe fruit-coloured heads. In flight they were mere motion, no more exotic than an apple but as beautiful as apples, flurrying and defining and redefining the air and the between tree spaces of the garden. They were transitory and then motionless for a few seconds and then gone. Even after so long, no morning passed but I saw a bird I was unable to identify, most of them exciting flashes of russet and of yellow. But the familiars of the garden at that moment were flocks of tiny sparrows that loved the ungathered mulberries; there seemed to be more of them every day. I was seriously tempted to buy a bulbul, a small fluffy grey creeper or flycatcher with a long black beak. They were for sale in the Kabul bird-market, a filthy and fly-infested place where only songbirds are sold. It is a caked sea of black and green stagnation and mud, the beggars squat in the mud and the children are smeared with it. I would have bought a bird simply to release it, but the chance that a roseate finch or a siskin suddenly released would survive is too small. The cheeping, bubbling and twittering of alarm and misery from darkened, imprisoned birds in that stinking place are terrible.

We were beginning to plan a journey into Nuristan,[1] the old home of the pagan Kafirs. When after Roberts's campaign the British finally achieved their object of a strong united Afghanistan with clear, defensible frontiers to serve as a buffer state between India and Russia, the agreements were made with the Amir Abdur Rahman.[2] It was then that Herat was refortified in the west and the frontier carefully charted. Already twenty years before in 1871 Kafir children were 'much sought after as slaves' and by 1876 the Afghan pressure on the borders of the Kafir territory was mounting.[3] Acting in the nineties on information gathered in the eastern mountains then called Kafiristan by George Robertson,[4] who was unable to speak the native languages, the British government had abandoned the pagan mountain people west of the Kuner river to be included in Afghanistan, reserving the similar tribes and similar country of Chitral and Gilgit east of the Kuner as a British protectorate.[5]

Abdur Rahman pushed east into the valleys of Kafiristan in 1895, with a powerful army, suppressed the continual raiding described by Robertson and forcibly converted the entire territory to Islam;[6] those not converted were executed, and the best of the magnificent wooden cult figures and grave figures which are now the pride of the ethnographic room in the Kabul Museum were brought back by Abdur Rahman in 1905 as trophies of his victory. Kafiristan was renamed Nuristan, paganism was stamped out and we found very few living traces of it[7] or of the art of woodcarving that went with it. Already in Robertson's time some villages in Kafiristan were Moslem and now the country seriousness of the religion we found there is as wholehearted as the country brilliance of the woodcarving used to be. All the same it is worth noting that one of the wooden figures at Kabul, which was brought down from the mountains only a year ago and was supposed to have been found under rubble in a cellar, still smelt strongly to us from an apparently recent anointing with goat-oil.

The upper valleys of Nuristan are utterly isolated and their traditions are extremely ancient. There is no path through the gorges that a horse or a donkey can climb and the only horses at the higher villages have come southwards across snowy passes from Badakhshan. In 1929 Morgenstierne met an old man in Chitral who could recite his own genealogy for fifty-four genera-tions, which is well over a thousand years.[8] The meagre evidence of a Jesuit expedition from Agra in the sixteen seventies already records the strangely persistent rumour that the Kafirs had once been or might easily become Christian:[9] the only foundation for this view seems to be their hatred of their Moslem neighbours and the fact that they drank wine and had European looks. Their looks are certainly striking, but the relationship to Europe is a long way back. The work of Grierson[10] on local languages in the mountains has shown that the Kafirs have preserved a very early branch of the Indo-European family of languages; if this is so, then the ancestors of the modern Nuristanis were the close cousins of the early peoples of Europe. Sometimes in Afghanistan we saw fair-haired and blue-eyed children, but in the only cases where we could question an adult about this colouring we found it could be traced to women who accompanied the British armies in the region of the Khyber Pass; it also occurs near the Russian frontier.*

More educated Afghans have accepted a strange version of the Aryan racialist myth from German theorists,† but the myths that peoples project about themselves arise from a need for national unity and racial superiority which is felt in the present; they have nothing to do with the real past, a much more interesting subject. I have heard of the existence of a small fair-haired community in an isolated village on the edges of Tibet in the nineteen twenties, and many Afghans believe in the existence of such communities in Nuristan; neither our own experience nor the evidence of photography or of the many published studies has confirmed their existence, which is not of course impossible.

There is a persistent rumour that the fine-looking village people of Nuristan are the descendants of Alexander's soldiers. This is certainly a story that the Nuristanis were telling about themselves not only during the nineteenth century but from before the time of Marco Polo.[11] It can be partially connected to Marco Polo's own interest in the Alexander romance, but also represents an attempt by these remote tribes to define themselves as Pre-Islamic.[12] Today, as we discovered, the same story is being told in combination with a story of their descent through 'El Khoresh' from the Prophet himself.[13] This seems to be a garbled version of Quraysh, the name of the tribe to which the Prophet himself belonged. Kafir myths and religion show absolutely no trace of Greek beliefs though some of Zoroastrianism; when the Greek colonies flourished in Afghanistan, Greeks everywhere were moving inevitably towards monotheism, and what evidence we have suggests that in Bactria they ended by freely identifying with Buddhism, with Iranian cults, or even with local Indian pagan beliefs. No Greek community withdrew into these wild mountains, which were already inhabited, as Grierson has shown, and where

* A doctor who worked on the frontier recalled to a friend of mine examining a tribeswoman and discovering she was a Scots girl who had simply stepped off a train because a dashing young Afghan had smiled at her; the train went on. At the time there had been an international fuss but she was never found. When the doctor asked what could be done to get her out of this frightful situation she replied tranquilly it was much too late as she had six children by him.

† Afghans believe that Nazi racial theory includes Afghans as part of the master race, and until recently the royal guards were dressed up as Nazi stormtroopers and the late prime minister used to wear a black shirt and knee-breeches and carry a whip.

they would have had the greatest difficulty in establishing themselves. It is an open question to what extent the Greeks in Afghanistan or their successors until Abdur Rahman ever did penetrate the more inaccessible valleys, and this was one of the problems we set out to explore.[14]

We decided to walk up the valley of the river Pech, starting from a village called Kamdeh to cross the Kungani Pass, and to go down another valley to a bigger village of a similar name but greater importance, Kamdesh. There was some difficulty about permission for Kamdesh, since it meant passing close to the frontier with Pakistan on the way home. Mr Heath of the British Embassy had the same trouble in 1963;* and Mr Barrington in 1960 was not allowed to go there and was forced to travel in Nuristan with an escort of police and soldiers. But the road to Kamdesh is now a comparatively usual outing; several embassy parties had driven there in 1968 and 1969, and when in the end we arrived there we found several foreigners, Kamdesh being the furthest point to which Nuristan can easily be penetrated by road.†

We set out as a party of four on one of the first mornings of autumnal cold, Bruce and Elizabeth, Mr Christopher Rundle who was Oriental Secretary at the embassy and our host in Kabul, and myself. Our plan was to be dropped by Land-Rover at Kamdeh, the highest point on the river Pech that any wheeled vehicle can possibly reach, even with difficulty, even with a Gurkha driver, and then to be picked up on a particular day at Kamdesh, at the other end of the walk. There was to be no mountaineering although we did take a rope, and on the map the stages looked easy and the Pass not difficult. We carried enough food for at least one good meal a day, and reckoned on finding porters in the villages who would also be guides. The maps turned out to be a poor joke and even the porters had their disadvantages. Bruce and Elizabeth took a tent which at a pinch would hold three, but I got on quite well without one. We were conscious of travelling in some luxury and I heartily recommend anyone else who contemplates spending time walking through Nuristan to do

---

* He seems to have got permission through powerful friends. Bruce had travelled in Nuristan in 1965; his friends were the same ones. Mr Eric Newby and Mr Wilfred Thesiger in 1965 were still in the heroic age of Nuristan travelling.

† The same road continues north; it is travelled by lorries, but it stops at Bargi Matal.

the same. Drugs and medicines are important, guides are essential; one should take very warm and waterproof clothes. A week after we returned from Kamdesh, an English mountaineer died in the mountains not far from where we had been. He had dysentery, must have been moving slowly and was caught out at night. During the night he developed pneumonia and died. In winter there are wolves, bears and leopards. Weather conditions are not predictable.

We drove down the gorges to Jellalabad on the morning of August the twenty-first. The overhanging cliffs and the mares' tails of falling water and the widening torrents and lakes below them were the same as ever; and we descended into a world of sand and blue with flocks of mountains in the distance. A lorry had overturned on the asphalt, and shaken-looking people were standing beside it, but no one seemed to be hurt. We stopped at Jellalabad to drink tea under ripening date-palms. Then we crossed the river and the asphalt died away. It was soon extremely hot. The approach to the mountains was like an entry to the mountains of the moon. We crossed a gravel waste and turned up away from the river between wizened crags, with some snowy mountains showing perhaps from the Panjshir valley which we never saw again. It was a bare, scorched pebble landscape with rock-faces of an ominous grey and brown. We passed pebble shelters and the ruins of a pebble castle, and then at once we were back in a cultivated plain. We threaded our way across it for fifteen miles to the river Kuner, which is brown and fast-running between mudflats and reeds, and up to three hundred yards across, but ice-cold. Here and there on an inaccessible crest above the river we could see a dark fur of deodars.

The road cuts over jags of rock and breaks suddenly into new landscapes where the river bends; I remember one of reed-beds with tall eery plumes and a very old woman in black reed-cutting, with grey hair plaited in dozens of thin little pigtails. Ten or twelve people were crossing the river on a goatskin raft with a wooden frame, with two men paddling. Naked children tanned as dark as old copper were jumping in and out of the small streams. An old man rode by on horseback, dwarfing his small pony with his beard and his turban and his dignity, very like the wooden figure of the mounted man from Nuristan in the Kabul Museum.[15] A small herd of water-buffalo on their way up from the river stampeded in front of the Land-Rover, grunting and cantering and eyeing one another like English hunting ladies. The clouds unwreathed and the crops and the rocks were burnished, but the mountains carried heavy moving drapes of cloud-shadow, and there were still a few travelling clouds as heavy as sea-clouds. We passed the first Nuristan graveyards; the monuments were formal flat wooden croziers almost purely geometric but still carrying visible references to the double horseheads from which they were descended fifty or a hundred years ago.

At Chagaserai, fifty-eight miles from Jellalabad, the bridge has a police guard to examine permissions, and this is the official entrance to Nuristan; Kamdeh is another thirty-one miles, by a broken, stony track up the Pech river, which runs down from its mountains into the Kuner river at this point. A quarter of a mile beyond the bridge we left the dust-road we had got used to, and turned off left along a track, that wound slowly upwards into the mountains. Bruce, who had been here before, had been saying all morning that somewhere soon we should have a surprise; what we saw could scarcely have been more astonishing.

We passed at once through an Islamic graveyard in which nearly every grave was built up with large and small fragments of a marble architecture, and all the elements of this architecture were classical. The marble was glittering white and it had been crisply carved. These amazing pieces were first described by the Danish ethnographer Lennart Edelberg, who believed they must belong to a Kushan Buddhist stupa.[16] He was certainly not right and has been corrected by Madame J. E. Van Lohnizen-de-Leeuw,[17] who showed with a wealth of north-west Indian parallels that the truth is even odder. They belong to an eighth- or ninth-century Gupta temple of the same pagan revival that produced the marble statues from Gardez and from Khair Khane to the north of Kabul. I did not at this time know of either of these publications, though Bruce remembered their existence and rescued me when I got as far as saying it was a marble temple. Most unfortunately, as we were in an embassy Land-Rover and the driver was supposed to get home that night (which turned out to be impossible), we had no time to do more than gape. I have the impression it would be possible with time and care to discover more than has yet been published, though perhaps not significantly more.

A little further on in another grave I saw three small column bases, a foot or eighteen inches in diameter, and a row of triglyphs about a foot long. There was an inscription in the Arabic script carved in relief on the circular section of one of the bases. The high quality of the handling of the marble and its confident classic style were a revelation that threw me off my mental balance for several hours. The site of the temple is not known and we were unable to guess it. Marble as good as that might have travelled some way, but the two places where the fragments are being within five minutes walk of each other suggest that the temple was also not far away, perhaps somewhere on the hill above the graveyard, or perhaps exactly where the graveyard now is.

The river valley narrowed, crops glittered, the river reflected a sun-glitter of sinister power. It was foam-marbled green water fretting over rocks and often crowded with naked little boys and older boys in loin cloths. Some children of nine were playing skittles with heavy stones, naked on the river sand. We passed black and grey boulders, and black and plum-purple old ladies, or sometimes the old ladies appeared in dramatic poses on the skyline dressed in vermilion and carrying axes like so many Lady Macbeths. The architecture was shabby, elegant and inventive: a house had two trees growing through it for shade on the roof, or it was crammed up under an enormous granite boulder like a big swallows' nest, or it had pillars with branching Ionic capitals. In the tree-shade of the last village before Kamdeh, we swept past the most elegant teahouse I have ever seen.

At Kamdeh we stopped at last, in a courtyard high above the river under a vast dark plane tree. Here we started to negotiate. A circle formed on benches and every new arrival formally greeted everyone present individually, kissing the grandees and their close friends. Most of the men carried rifles and one or two of them carried long-handled Nuristani hand-axes, one wore a full belt of cartridges and a single gold earring. Women, young men and boys wore blue eyeshadow. Thunder rattled and boomed, but almost no rain fell. I went down the hill for water, rather as an excuse to walk and be alone after the fearfully dusty and cramped ride. As I came back a flock of swallows flying low came swooping down-valley around my head. A big wind blew dead leaves from the chenar. The mountainside opposite was dotted with deodars high up, and its craggy folds had the look of petrified brocade. I sat alone under the chenar in the early evening in terrific waves of wind and dust, reading *As You Like It*. At dusk there was a call to prayer, a rough, cloudy voice that could be heard for a long way up and down the valley. It seemed to me at that time strangely musical, like the antiphonal mountain-calls of the early evening that are still heard in some parts of eastern Europe.[18] Those calls are the origin of European pastoral poetry, which is a far cry from the voice at the small, open, straw-floored shed which is the mosque in Kamdeh. What it was saying was this:

God alone is strong; I confess there is no god but God; Mohammed is his prophet. Come to pray. Come to strength. God alone is strong; there is no god but God.

CHAPTER

I I

We bargained late into the darkness. The Kamdeh people were terrified of the village of Ishtiwi,[1] the highest inhabited village in the valley, nor were they ashamed to admit it. They refused absolutely to contract to pass it, but they did agree to deliver us there providing we took a policeman, who was for their protection, not ours. We compromised about this and the village policeman came as one of the porters. At first it was hard to see which of them he was, since two or three men had guns, but when we came close to Ishtiwi he took on authority and the others relied on him. The hubble-bubble bubbled and a toad hopped in and out of the lamplight. We slept that night under the chenar in inspissated darkness, but one chip of moon was enough to wash the mountains stone colour. Late at night a sudden burst of hoarse chanting came from the mosque. In the morning the porters slowly assembled. An important part of dress in Kamdeh, particularly for the young, is a long broad white cloth which can be worn like a toga, wrapped as a scarf, or used as a bundle-cloth.

After long discussions and load-sharings we set out for Wamah, a gentle, easy walk at first up the track from village to village. The mountains were studded with hollyoak, but we caught glimpses of a high crest, mostly cloud-enfolded, and long ridges of deodars. By seven in the morning we were walking in stinging hot sun through strong-smelling fields of maize. An eagle drifted among the deodars. The river was a wide, cold, light green stream running fast. I went out on to a boulder to rest and drink and eat a biscuit, and was joined by a local boy, perhaps fourteen, who sat down at a polite distance to stare. We could talk a little and I offered him a biscuit. He looked at me with sweet and adoring eyes, and for most of that day's walk he stuck like a limpet. It was impossible to be rid of him without being impolite, and it was all I could do to stop him from carrying my bits and pieces of equipment for me. Eventually he carried Elizabeth's bag and trotted happily ahead.

It was clearly not on to keep him waiting at every bend in the road and anyway he thought it his place to walk behind me. Guided like a goat by his goatherd from behind, I began to accelerate; for a strenuous half hour I went faster and faster, but the boy still hummed and chattered. Finally, I did persuade him to go first over some rocks; he jumped up them like a gazelle and for a solid hour progress became a kind of light cavalry dash. We came to a shaded grove with great splashes of sun and boulder-shadow, where we flopped down under the trees to wait for the others. The porters stopped here for too long and the boy took his two schoolbooks and rushed away on his own. We sat about luxuriously while the porters smoked a mixture of mulberry leaves and a spiky hedge bush like a vetch. They rolled it into a pipe-bowl made of a rolled cabbage leaf pinned with a twig, and smoked it through their cupped hands.

All day the rocks were fine with strange sugary crystalline cuts into grey-textured boulders, splashes of shadow deeper than the splashes of sun, organ pipes of black rock cliff. The river grew stronger and more harmonious as the valley narrowed. Geckoes of prodigious length with blue-ringed scales took refuge on impossible overhangs. For an hour we moved through the mixed smell of old holly leaves underfoot and fresh ones overhead. Constantly we drank clear, pure water; it was the first time in two or three months we had followed a clean stream. Old men met the porters on the road and they gave each other presents of sweet-smelling rushes to hold in the hand; boys gave each other grapes.* Dark ripe pomegranates hung in the trees with dark children under them. I noticed a house wall painted with a vase of roses and a blue date-palm with yellow fruit, and a little later wild vines, wild figs and wild olives. There was one short piece of rock-climbing along a sloping ledge. Everyone else negotiated it easily but I found it tricky and a four-legged creature of any size would have found it impossible.

For some time you could see your own liquid shadow moving into the stationary shadows of rocks and out again. Then at about

* Wine has not been made in Nuristan since Islamic rules were imposed. Colonel Holdich, who drank it somewhere here late in the last century, says it looked and tasted like badly corked Chablis. The grapes are not the best in Afghanistan.

four in the afternoon a colossal storm broke over us. Thunder pealed continuously from peak to peak and echoed with an endless reverberation in the rocks. Tremendous rain fell and then hail. Between thundercracks and booms and watercurtains we gained very little ground in two hours. The cliffs streamed water and we were terrified of being caught in a flash-flood or a landslide.[2] The porters were behind and the rest of us crouched together under a rock where a young man arrived from nowhere to crouch with us. He wore eyeblue and his hair smelt strongly of goat's grease, and he had with him a pet goat, a young billy with intelligent, lustrous eyes and friendly manners and a most human habit of stamping and twitching with cold and then sneezing explosively.

Rain and hail slackened, there was a whoop like the hoot of a mountain train, and the porters arrived singing. They were not as wet as we were. Formal greetings were carried out as usual on the road, and we pressed on through the lowering evening towards Wamah. We were very anxious to see it, because it stands isolated on a high crag a thousand feet above the gorges, and the traditional life of Nuristan has survived there probably more richly than in any other village. As the evening drew in we entered a territory where the hand-axe habit had become general, and we began to see men and women with conical baskets tied to their backs, the men wearing leggings and walking with staffs. The path was a waterfall; it had a strong foxy smell of cannabis and of sweet reeds after the rain. Through the roaring of water at the loudest part of the gorge, I could hear the voices of birds singing exactly like nightingales. We scrambled and splashed through a tributary and over a slippery bridge into a long meadow on the floor of a dark, high ravine. Darkness began to close in; we could see the lights of Wamah very high up but we had little time left to choose where to shelter for the night, a night in which for all we knew there might well be another thunderstorm.

We decided in gathering shades not to try the climb to Wamah: it was across the river and the bridge was still a mile or two away, and we had no wish to arrive at a strange village after dark. When Bruce had been here in 1965 he was warned against the Wamah people, and in spite of all invitations camped beside the river. Some time after dark there came a shout and a glitter of flames from the villagers, who were slowly winding their way down the cliff-face. A procession of torches snaked its way to the camp. When it reached him it turned out to be a complete and elaborate dinner, sent down from the village course by course. The final touch was two young men to sing him polyphonal music,[3] and three little boys with solemn faces to do a tumbling act. But now it was too late for any hopes of hearing that singing again, and we blundered forward in the dark and rain to find a cave shelter that two of the porters knew about near the bridge.

We trailed backwards and forwards and up and down a precipitous hillside, sometimes following tracks and sometimes losing them. The shelters by the bridge were ruined and unusable. But the rain stopped again and we moved up to a cave on a ledge of the gorge about two hundred feet above the river. It was occupied; all we saw was an opening full of fire and beards. But next door there was an abandoned house built into the shelter of a cave, with the cave roof a few feet above the house roof. We climbed up and nested on a layer of last year's holly leaves. There was almost nothing to eat, since the porters had broken shoes, bad feet, a septic boil on the back, or had just gone missing, including the one with the food and the kettle. I had trouble climbing down to the river in the darkness to fetch water; the river was swollen of course, and so muddy it was undrinkable, but I drank it. I reached a low point of exhaustion on that muddy cliff.

Our dinner was ginger biscuits and brandy. We slept soundly, or at least I did. The porters all turned up during the night and woke at the moment of dawn, singing and banging on tins. The gorge was deep and narrow, and the sky looked very distant, but light blue. We made coffee, ate some pieces of a substantial cake, an offering from Chris Rundle's cook which I think was the heaviest item in the luggage, and set out to walk the stiffness and cold out of our bodies. Usually in the mornings I walked ahead for an hour or two, as the habit of being alone for at least a time in the day is not easy to break. Perhaps for this reason I have a strong impression, which my memory is only now running together, of that crisp and lonely morning; I can see the sunlight on particular trees and turns of the path and can still feel the growing heat as the shadow trailed away from the crests. We saw many more women in Nuristan than in any other Afghan villages, particularly near Wamah. We saw little old ladies with huge walking poles punting and scurrying along in plum-coloured stockings and black dresses with fine gold bangles and silver earrings. Some of the women wore tight silver-coiled hairbands and silver serpentine bracelets with knobby ends.* Men in Nuristan were often wearing one silver earring with a triangular silver plate. We saw a little tweed and an occasional glimpse of tartan.

The flowers were white hollyhocks. Two boys of eighteen with guns were travelling, as we were, up the path, and courteously stood aside to let us go by. Later they overtook us while we were resting and waited beside a spring for us to pass again. They fell in behind, but the pace of our porters was slow, and I insisted that they should pass us again. They were hard to persuade, but in the end they laughed and bounded past like wild animals; they ran for half a mile ahead and disappeared running up a cliff-path. The river Pech was stronger and clearer at every turn, even in the moss and melancholy of the deepest, severest parts of the gorge. By mid-morning the landscape and rockscape was blazing un-natural light; whether the light was mountainous or autumnal I am not sure, but when we stopped by another spring and I found in *As You Like It* a sentence 'Speakest thou in sober meanings?' it seemed a question to ask of the river and the mountains.

For the first time women spoke freely to us, shouting out questions from the fields. We held a long conversation with a patriarchal couple, both almost lost in the tall feathery tops of a crop of millet. The old man was cutting and loading his harvest into a conical basket on the old woman's back. We halted for shoe repairs for the porters, which they executed quite efficiently by the drastic use of murderous knives. An eagle like the tranquil godlike bird of Pindar's Zeus was flighting slowly in the high air-currents above the valley, in air so lucid and empty as to seem infinitely distant. Above this place we came to precipitous tall cliffs stuck all over with magnificent holly trees, much finer than the holly woods further down the valley; the leaves were dense, and glittered in dark green beards. High up we saw two men running over the rocks; they were hunting, I suppose, and we saw some very strange droppings on the path. I mentioned this to the others but the consensus was dubious and none of us knew what

* The heavy torques of coiled silver with turquoises at the two tips of the crescent which can be seen in the Kabul Museum are not now made locally, if they ever were. They are made in Peshawar for the Chitral and Nuristan market. We were offered one for sale in Kamdeh, and bought it for a friend for four pounds, the price of a cow in Nuristan – I was pleased to find that one was sold in the early sixties at Sotheby's for forty pounds, the price of a cow in England. Most of what seemed to be gold in Nuristan was really brass.

animal they might be. All we met on the path was a single old
lady in a local tartan mobcap, and a boy with an astounding
knife-handle in his belt. At this time we were climbing towards
the deodars. Springs dropped from the rock-face, there were salty
white rocks of a coarse marble in the river, and the hollyhocks
grew close around the path, even more massive and taller than
before. The roots of the trees grasping their way into the rocks
were thicker than vine-branches.

We came opposite to a high waterfall where a mountain
stream fell into the Pech from the crags above the right bank.
It fell hundreds of feet sheer down the rocks, sleeking its fast
white hair into green pools, and then down and down over
eight hundred feet of hardly discontinuous falls. It shot downwards in trajectories and mists and showered over broad rock
lips into the lowest pools. These falls seem to be unrecorded
and I am at a loss in what terms to describe them, but they
seemed to me one of the greatest natural wonders of Afghanistan. It was like the goddess Anahita, the incarnation of water
and of the Oxus in the Avesta, 'running down from a thousand
times the height of a man'. It would have been hard to cross
the river, though not I suppose impossible using a rope, and
we had no time to climb the opposite cliff, which would also
not have been impossible, so I am not even sure where the
abundant stream that fed the waterfall was coming from.
Perhaps this astonishing fall is one of many, though we never
saw another like it except perhaps the long falls of the river we
followed down above Kamdesh. Bridges over the Pech do exist,
usually simple cantilevered constructions of a few logs. At one
point we passed a rope runway with a sliding chair made of a
short plank hanging from the rope by a forked stick. Little by
little the valley was becoming wilder. We met an old man
wearing nothing but baggy trousers, a goatskin fashioned into
a kind of shirt and a round Chitrali hat, and carrying a
handsome longhandled axe. We stopped to eat at a beach of
pebbles shining with mica, by a deep sandy-bottomed bend of
the river, where the water was clear stone-green but still too
cold for swimming. Soon afterwards we entered the lowest
fringe of deodars.

Even the hollyoaks at this height were between thirty-five and
forty feet high. The first deodars were already like cedars; towering
conifers tufted like a larch with a stiff short fur of green on the

upper sides of their out-arching or in late age down-drooping branches. The fur was green or bluish green, and the trees grew everywhere; sometimes we saw them felled across the path, in a chaos of branches and gummy scented cones, and a tall sapling was sprouting from a cracked boulder in mid-stream. The small life of this part of the valley was vigorous: charcoal butterflies, small brown moths, a faint bird chirping almost river-drowned, and all the weeds of childhood, bootlaces and shamrock and wild strawberries. On the same afternoon the blackfly began. Blackfly are small, vicious gnatlike creatures which have very few homes in the world, one of them being the Pech river. They bite like gnats but the bump swells to an irritating blood-blister, and if they lay eggs in your bite you may catch elephantiasis, which *The Travellers' Guide to Health* informed us is more or less incurable. We were all bitten a number of times, and even the ordinary Pech gnats have amazing powers. Not all the insects were so vicious; there were lazy tan butterflies with tortoiseshell speckles and a huge, elaborate pale yellow and black one that moved rather faster.

We passed a village called Bini[4] on a left bank tributary, where we saw some cultivation, and soon afterwards a one-plank bridge. The single plank had nine-inch side pieces like inchoate balustrades, pinned with wooden pins some above and some below to prevent the plank from springing. At this bridge the Pech receives a broad tributary on its right bank, and the bridge crosses just below this confluence to a path up the other river. Where the two rivers join a hefty young deodar was growing; the river ran stilly and deeply below it. We looked back downriver on deodars below us, some in light and some in shadow; upstream cloud shadow darkened the ravine. It thundered tremendously but no rain fell; only the blackfly increased.

By now it was many miles between villages. As we approached the village of Chetah[5] we saw for the first time very high crests rearing above the treeline. Underfoot the vegetation was lush; I found a pink flowering balsam, vines grew in terraces on the hill away from the river, and there were unfamiliar flowers including a cluster of tiny vivid blue bells like a nightshade that the bees and the flies liked. Most of the people seemed to be woodcutters, some of them lived high up on the hillside, some in small isolated cottages built with logs and stones in alternate courses. We settled down in a level space between boulders not far from the river with a big open-air fire. We tried to buy a cooked chicken from the village but as it grew dark I settled rather deeply into my sleeping bag.

As You Like It was finished, but I had the Penguin Lorca and a torch. 'Why do you sleep alone, shepherd? In my woollen blanket you will sleep better. Your blanket is vague rock, and your shirt is frost.'[6]

Suddenly it thundered, with long flashes of lightning and some rain. Chris and I shifted in the dark to a tiny, smoky hut the porters had found, with straw in the corners and a fire blazing in the middle. Bruce and Elizabeth shifted their tent to the roof. We fitted ourselves into the jigsaw of bodies and began to cheer up. After an hour or two someone brought us two diminutive live chickens, but they both escaped and ran about the straw clucking with excitement; it was their last cluck, the youngest porter caught them and took them outside to their deaths. Among the flames and shadows and whistling draughts we saw them plucked and singed and seared and fried and boiled in a broth tasting of goat's grease in a round-bottomed black metal pot. It was a long process, and meanwhile we ate roasted corncobs and fresh thin bread. Lightning flashed against the opposite cliff. The porters were sharing an old pipe I happened to have. As the cooking meat neared its climax, their faces stirred forward in the firelight. It was a strange waking the next morning in the straw beside the ashes of the fire, among the bodies and bullet belts with a cold light on the cliff.

We were above seven thousand feet and the spring water was nearly freezing, but when full light penetrated the gorge it was the same intense blaze we had climbed into the day before. We set off through face-high weeds into a series of steep glens of deodars where streams ran down to the river. It was an easy stone's throw across now, with orange lichen and mossy boulders; dippers flitted across it. In the first half hour that morning, we came to the first long smear of snow in a fold of rocks. We walked through woods of walnut in yellow dropping leaf and deodars like pylons. We had a sense of snow-breathing shadow-covered air, a rock crest in the sun looked even colder than the snow, and looking down from where the path had climbed, you could see every pebble in the clear river. I lost the path and had to climb back to it through a tangle of boulders and trees and old leaves; I remember wondering what kind of small animals lived in holes under the rocks. The path descended, and we went by a one-pole bridge where we saw yellow-breasted waterbirds. Soon after this Elizabeth, who was walking last with Bruce, stopped in her tracks. 'Bruce,' she said, 'there's been some big beast here, I can smell it.' When Bruce had laughed her out of it they went forward again and found the porters stopped close by in a frantic huddle, fingering their guns. A snow leopard was streaking away into the trees. He was high up and I think Bruce hardly saw him. He must have been down on the path after Chris and me, and before the porters. To this day I have never seen a snow leopard except in a zoo, but it was something to have been in the same woods.

As we approached eight thousand feet we passed through swarms of butterflies and small moths of many kinds. For lunch the porters baked bread on a stove. We walked ahead of them for some time until we came to a bridge. As we started to cross to the left bank we saw a party of men with guns sitting in the open like a group for a Victorian photograph and watching us. Bruce became nervous. Elizabeth was in front as we balanced our way across the bridge and I was behind her; when we were halfway across the rifles came down suddenly to shoulders to point at our heads, and there was an unhurried clicking of bolts as bullets went into the barrels. Bruce said, 'Elizabeth, for God's sake stop, they're going to shoot at us.' I said she should go on slowly, and be careful not to change her pace, but the stream was noisy and I doubt if she heard either of us. We walked through a dead silence to a tree and sat down and I opened a packet of cigarettes and wandered across as casually as I could to offer them round. The rifles lowered, and fingers came off triggers. I hastily followed the cigarettes with Fribourg and Treyer's strongest snuff, which is common enough in Oxford High Street but like caviare in central Asia, and everyone was reduced to impotent sneezes and pleasure. We were accepted. Later, they banged away once or twice at a rock across the river; one of the guns was a British army rifle. A boy of eighteen or twenty had a slingbow, a two-stringed bow that throws stones. His eyes were carefully shadowed and he wore a coat of coarse off-white sacking cloth with red embroidery at the shoulder and the hem. He had a younger brother of eleven, barefoot, thin and shy, with enormous soldier's ankles. Two of the men set out across the bridge, one with a basket and a gun, the other with a baby and a gun, and the others dispersed through the trees.

We were in the country of fly-agaric,[7] and on this day I saw
agaric growing. The tree we sat under had fabulous tree-mush-
rooms. I went down to the river to wash and saw a huge tangerine
and black butterfly; we were at eight thousand feet and I think it
was the last one we saw before the final valley above Kamdeh.
We recrossed the bridge and climbed right out of the gorges to
where the upper Pech valley opens out into meadows. Orchids
were seeding in the grass between mellow fields of crops, children
were whistling and shouting in the walnut trees. The porters kept
us clear of Pushteh where they said the people were wolves. There
seemed to be a fortress wall above the village I would have liked
to see, but we moved obediently on through the meadows to
Sutzum, which is a small, shattered-looking settlement of about
two dozen houses on a hillside.

People in the fields wore woollen tunics and trousers like loose
old-fashioned underclothes, and met us with much greeting and
smiling. A terrified little girl of twelve gazed in admiration while
her younger brother, aged nine, suddenly stepped out and shook
hands with us. Babies carried smaller babies strapped to their
backs. We walked through birches and pink bog-heather and a
deep pink stonecrop. At Sutzum we waited under a group of giant
almond trees (*badam* the porters called them) in a pile of boulders
near the remains of a big stone circle until people came to speak
to us. It was like the place where we first camped and waited the
night before, and perhaps like the place by the bridge at Wamah,
but only at Sutzum part of the artificial stone circle has survived.
It was like the Rollright stones in Oxfordshire, a simple circle of
man-sized boulders of which the first purpose can never now be
perfectly understood. All one can say is that we were probably in
the sacred grove of Sutzum, and that this is where travellers must
wait. It was probably these groves and circles that no Moslem
was allowed to enter before 1895. In that case the destruction of
the stone circles will have been deliberate and if there were ever
gods in them the gods have gone.

We waited while the sun sank, watching the crows going home
to the last, highest deodars, only two or three hundred feet above
us. A cheerful, bearded man wearing a wreath of cranesbill and
buttercups on his head against the sun came and sang to us with
two or three friends. We crossed to the right bank and walked on
through the evening past a dead-looking village it was frightening
to approach alone. I spoke to an old man, but he was blind and

deaf, then to an old woman who scuttled away, then to a boy who stared without speaking; the mudbrick walls looked ghastly in the setting light and the houses were huddled closely together.

In the village square, when I found it, a mosque with an open balcony commanded the road. It had what must have been an old pagan temple pillar of dark wood, carved with a complicated design of interweaving straps. This kind of wooden architecture and more or less the same designs in woodcarving, and I believe also the same kind of jewellery, exist not only in Nuristan and Chitral and Gilgit but, I am told, in the forests of Paktya, in south-eastern Afghanistan, and certainly in the hill villages of the Swat valley.[8] The forest and its art and way of life must once have been practically continuous over that whole area. Even the folk stories of Swat still give very much the feeling of life in Nuristan, and to some extent in all Afghanistan, with their delicate savouring of sunsets, and their erotic fantasies of magic girls met at midday in wild places. They begin 'One afternoon, while I was lying under a walnut tree in my village I had a dream,' or 'It was some years ago, one day at the time of sunset when all was quiet and enchanting.'[9]

Above this village we came once again to a small gorge; a pair of hoopoes flew down it but the sun had set coldly and Chris came pelting along the track at full speed, running to keep himself warm. Carpets were laid out for us on a roof at Diwah and a pale three-quarter moon illuminated treeless crags. We ate the same thin local bread and a delicious crumbled cream cheese. The wind blew from the snow, we were contained by a sharp wild line of mountains, the river was almost too cold to brush one's teeth. All night, whenever I woke, starlight and moonlight were whitening the leathery cliffs. A heavy dew fell.

There were no chickens and no cock-crow in that village, but a chestnut horse that neighed at dawn and a donkey that brayed and hooted as the sun rose. By the time we had shaken ourselves awake the top crests were blazing with sun and the sky was icy blue; my first half-waking half-sleeping thought was a wish not to dive into such a cold sky. The bridge at Diwah was guarded by a gate and a kind of gate-tower, the village was a pattern of cubes, men in long cloaks and Chitrali hats stood looking at the river. The women were already in the fields; it was a hillside landscape full of figures with black-cloaked women in every cranny of it. Half an hour upstream on the right bank we came to a second village where we crossed a tributary perhaps half the size of the Pech itself. The cliffs were bare and rocky but the valley floor had crops and even a few groves of walnut trees. In the distance I could see a tiny village, with houses built of riverstones and the outer houses as tall and blank as a town wall, dominated by a high central tower like a rustic version of the Signoria tower at Florence. It was not really very far away, but it was Ishtiwi.

We had thought it would be further and I was ahead of the others, walking with a villager whose load I was helping to carry; the track was stony but he was barefooted. He led me into the village through a narrow alley without a gate but guarded by loopholes, and out into a small open square in the shadow of the tower. The sides of this square were a house wall, the solid base of the tower, a mosque with splendid, ancient, wooden pillars and a plank frieze decorated with geometric carvings, and an open balcony five or six feet above the ground, where each of us was installed as we arrived; it was already occupied by three travelling merchants from the village below Kamdeh. In the corner between the mosque and this *serai* was a powerful gate-tower leading out of the village in another direction. I have seldom felt such pleasure and astonishment. The sensation of crossing the square was like that of entering a small Italian hill-town in perhaps the eleventh century, only that there was no mortar and no cut stones, every building had been built up with wooden beams and big stones from the river.

We sat with the merchants on carpets on the balcony while people came to talk to us in turn. Men and then boys offered us pieces of *yakhud*, a red, dark crystalline gem I had never seen before: balas ruby. When we stopped buying it they gave it away. We were shown carpets and two large pieces of lapis lazuli taken from a sack of grain which had come to Ishtiwi from Badakhshan over the Anjuman Pass. The merchants had been at Ningalam, three days' quick travelling in one direction, and they said Kamdesh was two days' quick travelling in another. Ningalam is the nearest bazaar for pots and pans. We were shown Victorian and Edwardian Enfield rifles with British Army stamps, still in use and highly prized. Someone invited us to go shooting gazelle in the mountains, but the charge for borrowing a gun and ammunition would have been astronomic. When the hunters came in that night their only bag was a partridge. One of the young men who made this suggestion was wearing a spectacular yellow shirt which said Victory Inn, the reward of being a porter to an American shooting party. Most people's clothes were tweed or coarse woollen cloth with red or purple woollen embroidery. In the evening we saw brown tweed cloaks, and Kamdesh shoes of thin white or purple leather. The name of the coarse woollen weave with purple or blue lines is *Paroun*, which is also the name of the upper part of the Pech valley.

The children were chasing one another and the swallows across the rooftops, while the elder boys held a stone-throwing contest with heavy stones. Two boys of the same size and age both had suspiciously fresh black eyes. Very small children wore nothing but a Chinese-looking *Paroun* tunic.* A few of the Ishtiwi people had fair hair or ginger whiskers. Everything happened in the small square; it was the theatre of arrivals and departures, the meeting-place, the lounging place, and the main road. Outside the village an icy wind sliced across a landscape of pastures, green nut trees and pale gold barley.

The mosque was even better than I had hoped at first sight. It had clearly been converted from other use, not all of its pillars belonged together, and perhaps none of them was carved for this building. The outer portico had a little two-foot balustrade to separate it from the street, and two plain rectangular pillars to hold up the roof; inside this portico was a row of three older columns, square beams decorated with chip-carved designs, with lotus capitals and square bases, none of the three being the right height for the roof. The designs were coils and loops and wheels and stars and twining cables, and one side of the central pillar had a most naturalistic coiled snake in low relief with two horse-shoe torques end to end like a figure of eight carved above it. A doorway and two steps led into a dark and dusty inner mosque of almost exactly the same size, with six columns standing in two rows. The columns were gouty dark wood, like Jacobean table-legs, each of them a slightly different design from the others. They were beams rather than pillars, except that one had a round collar below its capital. Two stood on bases. The columns held up a heavy continuous wooden series of capitals under a beam like Ionic capitals flatly conceived and continued outwards into waves so that each one merged into the next. The same type of

---

* These tunics are a version of the tunic worn by the bearded foreigners in T'ang terracotta grave figures, but the T'ang figures have tunics with the same peculiarly sharp corners as Kushan figures.

continuous wave-like capitals occur in the Swat valley[10] and of course at Kamdesh. This design has certainly a Greek origin, but it entered Nuristan from India. In the Ishtiwi mosque the branching waves are carved from a different block of wood from the column below them and the roof-beam above them. The whole inner mosque was very dark; the only light came from small windows under the eaves, just above the roof level of the outer mosque. There was no *mihrab* to pray towards except an insignificant niche.

As evening drew in a long, heavily armed procession of about fifteen men filed into the village with grave faces and was greeted. The mountains wrinkled their cold snouts. At sunset the entire village crowded into the mosque for prayers; it was so crowded that people had to stand outside in the square. The atmosphere was curiously reminiscent of the gravity and naivety of night prayers at school. After prayers an elderly grandee of immense prestige in a tartan hat came to see us. Once again everyone had a collection of gems, but his included a great splinter of rock crystal. Ishtiwi had turned away our porters as soon as we paid them, and now we were forbidden to take on two young men from Kamdesh we had made friends with. We settled after what seemed endless agreements and re-agreements to pay two thousand afghanis to five local men for the rest of the journey. By now the mountain crest above the village was in cold grey moonlight; the moon was nearly full. Our balcony was crowded with faces of all ages and the boys sang lustily in a not very subtle polyphonic chorus. Little children crept closer across the square, and invented a game of dashing in and out of the light of my torch, which enthralled them. Chris and I slept where we were, stretched out between rifles and merchants, in shelter from the wind. Elizabeth and Bruce slept in their tent on the hillside; it was a green, beautiful spot but at nearly nine thousand feet it seemed an unattractive bedroom.

Dawn broke with singing from the mosque, and by half past five men were perched on the railing outside it in long woollen cloaks like long-plumaged birds. We made a slow start as one of our new porters went missing, and it was obvious from the beginning they were all good-humoured villains. At the last moment there was a confusion about the route and how long we should take; the grandee in the tartan hat decreed three days and we agreed, although when we told our two Kamdeh friends, who set out walking with us, they said it would only take two. A hawk went up from a crop of barley and wild peas. (This crop is a very ancient mixture that goes back to the beginnings of settled agricultural communities.) When we came to a right bank tributary and crossed it, and our porters insisted on following it down to a bridge over the Pech and crossing over to the left side, the Kamdeh men were horrified, but by now there was nothing either party could do about it. I went on with them for a little and then got myself soaked to the waist trying to ford the Pech higher up; I was pleased because the sun was very hot, but abandoned the attempt to ford the river for fear of worse, and went back to the bridge.

On the left bank we climbed straight up a steep green hillside into a new kind of world of wild flowers and young birches and fresh, bright light. The hay and the flowers were intoxicating and another young tan-feathered hawk went up from below my feet to hang level in the air. We were saying goodbye to the tiny, brilliant Pech in its open valley. The air was still fresh and clear but it smelt of snow and we could easily see the snowy range that closes the Pech valley to the north. We moved into a wood of big birch trees hanging high up on the hillside,* below a high canal that we were following. Sweet herbs put out to dry were strewn here and there beside the path. This canal had splashing falls and sometimes ran among boulders but there was no doubt it was a human construction. As we followed the curve of the canal and of the hill we came on a place where the trees cleared a little and we sat down for a rest. I began to notice the stone below my boots. We were sitting on two smooth grey boulders, pocked with dark balas rubies like a rain-spattered pavement. When we threw water on them they glittered and where the stream ran across the boulders they glittered underwater among pebbles and fallen leaves.

After the woods we left the path and clambered down into a rock-strewn valley; there we crossed a left bank tributary of the Pech; it came splashing and foaming down over fall after fall and vanished over the lip of the valley. Quite a high mountain confronted us; a few junipers grew on it and the top was crowned

---

* At nine thousand six hundred feet it may well be the highest birch wood in the world and the furthest south. This wood may have been deliberately planted to hold the hillside together at the point where it supports a high canal, but birch trees are certainly native very high up in the valley above Kamdesh. But Kipling has Himalayan birches.

with crags and jagged boulders. We could hear the small river and then the Pech first very loudly as we climbed, then like a distant noise of traffic, and then it diminished into silence. We settled down to climbing. We all went different ways up, and I remember meeting Bruce under an enormous shattered juniper. The air around the tree smelt pleasantly of snow and gin. Higher up I found myself climbing up a difficult waterfall like the inside of a drainpipe; the ground on both sides was soggy and festooned in rose bushes. We all climbed too high, and had to go back to meet the porters at a track curving round the Pech side of the mountain. Bruce and Elizabeth moved along the track while I went on up the mountains to look for Chris, who had climbed so fast he seemed to have vanished into mid air. I found him on the top among the boulders, very pleased with life because the moment before he heard me calling he had been face to face with another snow leopard. It had vanished somewhere near among the rocks.

CHAPTER
12

We came down from the mountain into a still more desolate valley full of rocks, with a stream in it that must have been one of the uppermost tributaries of the river Pech. It had now started to hail very heavily. We ate a hasty lunch of cheese and brandy, under a rock, with cold fingers; the porters took refuge in a hut and we moved up the valley into misty weather. The porters had told us we should find a shelter for the night one hour's walk ahead. As we walked it started to snow and we were soon in a heavy snowstorm. After ten or twenty minutes we came to some sheepfolds and a steading; we exchanged greetings with the shepherd and moved on, scrambling away into the snow over a boulder path. After half an hour the snow stopped, and we saw blue sky and sun. Out of the last of the storm came a bearded man with a skin-coat walking barefoot with a gun. He was on his way up to the herds, and we talked a few minutes; he was a sweet and happy man. The herd near the farm in the snowstorm had looked like red and white English Herefords, but later two long herds came trailing down through the extended shadows and some or all of them seemed to be a cross between Herefords and Indian hump-necked cattle.

They came wandering down alone and were so friendly or curious that they were hard to get rid of, and I had to leave them breathing heavy passion after me, by clambering up a scree of boulders on to the mountainside. The air was bitterly cold and when the sun went down it was going to be colder; meanwhile the afternoon was spectacular. The snow had melted leaving only some of the rock-faces sugared with snow, and we could see forbidding mountains far away to the north with their black sides draped in snow. They carried clouds on their peaks and they looked very high. Up the valley some unnamable shrub was in blazing yellow coloured leaf.

We were now at a goatfold with tiny huts like kennels, at twelve thousand four hundred feet, and the Kungani Pass, which we still assumed we were going to cross next morning, ought not to have been much higher.[1] We had climbed circuitously but steadily from Ishtiwi, following the contours of the hills without descending far. The stream we were now following towards its source, which could hardly be far away, was called the Uchuk. We were in a valley of staggering grey crests ending in a snowy col, and none of us could see a way out of it. The sun cast its last intense light on the shrubs and the boulders. It was the almost absolute solitude of the highest mountain pastures, where the only events are the screaming of a hawk and the rising and sinking of the sun. The bearded barefoot man came back downhill with a shepherd carrying a young kid in one hand. The sun had sunk and it began to freeze underfoot. We hastily got together the few twigs left over from earlier fires while Bruce, who had suspected from the start we were in the wrong place, went running back to find the porters.

Sure enough they were happily installed in the steading, and they took a lot of moving. Bruce, Elizabeth and Chris crammed themselves into the tent for the night, but I slept with the porters in a domed drystone kennel like an igloo. It had a stone central pillar to hold up the roof, which was about four feet from the ground, but the pillar was almost indistinguishable from a rough version of a Doric column. The rectangular stone for the body of the pillar was the only cut stone in the whole valley. The capital was simply one broader stone set on another to distribute the work of the pillar and concentrate the weight of the roof; it was quite functional and its relation to the shapes of formal pillars is probably only in similarity of function; we are not dealing with inherited decorative elements but a traditional engineering principle. And yet it was surprising.

We all crept under the dome together, and after many attempts we lit a fire of the frozen twigs against the pillar and Bruce cooked soup. I chose the darkest corner of the igloo, moved most of the stones from under my sleeping-bag, wrapped myself round in a mosquito net hoping it might be warm, and fell deeply asleep. I woke to a pleasant surprise which I took some time to understand. The porters had used the last of the little twig fire to light a dung fire against one wall. It was a massive bank of heat and the whole place was as warm as toast. The smoke had a sharp, pungent smell like that of coarse snuff, but for the sake of such luxury, I would have willingly wept twice as many tears and been far worse flea-bitten than I was that night. At dawn the bodies shifted and the men woke like birds and went to wash and pray. The ground was thick with hoarfrost which I thought at first was another fall of snow. We snuggled back into the smoke to warm ourselves, and the mullah, who had ginger whiskers and was called Mohammed Afzal, started to sing. He had a strong voice, and the songs were much finer than anything we heard in Ishtiwi. The first was an elaborate song in Persian calling on God to defend Nuristan; musically it seemed to be a folksong, and one would have said it was old, but that seems hardly possible. He sang a ballad or two and an impromptu comic song.

We lay chatting until the sun was well up, and the porters refused to move until eight because of having been moved the night before. We now discovered Mohammed Afzal had never been to Kamdesh, and nor had any of the others; all he knew was a pass over the mountains to the house of a friend who came from Ishtiwi. But the house was in the valley that led down to Kamdesh, and anyway there was now little we could do but follow Mohammed Afzal. He smiled villainously in his ginger beard, and said the journey would be four days. About this we were adamant. We should make it in three even by this new route unless we dropped in our tracks. We badly wanted a free day at Kamdesh before the Land-Rover arrived there, and this was now at stake. We won the argument in the end, but only when I had bribed Mohammed Afzal by promising him a hundred feet of climbing rope at Kamdesh which I would of course have given him anyway if he wanted it.

It was all a game, I think. Meanwhile a hawk screamed and the youngest porters stood grinning in the sun and sang a song over and over again which means 'O how many minutes? O how many minutes?' I remember the cheeping of a bird in the scree, and the purity and tranquillity of everything in sight, the intensity of the simplest colours and sounds. We started out in a long slow file towards the head of the valley. It became clearer and clearer that no pass existed; a pass is a low neck of land between two valleys, but as the snow and rock barrier at the top of the col came closer it was hard to make out even a practicable goat-track over the crest. We stopped for a rest below the banks of permanent snow that rose forbiddingly above the source of the Uchuk. A colony of wild delphinium was growing in the scree. Mohammed Afzal picked ice from the rocks in midstream and chewed it. At this snow-fed pool we found fresh-looking leopard tracks and the tracks of a mountain fox.

It was now evident we should have to climb above the snow-banks and scramble somehow up the steep cliffs of the col; we were nervous about time, and Bruce kept trying to apply human reason to the route, but there are no footholds for reason on an unfamiliar cliff and we followed the porters. We climbed labori-ously above and sometimes across the frozen snow-bank for about an hour or two, through profuse wild onion and sorrel growing out of a rocky wall, and then sheer up the rocks and scree. At a certain point Elizabeth got scared of the rocks, and we mentioned the possibility of turning back, but I was against that course because it would land us in other difficulties, so we agreed rather heartlessly that Elizabeth should go on until the rocks simply halted her, and then we should pull her up on a rope. Still, the cliff did end like every cliff, and we came out on the ridge of the col very high above the snow and not far from the peak of the mountain.

It snowed gently. The ridge commands a vast wilderness of mountains. We were not on the lowest point of the ridge, which was inaccessibly steep, but we seem to have been at about sixteen thousand five hundred feet,[2] and we could gaze on equal terms at the sombre masses of snow and rock rearing up into peaks and punctuating the distance. We looked down towards the Anjuman Pass;[3] it was a long way below and surprisingly close. We ate in an exhilarated mood, and dropped as quickly as we could down the other side of the ridge. We were climbing down into an enormous glen like an amphitheatre with other glens running down to join it. We slid and scrambled down a streambed and down endless scree and the first small snowfield with wild roses growing just above it in the rocks; after the scrambling we reached ground where you could run, and then ground where you could walk. It was a mountain pasture valley or rather a meeting of valleys where four streams run together into a boulder-strewn meadow to form the Nichingul. The whole vast glen was enclosed by tall green and rocky hillsides, every hillside streaked with streams and flying falls. The air was full of the low drumming of all this water. Hail fell and low cloud pressed overhead. The landscape was like a craggy, apocalyptic version of Yorkshire in which all the heights were exaggerated, the streams redoubled and the green intensified.

The weather cleared and a rainbow appeared beaming clear pink and violet between two hillsides. We waited for the porters near a steading on the left bank of the young Nichingul. Its ramshackle buildings were invisible at first, they stood well back on the hillside between two spurs in whatever shelter there was. It seemed to add to the isolation. The meeting of the valleys was lonely and idyllic, but this rough, wild farm with its drenched, rough walls made it easy to imagine what life would be like at such a height. As the sun went down huge herds of cattle and goats came streaming down to the farm. Three or four guard dogs attacked us, so we withdrew to wait for the porters in shelter of a hill. They came and started to bargain for their supper at the farm. They waited like strangers at a village, at some rocks well away from the buildings but in clear sight. It was a nicely calculated distance but it infuriated the dogs. They came galloping and barking at us like berserk huskies; we sat still and the porters went on eating. The dogs sat round us in a circle, snarling and edging closer. Mohammed Afzal tried chasing one away with a stick but by now it was madly angry and it nearly bit him. He withdrew, and went on with his supper, then suddenly wiped his whiskers, put his stick between his teeth, and charged the dog on all fours, barking back at it. The dog fled with its tail between its legs.

We went on to a second steading lower down the valley. When we arrived it was darkening, the dusky flocks undulated like a sea and half a dozen guard dogs were making savage noises here and there among the boulders. The farm people were strong and tall with dark, sober faces and clear eyes; I do not think there were any women or young boys, the men were friendly but very silent. These steadings in the highest pastures are used only in summer and from a distance they are almost indistinguishable from a boulder scree. The snowstorm we were caught in was the first of the winter; in a week or two the herds would be moving down to their villages, in a month or two the mountains would be impassable. There was nowhere much to sleep. The porters slept on the roof of the cowshed which was built on to the cottage of unworked stones where the family lived, and Bruce, Elizabeth and Chris put up the tent in a ruined goatfold. There was a tumbledown kennel attached to it, too dark, dangerous and stony to sleep in, and we were warned it was unsafe, but there was no room anywhere else so I slept on its roof.

Bruce had a cold, so we sent him to bed with the last of the brandy. The farmer built us a fire and brought a long splinter of juniper through the dark, burning with a steady flame. Chris and Elizabeth made coffee and I cocooned myself in all my clothes on the roof of the kennel. As the sunset drained from the west an autumn full moon came sailing up in the east into a clear sky through a yellow mist almost as dense as dawn. I could hear the squeak and flitter of a bat. The sky was quite empty except for two puffs of moon-illuminated cloud. The valley was a wind-tunnel and all night long the wind blasted out of the east between the mountains with a monotonous whistling rush. In the west you could see the snow glittering on the black peaks; it already seemed incredible we could have come down from that world. The moon moved swiftly overhead and the wind cut like ice.

Suddenly a drum was beating and a flute was playing, always repeating the same theme. I heard singing and I could just make out from my rooftop that someone was dancing and being cheered. Dogs started to howl, and I could get no closer to the dancing because some of the howls were moving. The music died out and started again, and after an hour it had become very wild, with mysterious imitations of animal cries[4] against the real howling of dogs. All this time there was the steady rush of the wind and the full moon shone. It was several hours before the music died away, first the voices as one by one they fell asleep, then the flute, and the drum last and very late. I fell asleep myself several times, but the moon and the wind and the snow were too much; whenever I woke I heard music or dogs howling. At one moment when the moon was directly above us I woke to very loud howls and the goats were stirring about as if they smelt some wild animal; I heard them running among the stones and then the roof I was lying on began to shake and a stone rumbled off it. I remember thinking they wanted to get in and we were being stormed, and in fact the next morning we did find one or two goats crouching in shelter in the foot of space between the kennel and the tent. I thought my kennel was probably going to collapse, but I was so tired that I decided to lie there until it did; at least I was likely to fall on top of it. The monotonous noise of the wind sent me to sleep in spite of the cold, but the dogs howled almost continuously all night and when I woke again the kennel was shaking as badly as ever, but the moon was declining. In the morning I discovered it had been an earthquake and everyone had lain awake frightened by it. The sombre, richer texture of the hills and the black handsome crests began to alter, the moon sank yellow and the sun rose yellow through an even yellower mist than the moon, and the sky turned blue above the first movements of the shepherds in the flocks. Then prayers, the chaining up of dogs, the whole herd of goats flocking uphill and moving away to pasture, then the lighting of a fire.

I went across to talk to the porters and see about hot water. The farm kitchen had a central pillar exactly like the one in the drystone hut by the Uchuk; it was taller but the room it could hold up was no bigger, and built only a little better in the same technique. Every plate and bowl and spoon was wooden, and butter was being made by shaking and turning the milk in a leather skin. There was no kettle and the only metal in that whole steading must have been one pot, a knife or two, an axe and maybe the metal parts of a gun, although I saw no gun. We bought a solid round goat cheese about a foot across and two inches thick for something like ten shillings; it was one of the best country cheeses I have ever eaten.* The family lined up to say goodbye to us, dour, friendly and very correct. We left the porters and set off at half past six.

We had no way of being certain how far Kamdesh was, we thought above thirty miles, but no European had ever crossed the Uchuk Pass before and we were not sure, nor do we know for certain to this day, where the Kungani Pass reaches the Nichingul valley. We decided to make what pace we could and leave the porters to follow us. Bruce was well again on that morning, but Elizabeth was not, and by nightfall she must have been near to complete exhaustion. Chris and I were in rather rude health. We set out walking through the same kind of world of remote upper pastures, but wider and richer than before. We went down over snowbanks and passed abandoned steadings, and through waist high groves of eremurus in seed: long stalks with baubles of dried grape-shaped seedpods. From that first hour or so I best remember

---

* 100 afghanis. It was quite impossible to buy in Kabul and seems not to be marketed at all. Yet it would hold its own even in Paris. Considering all that is being done for less interesting communities in Afghanistan, it seems a pity no one has thought of marketing Nuristan cheese.

the rich colour of crows flying through bright light against a hillside, and the way in which a flock in the early morning carries its shadows like a flock of shadows. We found strange patterns of stones left by shepherds, they could have been a language, a signature or a game. Once again we saw fresh leopard tracks beside a pool of the river.

At first we crossed and recrossed the river as we wished, but long before mid-morning that was impossible. After two hours' walking we came to a column-cairn of heavy stones on a crag above the first deep defile. The first junipers were growing near this place among the rocks, and you could already see the topmost deodars further down the river. Butterflies again. A black redstart flew across the river, flirting his white cap and his red tail. Lateral valleys began to open out in vistas of fine trees and toppling grey crests that lashed their own rock-faces with waterfalls. We passed from boulder-scattered meadows and long screes down to a height where there were tall native birches. We saw no more empty steadings after we left the upper river, but now we passed herdboys and two boys with donkeys going up with empty panniers. There was a smell of saffron and catmint underfoot and of junipers in the hot gorges. By eleven that morning we were down to nine thousand feet. We crossed a bridge to the right bank and soon afterwards the path climbed across a surprising scree of huge fragments of the finest cream-white marble. It was exactly like Pentelic stone, and some boulders showed the same blue-grey band that occurs in Attic marbles. This marble seems to be a thick vein in the schist; it was exposed here by a landslide. It will never be quarried, I suppose, because no block of any size could ever be taken down the Nichingul; yet if you saw a piece of it on the Athenian Acropolis, you would certainly think it was a fragment of the Parthenon.

The river plunged into deep pools, sometimes under high overhanging cliffs, wheeling from one waterfall to another in streams of pure, strong water over broken marble. Several redstarts were busy up and down these falls and pools. We crossed back to the left bank where we encountered a shepherd in a catmint wreath. By this time it was past midday and everyone we met gave us different advice about how far it was to Kamdesh. I think we were all stiff, and I was walking in a dream. I remember passing splinters of coloured rock, and suddenly and most surprisingly a small bank of frozen snow. Beside it stood an enormous split rock of marble with a black and white whirling texture that could have made a dinner table for Nero.

Almost as suddenly the gorges seemed to be over. We came out into a sunny field between trees and found some men with loaded donkeys who had just come up from Kamdesh. The sky ahead was full of all the highest mountains on the imagination's map. It was the big Chitral ranges, sharp and snowy and very high up, outlined in a slightly livid light against a formidable cloudy distance. We stood at the top of an enormous waterfall where the river, which was broad and powerful now, fell in a continual series of mighty jumps and leaps and roars down many, many hundreds of feet. The little track became a cliff-path and we went down with the water to a bridge over the lowest pools where the force of the eddies had hollowed the rocks in all directions into deep cups and bowls and hollow recesses. We were down to seven thousand feet and back among walnut woods, big nuts and yellow leaf; autumn among this rich undergrowth and these interlacing trees and springs was like a season we had forgotten for a long time and now rediscovered.

As we walked down through the woods the edges of a dense rainstorm came sweeping up towards us and we sheltered under a rock. The rain started to fall and one by one a whole string of people from the path congregated under the same rock. We thought of waiting for the porters, having seen them only once in the whole day, moving fast down the upper river, but it seemed best to find a shelter for the night; it was mid-afternoon but we now felt that Kamdesh could not be far off. It was further than we imagined. I started off alone before the rain finished, as I had knocked one of my knees on a rock and it was slightly swollen, so I was anxious not to let it stiffen. The track descended into a green world of riverspray and rainspray and leaves and streams, above the first cottages embosomed in maize and water melons.

I found myself following a donkey foal and a cheerful young man who capered about barefoot across smooth, streaming rocks. I followed the foal along safer routes in spite of all the young man's encouragement and challenges. He told me proudly he had just left the army after two years as a parachutist. He went on to utter judicious generalities about world politics and the greatness and goodness of both our countries; this was fine and I was almost ready to go slithering across the boulders to keep up the good

impression, but it turned out he thought I was a Russian. At last
we came to a mosque with elaborate fretted wood, and to the rich
hill-village of Kushtus, which hangs above the lower Nichingul a
few miles before it runs down into the Kamdesh river.[5] But we
were too hopeful too early, the track lengthened and we lost it
several times. Kamdesh is a mile or two downstream from the
confluence, and it looks east across the gorge of its own river. We
crossed the rich fields to a thick pelt of deodars, dusk fell,
Elizabeth was terribly tired, there was no sign at all of Kamdesh,
and we began to think we might be badly lost and would end by
sleeping in the forest. I recall observing secretly and with some
relief that there were no wolf-tracks. We must have been stupefied
with tiredness; by later calculations we had walked well over forty
miles, perhaps forty-five or forty-six. The porters reached Kushtus
and bedded down there for the night. In the last moment of light
before night closed in we came out above Kamdesh on exactly the
right path.

    We ate an exhausted meal outside the first house we came to
which belonged to a schoolmaster, and spent a strange, uneasy
night on very short mattresses, which we borrowed and shared.
In the morning, cocks crowed all over the hillside and prayer was
chanted in the mosque opposite the house. The porters arrived
looking happy and rested while we ate breakfast. I was sorry to
say goodbye to them, but they kept reappearing full of glee and
weighted down with the spoils of Kamdesh in mysterious bundles.
Later I sat in the mosque balcony as the sun rose, watching while
it unpicked the dark and misty folds of forest and coloured the
Bashgul river. We were all overcome by the fabulous richness of
the landscape, the opulence of the wooden architecture, the
yellow-green combes of ripening corn, the glistening trees. We ate
our first bread since the Uchuk valley and drank our first sugared
tea since Jellalabad; the smell of dense vegetation, the heat and
the flies were things we had forgotten.

    Perhaps no one can grasp the way in which a fertile hill town
on a trade-route can seem a kind of heaven to mountain villagers,
without approaching it more or less as we arrived at Kamdesh.
All day we roamed around the streets, which were really field-
tracks between little colonies of houses built into one another on
the hillside. The mosque balcony had frescoes in faded colours on
flaking plaster, a tiny motor-car and a huge knife in a pomegranate
as big as a melon, flowers, and a trophy of arms, two rifles, two

daggers, two swords, and a tall axe in the centre. The flower-paintings are always two dimensional and the relative sizes of flowers have more to do with design than with nature. The whole of Kamdesh has an air of solid and majestic ease. I was shown a shower-bath in which every single fitting was carved in wood and the water emptied through a hole in the house wall. We saw white hollyhocks that turn mauve in late autumn, apricots were drying on rooftops, old men as well as boys carried sling-bows. In the gorges we had seen the carcase of an animal left untouched after several days, but here we saw a vulture. The carved pillars of the lower mosques were like a dark grove repeating the living grove of walnut trees it stood in. Yet even the grandest house in Kamdesh has a cooking hearth in its living room, though the same house has an Edwardian steeple in the style of Switzerland or France.* The people here believe that all Nuristanis are descended from the Prophet through his son El Khoresh. Some of them have been to Jellalabad. It was only in Ishtiwi that we were told that El Khoresh's tribe moved to Greece after the death of the Prophet and came to Nuristan later with Alexander.

We took a long path down through the groves and waterfalls towards Kamus,† in the hope of meeting our Land-Rover as it came up from Kabul that evening and driving to the Kamus resthouse; we were due to be collected in any case the next morning where the rivers met. On the way down we noticed a huge drum of stone sticking out of a hedge; I have seldom seen a stone that looked more like a carefully worked column drum; it was not pierced, but I think one must assume it was an unused, unfinished millstone, abandoned perhaps in 1895. Nearer the river I saw something far stranger. The Land-Rover had not come and it was early evening, so I walked up to the police station at the confluence to make sure it had not arrived there early in the day. About a quarter or half an hour's walk from lower Kamdesh, close beside the road, below the hill and not towards the river, I found the foundations of strong stone

---

* Via British India I suppose. This house and the houses around it must therefore have been built after the old Kamdesh was destroyed by Abdur Rahman.

† Our path was not the usual one from the road to Kamdesh; it descends gradually and meets the road and the Bashgul river about three miles downstream of the confluence and the stone bridge and police station. It is a good route only if you are walking to Kamus. We were misdirected by the schoolmaster who was a foolish fellow and had a complicated plan to profit by the situation. Kamus is about six miles downstream from the confluence.

walls of big squared blocks, including some marble. The building cannot have been a fortification, since it stood in a hollow dominated by spurs of hill which were not fortified. It must therefore have been a temple, and some of its blocks seemed to have been re-used. There was no clue to the style or date of the building, but it was extensive and ambitious. It was not the grove of Imra, which Heath reports was at Kamus, below the place where the resthouse now is. Robertson says nothing about it. The motor track which passes it is modern, and the old path may not have passed so near. Nothing is known of any architecture in Robertson's time which remotely resembles it. To my great regret I was unable to examine it thoroughly or even to draw it. I had been swimming or washing in the river at the foot of the path, and had left most of my clothes and baggage and had no paper with me, and I was in a hurry. Before I got back to the others the Land-Rover arrived.

We stopped that night at the peculiar hotel set up some years ago when it was proposed to open up Kamdesh to tourism. Since then the hotel, which is extremely hard to find, has sunk gradually into a delightful decay. There was a huge spider in the lavatory and a dead mouse a week old in one of the bedrooms; the bathrooms were well fitted but no water ran anywhere as the pipes had never been connected, and there were not enough oil lights to go round; still, we got an excellent dinner of chicken and rice cooked with apricots, and I sincerely recommend this hotel to anyone intrepid enough to reach it. Next morning we drove down the Kuner, past a broken bridge, fortresses and fortified villages, through cultivated land where we saw several orioles in the fields above the broad muddy river; beyond the river we could see well-kept villages and neat, glittering terraces in Pakistan, but our side was seedier. The landscape sank into a daze of heat and a haze of dust. As we came into Kabul we passed two Hazara porters, one of them an old man, pulling with tired, dignified faces at what would have been a big load for a horse. We passed through the dusty warmth of Kabul into the preserved peace of the embassy garden, and into the quiet house.

I spent the early evening in the bath reading letters and newspapers. The mayor of Hunza was reported to have given two camels to a visiting Chinese trade delegation. The chief of police at Peshawar asserted that about two thousand wanted men were hiding in tribal territories near the Khyber Pass.

One day merged into another. Every day now there were boys kite-fighting on waste ground.* It was the end of the season and summer visitors were leaving. I was staying on in Afghanistan in order to get to Ay Khanoum and the Oxus in ten days' time when the French started their winter's work; Elizabeth and Bruce were leaving at once for Pakistan. The night before they went we settled our bills and dined together at a brand new hotel. The entire expedition to Nuristan had cost 2,174 afghanis each for four of us, that is about nine pounds each.

The hotel offered provincial German cooking in American surroundings at New York prices. The wine list had ten kinds of champagne and no claret, the muzak had been mysteriously crosswired with the telephone system, and an attempt to put this right had electrified the windowframes and doorhandles. Bruce and Elizabeth went and I half wished I was going with them. There were no more hoopoes in the embassy garden and the snow was gone from all the mountains round Kabul; they were left with toothless gums. I went for several expeditions on my own but I felt the onset of tedium like the condensation of a heavy waterdrop. I wanted badly to see Ay Khanoum, but after so many official disappointments I hardly believed I ever would, even though I had the permission in my pocket.

* A seasonal game recently forbidden by decree. Kitestrings are soaked in ground glass or carry jags of metal, hands are wrapped in old tyres; the aim is to cut strings or wrists.

PART SIX

❀

Ay Khanoum

CHAPTER

13

Ay Khanoum* stands on the east back of the Kokcha, just at the point where it flows into the Oxus.† It is the site of a Greek city founded soon after Alexander the Great reduced the easternmost province of the Persian Empire and left it as a Greek province held down by Macedonian garrisons.

It is extremely likely that Ay Khanoum was originally a city called Alexandria on the Oxus, founded in the name of Alexander himself.[1] If that is true, it was probably founded in the twenties of the third century B.C., when Alexander was about twenty-eight years old, and within five or six years of his death. But it now looks almost certain that Ay Khanoum was a Persian city before it was Greek. Some of the stone elements in the great Hellenistic palace of the ruler were older stones re-used, and among the foundations of the palace is an undisputed bell-shaped Persian column-base. The site of the city is defensive. It stands on the only unfordable stretch of the Oxus for miles in both directions, opposite a short range of steep rough hills on the Russian bank, although this is not the ideal spot to guard either the crossing of the Kokcha or the road from east to west along the south bank of the Oxus.

The Greek city is protected by a gigantic mound on the south which once must have been the acropolis, the Kokcha washes it on the west and the Oxus on the north; the lower town is penned in by this mound and the two rivers, on a long, almost triangular, swathe of ground between the acropolis and the Oxus, with the top of the triangle closed by a powerful wall. To put the first

* The place name means The Moon Woman. The official reports on the excavations at Ay Khanoum are to be found in *Comptes Rendus de l'Academie des Inscriptions*, annually from 1965.

† The local name of the Oxus is the *Amu Darya*. Along most of its length the Oxus is the border that divides Russia from Afghanistan. This is not at all a heavily defended frontier, but both sides are very sensitive about allowing foreigners anywhere near it, hence my difficulty in reaching Ay Khanoum.

question first, what was the military or mercantile importance of this site for the Persians? It must have been close to the furthest eastern extent of Persian penetration, it was in shelter from the nomads north of the Oxus, the 'princes of felts and furs' as the Chinese called them,[2] the townless forest-living and cave-living herdsmen of Ptolemy,[3] whose pressure from the north-east on the Persian Empire was already known to Herodotos.[4] It was not on any trade route the Persians are likely to have used to India, but it faced the way down from the Kokcha, the source of lapis lazuli and balas rubies, the entrance to the Wakan corridor and the pass that led to China, and it was the effective presence of Persia in the grazing-grounds of the upper Oxus. It is hard to believe it was not a 'royal fortress' to control the frontier like the Persian fort on the Indus which separated the Opiai from the Indoi and was refounded as Opian Alexandria.[5] What Alexander occupied was not virgin territory or an untamed barbarous world, but the eastern Persian Empire, including of course its frontier fortresses.

I went north in a hired Land-Rover so battered that it wore holes in my trousers. The mountain crests were powdered with freshly fallen snow and in the winter clarity you could see the site of Kapisa, which I had failed to reach so many times, quite clearly. In the mountains the shadows were more definite than the trees, and the sunlight was so bright it seemed to be dying like a leaf when it turns colour. Near the top of the pass a soft barrage of clouds hung on the mountainside with the taller peaks showing naked above it. Soldiers stood shivering over their spades and picks. The cloud was a dense, snowy vapour leaning on the crest of the mountain from the north side and hardly overflowing to the south, so halfway through the long ill-lit concrete bunker of the Salang tunnel we ran into freezing fog. The windscreen froze faster than it could be cleaned, and the world outside the tunnel was almost as obscure as inside it, dark grey fog, grey ice and snow on the road, and glimpses of glittering white snow and ice whenever the fog lifted. I saw an eremurus crystallized in ice, and as the clouds lifted or we passed below them a herd of goats moved down the hillside with snow and ice in their fleeces. The driver and I were both shivering, and when we drove through the avenue of catalpas at Baghlan an hour or two later, it was still cool. Swallows and mynahs were in big flocks, and by the river south of the last gorge before Kunduz I saw fifty or a hundred horses grazing together and a whole village of black tents.

In Kunduz I went to see Tawab. A general election was nearing its climax. There are fifteen days of voting, and on the first day at one at least of the Kabul voting stations only four people voted. Parliamentary government was a new idea in Afghanistan, and the king still appointed the ministers without reference to election, although members of the royal family had in 1964 been debarred from holding these positions, perhaps because a cousin as prime minister rather weakens than strengthens the king's position. There were no parties in the European sense. I saw villagers being led to vote at Ghazni in a procession with drums and flutes, and in several places I met lorry-loads of voters travelling with ancient flute-players on the roof of the driver's cab. The Nashir family headquarters was as busy as the stock exchange. Four hundred voters had to be fed at midday and another four hundred in the evening. A count had been announced at Chardara, where a cousin of Tawab's got in, but there were five more days of elections. When the results came through, word was passed outside and four or five guns went off in the air. A powerful-looking, tense group of lieutenants came out of the room where the wireless was, followed by Tawab's preoccupied uncles, and finally Mr Nashir himself, looking cool and businesslike and remarkably young, and wearing a brown European suit and a bow-tie. More rifle shots went off further away. Tawab had been pressed into service and was longing for it all to be over; so was the driver who took me to the Spinzar hotel – he said it was his hundredth errand that day and his jeep was overheated.

The next morning I insisted on setting off extremely early; we drove north through the dark on the asphalt road towards the Russian frontier where I waved a paper at a sleepy soldier, and we turned off into the desert some way north of the Archi bridge. Dawn broke slowly and coldly in the desert. The sun came up brilliant over a sand-dune exactly ahead of us. Before and after dawn long caravans of camels passed us going west, otherwise there was nothing. Most of the birds were hawks and when we stopped for breakfast after sunrise the silence was absolute. We were following a broad tangle of droving tracks between the dunes, which brought us out to a small fertile oasis and a village called Dasht-i Archi.* A dozen donkeys were drinking side by

* This name seems to mean Archi desert, but *dasht* can also mean a desert grazing-ground. The Archi is a little river that runs into the Kunduz river between Kunduz and the Oxus.

side under a bridge, and a villager was leading an ape along the track like a dog on a lead.

In another hour we were among semi-desert hills in an even more purely central Asian landscape of very bright yellow stubble and toasted thistles, the tents and herds of nomads, and children who waved and jumped and shouted at the sight of a car. Driving on through sun and silence and resigned to another several hours' travelling we came suddenly down to Hodjigar, a village with trees and a watersplash where more than half the men we saw were riding horses. I noticed with some horror the fearful condition of the track I might easily have taken from Taliqan.[6] As we came out of the village into the Kokcha plain I could see Russia; the mountainous hills a few miles away to the north were the hills that marked the course of the Oxus opposite Ay Khanoum.

We bucketed along for a mile or so over the plain to the lowest Kokcha bridge. Beside this bridge is one of the new stations for sheep-dipping, a proof if any were needed that this is one of the routes that the nomads use to move their animals in and out of the summer grazing-grounds. It is impossible to say whether there was always a bridge here. It may be possible to ford the river with camels or horses, but I should not like to have to do it with donkeys* or a flock of sheep, unless perhaps in winter when the snow freezes and the rivers are low. In the plain east of the Kokcha, nomads were encamped in their black tents. I noticed several mysterious bumps; one of them was the ruins of a long canal, which seems to be connected with the Ay Khanoum mound. It is not certain when this canal was dug or whether it was simply for irrigation. Canals did exist in Russian Turkestan as early as the first half of the third millennium B.C., and with just the same measurements as canals that are still in use today, and the Ay Khanoum canal has been explored but not yet excavated.[7]

At the end of the plain we came to a sleepy village called Dasht-i Qala, where a single dusty hoopoe flittered through a melancholy graveyard. I was taken to the chief of police, a fat man in civilian robes bargaining lazily in the bazaar. He knew nothing about me and went away to telephone. Meanwhile I found the liveliest and strongest frescoed room I had ever seen; its whole wallspace was covered in big red painted flowers, red and blue architectural

* Herodotos in fact remarks that the Scythians have no donkeys or mules (4, 28) and this might be relevant.

drawings and geometric decorations, wheels and running spirals, and some of the motifs were not unlike the chip-carved designs on wooden architecture that we saw at Ishtiwi and Kamdesh. The village market square seemed to alter while I waited for the policeman from an almost laughable tranquillity to an atmosphere of tensity and dust. I begged a mug of hot water and shaved to keep my spirits up. He came wandering back, poking at the vegetables, and it was all right. We were given a policeman to guide us finally to the hamlet of Ay Khanoum, on the banks of the Kokcha below the south bastion of the great mound, and up the track through the barricade of the ruined walls to the excavation. The track enters the city through the space in the walls where its gateway once stood.

The general history of any site can only be the last result of a long excavation and it looks as if Professor Bernard will be at work for many seasons to come. This is the only Greek city in central Asia ever to have been scientifically excavated; it holds the answers to old questions and the beginnings of new ones. Its central building is an ambitious Hellenistic palace of the Seleucid period with some important Persian features and possibly an earlier Persian building underneath it; another smaller house near the Kokcha at the western extremity of the city has the same ground plan, which seems to be Persian since it occurs also at Persepolis but never in the west. The palace has an open outer courtyard with long colonnades, but the central courts of the palace buildings are roofed rooms with a huge roofspan, surrounded by corridors giving on to smaller rooms.[8] The reason for this roofed grandeur may possibly be a magnificent style of living; but it is more likely to be coolness in summer and warmth in winter; one should remember the climate. As an engineering feat it depended on fine timber, very likely deodars.

Some reconstruction, for example in the temple now being excavated which dominated the city from below the acropolis, took place in the Greek period. The whole city seems to have been destroyed by fire, but it was later occupied by squatters whose origin is hard to place. Later again the bricks and stones were pillaged and the surviving pillars felled like trees probably for the bronze bindings of their bases, so that bases survived like tree-stumps and capitals like broken fruit or the fragments of branches. The hero-shrine outside the palace gates, which is older than the layout of the palace, was broken open by tunnelling; and three of its four tombs were looted. In modern times a few huts stood on the abandoned ground, and the Uzbeks used it for encampments; it was also used for *buzkashi*. The mound of the acropolis, which is not unlike Aliabad, is about two hundred feet high and the abundant fragments of pottery include some Islamic wares; it is easy enough to trace its defences, but trial trenches in selected spots have not yet revealed anything of interest.

At the time of my visit the most interesting building was the temple. It was a square building not exactly oriented, probably because of the lie of the land and in order for it to face the acropolis. Its outer walls had originally a series of recessed squared niches like window-frames, each niche recessed in a series of three diminishing rectangles one inside the other; this is an Achaemenid Persian style but when the temple was reconstructed these smart and elaborate walls were cloaked in massive claybrick. The base of the Achaemenid walls was a pair of very tall rounded steps like the shapes of old-fashioned jellymoulds. These walls were painted white but not stuccoed. The inside was T-shaped, with the entry at the base of the T and an outer room in the upright with two subsidiary store-rooms or sacristies beside it. The mudbrick of this outer room[9] was strengthened by vertical beams and some traces of burnt stucco have been found there. The right-hand sacristy was full of scraps of ivory and small carbonized fragments of wooden ornamental mouldings and Professor Bernard himself has recovered a carbonized wooden Ionic capital here almost complete.* The cult statue stood on a bench-like platform in the inner shrine; one of its marble feet has been recovered; it was the sandalled foot of a male figure that must have stood some ten or perhaps fifteen feet high. Maybe only its white parts were marble, but the workmanship is rich and the design crisp. Its ornamentation includes a thunderbolt, which suggests Zeus or a king identified with Zeus. My own guess is that this monstrous work of art represents the rebuilding of the temple with a new and atavistic dedication. I find it hard not to connect the original dedication with the goddess on a silver-gilt plaque found in the left-hand sacristy hidden under storage jars on the second day of the 1969 excavation. The goddess is Kybele.

The plaque is a repoussé disc of silver about a foot across, with

* It was the Asian and Indian type of Ionic capital, with a deep dip and a pronounced curl, something like a pair of ram's horns. It is from this kind of capital that Swat and Nuristan wooden capitals ultimately derive.

the figures gilded. The workmanship is extremely fine. The head of a young Greek sun-god with thirteen rays sprouting from behind his head, a crescent moon and a sixteen-point star of rays look down on a mountain landscape indicated by rocky ground. A chariot drawn by two soberly prancing lions, and driven by a girl in Greek dress facing forwards, is carrying a robed woman with a chimney-pot head-dress (she is wearing a *polos*) and more flowing robes, who faces you. She is the goddess Kybele. Behind the chariot walks a priest in a Persian hat and a long tunic holding an umbrella above Kybele's head. This honorific shade is sketchy and the priest when I saw the plaque was a little indistinct. The chariot moves to the right across level rocky ground towards an altar which is purely Persian. It consists of six steep steps like separate blocks of diminishing size, with a straight front towards the lions. A priest in a long tunic and girdle and a conical hat has mounted to the third step, his waist is level with the top and he makes an offering in or on a small vessel which is like a seventh step of the altar. He is facing the goddess.

A mixture of religions can seldom have been so clearly expressed in a mixture of styles at such a high level of art. Kybele was the Persian mother-goddess adopted by the Greeks in Asia Minor; she was easily identified with Rhea, mother of Zeus, and with the vague Mother of the gods, whose cult in Athens was very ancient.[10] But Kybele was not publicly worshipped in any city in mainland Greece until the time of the Roman Empire; her worship in Greece began as a private religious cult imported by foreigners.[11] Still, she was of all Asian goddesses probably the only one the Greeks in Asia knew already in the early third century B.C. It is at least not impossible that she had a cult at Ay Khanoum before the Greeks arrived, but this silver-gilt disk is a perfect fusion of Greek and Persian elements in a Greek setting. It is even possible the goddess may be not Kybele, but Artemis Nanaia, an offshoot of Ishtar: without written evidence it is impossible to know. Artemis Nanaia is sometimes identified with Anahita the goddess of the Oxus.

Whatever else we know of the religious and the public life of Ay Khanoum is Greek. There was a typical Hellenistic palaestra near the river, which has yielded a grave and ageing head of Herakles.[12] The hero-shrine was two or three times rebuilt; it was a small chapel with two brick graves and two sarcophagi, with a pair of columns at the entrance to the outer room;[13] the mound it stands on is perhaps the grave of the founder of the city. The most interesting of the few Ay Khanoum inscriptions stood outside the chapel, which it refers to as 'the sacred enclosure of Kineas'.[14] Kineas seems to be a man and not a god, and the graves in his shrine suggest a dynastic cult. It is hard to see what except founding the city could make a man otherwise unknown to history so important here. If Ay Khanoum was really Alexandria on the Oxus, it is probable that Kineas founded it in Alexander's name, just as the Egyptian Alexandria was founded, but this is a problem we shall never solve without written evidence.

The inscription, which is written in verse, in lettering of before 250 B.C., records that Klearchos copied out the precepts of the famous men of ancient times, which he saw at Delphi, and has inscribed them here, in the sacred enclosure of Kineas. The stone tablet with the Delphic inscriptions has perished; only one maxim survives on the same stone as the first inscription. There is a third inscription encouraging people to the various virtues proper to the different ages of human life.[15] To preserve this peculiarly Greek wisdom cut in stone in so remote a spot must have been a conscious and purposeful act. Can it posssibly have been Klearchos, the pupil of Aristotle, who was responsible?[16]

Ay Khanoum was a rich city, and today it is a heady site. From the mound you can see the shining pebbly Kokcha where it runs into the Oxus. The Kokcha is much deeper and stronger and faster than it looked from a distance; it ruffles the Oxus where they join with a noise and glitter like the tide. In the evening I swam in it; it splits into three streams between pebble banks for a few yards, and I was told I could cross the first and swim in the second, but if I entered the third I would probably be shot by a Russian sentry. There was no Russian sentry for several miles and both sides of the river are undefended.

Since I had only two days I walked indefatigably around the monuments through a golden crop of vicious Greek thistles; the city was about the size of Sounion or Delphi, with a disproportionately big palace. The pink and grey Russian cliffs rise to about four hundred feet, the Oxus is a hundred and fifty yards across and licks its stones noisily, but there are traces of ramparts facing the river. The main city walls facing the plain have a deep fosse and a series of towers thirty or forty feet high constructed entirely with small mudbricks; the substructure of the walls is a mixture of pebbles and clay. The exact shapes of these walls as of everything else stood out most clearly in the earliest sun of the day.

Upstream but plainly visible from Ay Khanoum stands another site, right on the edge of the Oxus opposite some fertile woody land. It seems to consist of a large round tower-like mound on a flatter base. It is said to be Kushan but there seems no particular reason for believing this, and in fact the site has never been properly investigated.[17] To make things worse the same pottery occurs almost everywhere, and some of the ancient types can be exactly matched from the modern kiln which was found on the site of the palaestra. A mass of interesting pottery is coming out of the house by the Kokcha, including some quite fine and thin fragments of black glazed cups, but the classification of all the pottery of Ay Khanoum is going to be a long and intricate task.

The luxury of the palace is hard to describe. Its floors were tiled and its weight-carrying walls were massive mudbrick; no art has come out of it except its architecture; the spiny nodding leaves of stone acanthus. There were traces of old rose on its upper mouldings like the deep rose pink of the walls in the house by the Kokcha. These decorations were exactly worked, and the Corinthian column-bases were not only elaborately designed but also perfectly regular. Admittedly the surface skin of the column drums was less fine than marble would be, but there were traces of white plaster on them which alters the picture. The stone seems to be local and the Russians claim to have found the precise quarry it came from about thirty miles upstream. If this is right it has the implication that Greek influence must have reached at least that distance to the north-east. The road from the main gate travels north-east; I traced it for some way over the plain, and near where it must have reached the first barrier of hills I could see drovers' tracks; it would be an important contribution if someone could tell us where it went.

At night there was a sand of stars, in the morning before dawn a schoolmaster's bell. I was asking myself so many questions of detail that I almost forgot where I was. *Vedeva Troia in cenere e caverne*. A continual plume of dust blew from the excavations. Swallows skimmed and little green bee-eaters uttered their strange cries. I admit to hoping it was called Alexandria; it would be a good place to be remembered by.

As we drove back through the desert it was full of birds: vultures, bee-eaters, hawks of various sizes, a buzzard and one splendid hoopoe. The journey seemed swifter than before, and now that it was light I could see the mounds north of Kunduz; they seemed less surprising than they would have done three months ago. We reached Kunduz in a yellow haze of sunset and cattle-dust and I remember that there was a smell of bread and smoke and melons. Wazir Mohammed was sad. The theatre company had quarrelled and broken up, and he told me he had decided to leave Afghanistan. His first idea was to go to consult with Charlie Chaplin about the state of the theatre all over the world, and then to become an actor in another society and another language. He asked if I had heard any classical Afghan music. Then he sat down cross-legged in Tawab's house and someone brought him a portable harmonium with an oversweet tone. He played and sang a long lament for dead kings. It was a desert of warbles and groans. After two hours he finished and Tawab nodded. There was nothing more that any of us could say.

Next day I went to Kabul, then to England, and unloaded my pebbles on to my desk.

NOTES

CHAPTER ONE

1. There are eighth-century Turkish inscriptions from the territory south of Lake Baikal in Siberia, but for most early references to the Turkish tribes we depend on Chinese sources. Their first explosion in Asia was in the sixth century A.D.; by 567 they had beaten the Ephthalite Huns, reached the Oxus, and sent an embassy to the Emperor Justin II to reopen the overland silk route to China. In the tenth century the Seljuk Turks effectively took over the Islamic Caliphate at Baghdad and in 1071 at the battle of Manzikert defeated the Byzantines and established dominance over Asia. Genghis Khan was a Mongol khan controlling Turkish tribes; the highwater of Turkish expansion into Europe and Africa was reached in comparatively modern times; it was the work of the Osmanli or Ottoman Turks, dubious cousins of the Seljuks who had been left behind near Brusa, where they had suffered little from Genghis and Tamburlaine.

2. Cf. E. W. Bodnar, S.J., *Cyriacus of Ancona and Athens*, Brussels, 1960, pp. 66–8.

3. Sir Aurel Stein's books and Yule's *Marco Polo* were the foundation stones; the work of the Délégation Archéologique Française en Afghanistan since the nineteen twenties has in the end built up a full treatment of most archaeological problems. The greatest single change in knowledge was the discovery and excavation of Ay Khanoum (cf. Chapter 13).

4. The Parthians of course were not savages: from the point of view of Tacitus, as Professor Momigliano has pointed out, they 'had the deplorable quality of not being barbarous enough' (*Studies in Historiography*, 1969, p. 122). (The revived Persian Empire is also called the Sassanian Empire.)

5. For a full account of what is known of the political history and the complicated civil wars of the Bactrian Greeks cf. W. Tarn, *The Greeks in Bactria and India* (1951). There is a more readable but less professional account by George Woodcock in *The Greeks in India* (1966). The son of the last reigning monarch of the Seleucid dynasty was the Philopappos whose gravestone is the Monument of Philopappos at Athens.

6. The Mediterranean could be all but reached by sea from the Indus and the Persian Gulf. The influence of the city of Alexandria on the Buddhist art of the first centuries A.D. in northern India reflects this route. (For the question of Greek coastal cities cf. J. Innes Miller, *The Spice Trade of the Roman Empire* (1969), pp. 173–202 and 211–12.)

7. There is a brief but able statement of the evidence for Hekatompylos as it was known a hundred years ago in Smith's dictionary of Greek and Roman geography (1854), in an article by W. S. Vaux.

8. Cf. Karl Jettmar's article on Dardistan in *East and West*, New Series, 17 (1967), based on the Russian publication.

9. The best study of this process is by G. Le Rider, *Suse sous les Seleucides et les Parthes* (*Mem. Miss. Arch. en Iran*, vol. 38, 1965), on the city of Sousa. For the mixture of populations cf. p. 280. At Sousa the Macedonian Greek calendar was still in use after A.D. 21.

10. *O.G.I.* 431, cf. *Klio* 9, pp. 352–63. From a small Parthian temple at Orchoi; reported by Le Rider.

11. Cf. R. F. Hosking and G. M. Meredith-Owens, *Handbook of Asian Scripts* (British Museum, 1966), p. 14 and plate 4. For Parthian Greek script cf. *Journal of Hellenic Studies*, 36 (1915), p. 25, n.5.

12. On Greek law and language in western Asia cf. Polybius 10, 24, 3. On the lawbook cf. *J.H.S.* 36 (1915), p. 60, mn. 128–9.

13. The inscription is in lines of dots. It was dedicated in the reign of the Kushan king Huviska, 'in the month Artemisios in the year 51' of the Kushan era. What is exciting is not simply that it should be Greek but precisely Macedonian.

14. Cf. Tarn, *The Greeks in Bactria and India*, p. 388. The Swat vase records a dedication in about 100 B.C., by 'Theodoros the meridarch'. It is the clearest evidence we have of the existence of Greek Buddhists in the period of the early stupas, when Gautama was beginning to be worshipped in reliquaries enshrined in enormous mounds, and to be assimilated to a god, but before the beginnings of Sanchi and Gandaran Buddhist art. The Greek inscriptions of Asoka are of course much earlier. Perhaps it is worth pointing out that in the absence of literary evidence and of figurative art, an occasional inscribed dedication is the only kind of evidence of Greek Buddhism we could expect. For the shaky literary evidence of the *Questions of King Milinda*, cf. Tarn, *The Greeks in Bactria and India*, pp. 414f. For Buddhist inscriptions of Asoka at Kandahar cf. Louis Robert in *Comptes Rendus de l'Académie des Inscriptions* (1958) and again in 1964.

15. To deal with the east and the silk road, Ptolemy draws on Marinus of Tyre, whose works are now lost, and Marinus of Tyre relies on Maes. In general cf. Sven Hedin, *The Silk Road*, and C. G. Simkin, *The Traditional Trade of Asia*, pp. 35f.

16. In the eighteenth and early nineteenth centuries the tower stood

among the other ruins of some grandeur; cf. the picture by Flandin and Coste reproduced in Sir Percy Sykes's *History of Persia* (vol. 1, p. 540).

17. The chapels of the Bagnio slave prison in Istanbul in the eighteenth century had a fine set of bells. 'Il y a cinq ou six ans qu'on les leur a enlevées; parce que, disaient les Turcs, leur son reveillait les Anges qui venaient dormir la nuit sur le toit d'une Mosquée bâtie depuis peu dans le voisinage' (*Nouveaux Mémoires des Missions Jésuites dans le Levant*, 1753, vol. 1, p. 163).

CHAPTER TWO

1. There is a well-balanced and readable account of the British invasions of Afghanistan by Arthur Swinson, *Northwest Frontier* (1967), with a full, learned bibliography.

2. The link is the *murus Dacicus*.

3. There seems to have been a similar breakdown of sanitation at Bokhara at the time when it was taken over by the Arabs. For a series of vividly coarse disparagements of Bokhara cf. *The Lata'if al Mara'if of Tha'libi* (ed. C. E. Bosworth, Edinburgh, 1968), pp. 139–40f.

4. The best account of Pathan history and origins is in Sir Ola Carol's *The Pathans* (1965).

5. Cf. Chapters 11 and 12.

6. They have a slightly Chinese or Mongol appearance, but the hordes of the Mongol invasions seem to have been largely Turkish. Can it be that the Hazaras descend from a Turkish tribe which reached Afghanistan earlier, and that the Chinese-looking soldiers at Tapa Sardar, the Buddhist site at Ghazni, are the ancestors of the Hazaras? I am very doubtful about this suggestion. For the soldiers, cf. *East and West*, n.s. 18, 1968, figs. 64–5.

7. Cf. *The Baburnama*, ed. A. S. Beveridge, 1922, reprinted 1969 (Luzac, 46 Great Russell Street, London).

8. References to all French excavations and reports are to the relevant volumes of the *Mémoires de la Délégation Archéologique Française en Afghanistan* (D.A.F.A.) vol. 1 (1942) ff.

9. There are some photographs of the interior of the castle in 1879 taken by P. V. Luke, C.I.E., now kept in the British Embassy at Kabul.

10. Mem. D.A.F.A., vol. 1 (1942).

11. This immensely important site has been investigated and a trial excavation took place, but it has never been thoroughly uncovered. The famous Begram treasure was found there, cf. Ghirshman's *Begram* (Mem. D.A.F.A., 1946).

12. Ghirshman, *Begram* (1946), p. 9.

13. John Wood, *Journey to the Source of the River Oxus* (1872), ed. by Yule, p. 233, n.1.

14. Cf. in general F. Pfister, *Alexander der Grosse: Offenbarungen der*

Griechen, Juden, Mohammedaner und Christen, Berlin, 1956. Jewish Alexander traditions are noted by D. J. A. Ross in *Alexander Historiatus* (Secker & Warburg, London, 1963), pp. 33f. There was already a Syriac version of the Alexander legend in the sixth century (*ibid.*, p. 47).

15. Babur asked to have no monument, but to be buried at Kabul in a tomb open to the sky. He died at Agra. Cf. *The Baburnama*, ed. A. S. Beveridge, pp. 708–11, with photographs at pp. 367 and 445.

16. The restoration and inscription are described in a short illustrated pamphlet issued by the Afghan Antiquities and Museums Service and the Istituto Italiano per il Medio ed Estremo Oriente in 1966.

17. *Description des Médailles Chinoises*, Paris, anno 13 (1805). The phrase 'silk road' was probably invented by Baron von Richthofen (*die Seidenstrasse des Marinus*) in the nineteenth century.

18. Cf. Miller, *The Spice Trade of the Roman Empire* (1969) chapters 11 to 13, and in general C. G. Simkin, *The Traditional Trade of Asia* (1968).

19. There is an excellent study of western influence in early medieval China by E. H. Schafer, entitled *The Golden Peaches of Samarkand* (California, 1963). It was not only Buddhism and Gandaran Buddhist art that sparked a native flame in China; there is a strong and clear influence of Hellenistic and western Asian originals on the small terracotta figures found in tombs at least as early as the sixth century A.D. A particularly interesting collection is to be seen in the Princeton Fine Arts Museum, where there is an earlier doll-like wooden figure to compare them with, but these terracottas are in many western museums.

20. Illustrated in *Account of the Kingdom of Caubul* (1839), vol. 1, p. 108. This is the second edition of Elphinstone's book, published thirty years after his visit.

21. Elphinstone's *Caubul*, pp. 106–8, with the note on p. 180, dated 1838.

22. Leitner was a distinguished Orientalist, cf. Schuyler Jones, *Bibliography of Nuristan* (Copenhagen, 1966), nos. 170–75. He attacked Robertson's *Kafirs of the Hindu Kush* in memorable terms in a letter to *The Times* (26 Dec. 1896). For Luke's photographs cf. note 7 above.

23. S. Piggott, 'The Earliest Buddhist Shrines', *Antiquity*, 17, n. 65, March, 1943.

24. R. E. M. Wheeler, 'Romano-Buddhist Art', *Antiquity*, 28 (1949). This article is the classic statement of the view that Buddhist art has nothing to do with any Greek survival. Its arguments are still fundamental to this subject. One should also consult D. Schlumberger, *L'Orient Hellénisé L'Art grec et ses Héritiers dans l'Asie non Méditerranéenne* (Paris, 1969).

CHAPTER THREE

1. Michael Sullivan, *The Cave Temples of Maichishan* (1969), reporting a 1958 expedition.

2. *Musée Nationale d'Afghanistan, Guide* (1964), p. 19, cf. p. 18. Bamiyan room, case 4, side B. Illustrated in *Guide to the Kabul Museum* (1968).

3. All these figures are in case 4, side B, except for a kouros-like stone body in the Fundukistan room.

4. Mem. D.A.F.A., vol. 7 (1936). Nancy Dupree in her small guide-book *Bamiyan* (1967 edition) calls Khair Khane a Buddhist settlement which was active during the fifth century A.D. There were three sanctuaries each with the same plan and a number of fragments of white marble sculpture. The terrace in front of these sanctuaries covered the site of a simple temple already disused. There were steps and a ramp. It is very hard to know to what extent a Buddhist community in the fifth century A.D. would be tolerant of a sun god, or in what sense such a community would be Buddhist (cf. in general Getty, *The Gods of Northern Buddhism*), but it is surely significant that in the autumn of 1969 the Italian excavators at Ghazni found a large figure of a pagan Indian mother-goddess riding on an elephant among the ruins of what is certainly a Buddhist monastery. At the time of writing it has not yet been published.

5. Cf. Mem. D.A.F.A., vol. 1 (1942), *La Vieille route de l'Inde (de Bactres à Taxila)*. There is information about other routes in E. H. Warrington, *Commerce between the Roman Empire and India* (1928). The modern road directly north from Kabul and Kapisa to Kunduz and the Oxus crosses only one barrier, the immense obstacle of the Salang Pass. I have seen horses crossing this pass by the modern road and the tunnel; they used previously to cross by an old road apparently built by Abdur Rahman, which must always have been a route of some kind at least during three or four months of the year.

6. Sir Henry Yule, in the introduction to Wood's *Journey to the Source of the River Oxus*, p. lxxvi.

7. Dr Gerard in the *Journal of the Asiatic Society of Bengal*, vol. 2, p. 8.

8. Capital of the province; Pliny says '*Capisene habuit Capisam urbem quam diruit Cyrus*', (N.H. 6, 92), but we know that Darius rebuilt it.

9. The suggestion that Alexander's garrison was installed in a new city some miles away is quite unfounded. The site sometimes named for it near the mouth of the Salang Pass rests on no ancient literary evidence and no archaeological indication, but on some coins that were not published and have not been preserved. But already in the eighteen forties, the coins found all over the plain numbered many thousands. Kushan Kapisa was described by Chinese Buddhist pilgrims, and its monasteries and several stupas have been identified. For Borj-i Abdullah cf. Ghirshman, *Begram* (1946), p. 4.

10. *Musée Nationale d'Afghanistan, Guide* (1964), pp. 4f., *Guide to the Kabul Museum* (1968), pp. 40f. Ghirshman, *Begram* (1946). The mass of the treasure is unknown to most scholars; what is exhibited at Kabul is only the tip of the iceberg.

11. In the sixth part of the Quaker Graveyard at Nantucket, called Our Lady of Walsingham. The seagulls blink their heavy lids in part two.

12. Cf. Edward Conze's introduction to his *Buddhist Scriptures* (1959), p. 14. As Buddhism became more popular it became polytheistic and in the end superstitious. The early teachings have interesting analogies with Roman stoicism. The class structure expressed in Gandaran Buddhist narrative art is notably aristocratic. It is possible that at one time Buddhism was the ideology of a rising middle class, but by the Kushan period all the elements of the ruling class had consolidated their position.

13. E. Conze's translation from the Acts of Buddha (first century A.D.), *Buddhist Scriptures*, p. 48.

14. E. Conze, *Buddhist Scriptures*, pp. 146–7. Tarn believed the Milinda panha depended on some lost variation of the Alexander romance (*The Greeks in Bactria and India*, 1951, pp. 265f. and 414f.). It certainly has little to do with the historical Greek king Menander, and it might possibly be a version of a story originally told about Kanishka (Tarn, cf. Demieville on the Chinese versions, *Bull. Ex. fr. Extr.–Or.* 24 (1924), pp. 43 and 26). But the form is clearly Greek and so is the principal character. The nearest analogy for the form is in the Greek writings of the early Christian apologists.

15. Fa-Hsien, translated by James Legge, 1886, quoted in Nancy Dupree's guidebook, *Bamiyan* (1967), p. 53.

16. Hiuen-Tsiang, from S. Beal's *Buddhist Records of the Western World* (1884, and recently reprinted), p. 50. The 1969 reprint of this vital book is distributed by Munshiram Manoharlal of Delhi.

17. Ria Hackim et Ahmad Ali Kohzad, *Légendes et coutumes Afghanes* (Musée Guimet, 1953), pp. 5f.

18. Cf. K. Jettmar in *Proc. Amer. Phil. Soc.*, 105 (1961), pp. 87f., in a report on research in Dardistan in 1958.

CHAPTER FOUR

1. I mean the conical hill covered with ruins. The Mongols called it Mobalig, the cursed city, and never rebuilt it. It was the akropolis if any of ancient Bamiyan. Cf. N. Dupree, *Valley of Bamiyan* (1967), pp. 6of.

2. Tarn, *The Greeks in Bactria and India*, pp. 82 and 117. The nomads were being bought off with tribute even before the age of invasions; hence also it seems the coin at Kunduz.

3. *Geog. Journ.* (1916), pp. 63–4. He speaks of 'a close line of ancient

watch-stations stretching right across the desert' from Hamun to the Helmand.

4. For these buildings cf. Wheeler, *Flames over Persepolis* (1968), pp. 33f. He is not responsible for the suggestion that they are tentlike.

5. Plutarch, *Perikles*, 13, 6.

6. Bk. 1, c. 57, bk. 2, c. 16.

7. Printed in the ninth and last volume of the *Nouvelles Lettres des Missions de la Compagnie de Jésus dans le Levant*, in the second decade of the eighteenth century. (Second edition: I have never seen the first.)

8. *Journal of the Royal Central Asian Society* (1944), pp. 15–16; cf. also the Alicur II necropolis. As for imports at this period in this area, Indian cornelian has been found in the Pamirs and shell-discs of Indian ocean seashells were used in the Pamirs to cover the eyes of the dead.

9. Illustrated in the exhibition catalogue, *Ancient Art from Afghanistan* (Arts Council 1967–8), plate 7.

10. M. Leberre intends to publish a study of the castles of the Hindu Kush for which he had already collected a mass of material; his work will certainly be authoritative. Meanwhile it is hardly possible to discover anything about this field of architectural history without consulting him.

11. I mean the British War Office maps, available in England. The paths and tracks are sketchy and misleading and one valley merges with another. Better maps exist at the Cartographic Institute in Kabul but are hard to obtain.

12. Conze, *Buddhist Scriptures*, p. 111.

13. *Harshacherita*, Cowell's translation, p. 101.

14. Conze, *Buddhist Scriptures*, pp. 232–3.

15. Dupree, *Bamiyan* (1967), pp. 50f.

16. Peers Carter's fine hound Chipak died in Sussex in 1982.

CHAPTER FIVE

1. It is now the subject of a short book of adventurous travel in Afghanistan by Freya Stark – *The Minaret of Djam* (1970).

2. Ibn Haukal's map of Khorasan shows the Jibal-al-Ghur in this way, and makes these observations. The border was six and a half marches from Herat.

3. Fully published with photographs by Gherardo Gnoli as No. 30 in *Serie Orientale*, Roma (Istituto Italiano per Medio ed Estreno Oriente, Rome, 1964). This publication is the source of my next paragraph.

4. These regions seem to have been first mapped during the negotiation of the Russian–Afghan boundary; the map we were using was based on the Survey of India map, 1941. Better maps exist at the Cartographic Institute in Kabul, but they were not easily available to us at the time.

5. Satires 1, 6, 104.

6. There must be a path somewhere here northwards to the Murghab

river, which runs north-west into the Amu Darya (the Oxus). The British map marks such a path, but in a schematic and obviously unreliable way.

7. In the case of Horace I am thinking of Satires 1, 5; I am not sure whether the *Odyssey* is or is not about a journey.

CHAPTER SIX

1. Behzad, greatest of all Persian miniaturists, was born in Herat in 1440 and worked for Husain Baiqara.

2. Lt.-Col. Stoddart of the military mission at Teheran. Cf. A. Swinson, *Northwest Frontier*, pp. 36–9, and in general Lord Curzon's *Russia in Central Asia*, 1889.

3. It was touch and go whether Herat would remain independent, as Samarkand and Bokhara had been until they were swallowed up by Russia. Dost Mahommed died soon after taking Herat and is buried there.

4. In the article 'Herat' in the eleventh edition of the *Encyclopedia Britannica*.

5. The *Avesta* calls the oasis Hairava, the Greek or Persian name was Artokoana.

6. Alexander's city was called Alexandria of the Arians (cf. *Amm. Marc.*, 23, 6).

7. Almost none of this is left; what remains is mostly 'pseudo-kufic', that is ornamental, resembling inscriptions.

8. One should use the Afghan Tourist Organization's guide, by N. H. Wolfe (1966). It is of interest that in about 1810 Herat had a population of 100,000, but by 1838 only 45,000 (Elphinstone, *Kingdom of Caubul*, vol. 2, p. 216).

9. I am reminded to ask whether it was the American Indians or in fact the people of north-west India who persuaded the English gentry in the Duke of Wellington's time to exchange their knee-breeches for trousers. Vasari records that a Venetian lady painter in his time used to wear Persian trousers, and in the great onset of Turkish fashions in China under the T'ang in the eighth and ninth centuries, Chinese women discarded their veils and took to riding astride wearing Turkish trousers. There are T'ang terracotta figures of Chinese women polo players now in Kansas City and in the Princeton University Museum; the one at Princeton has a strong western resonance in terms of art history as well as of fashion. Another was sold in London in 1972.

10. She was called Bibi Nur, and her sister was called Bibi Hur. They are buried side by side in a shrine in Herat built over them by Shah Rukh. Mongol women were emancipated and active. This bridge may be related to the conscious mercantile policy of Tamburlaine (cf. C. G. F.

Simkin, *The Traditional Trade of Asia*, 1968, pp. 170–71). What central Asia sent to India was horses. What came back was slaves and candy.

11. Cf. Swinson, as in note above, p. 182.

12. Cf. K. Fischer, 'Zur Lage von Kandahar', in *Bonner Jahrb.*, 167 (1967), with map at p. 136.

13. There is an excellent account of all Asoka's inscriptions with a composite text in N. A. Niksam and R. McKeon, *The Edicts of Asoka*, including an invaluable map of the places they were found. There is a fuller discussion with a bibliography by J. Bloch, *Les Inscriptions d' Asoka*, Paris, 1950. The furthest north-west apart from Kandahar are Shabbaz-garhi and Mansehra, north-east and north-west of Taxila. The smuggling of Buddhist antiquities at least in Swat (that is Gandara) started before the 1914 war and has of course increased in volume (cf. Lt.-Col. S. H. Godfrey in *Journal of the Royal Central Asian Society*, 23 for 1926, p. 462). When one recalls that the first excavators at Hadda threw away 3,000 heads as being substandard and not worth keeping, one sees that the tragedy is not so terrible as it seems. The removal of an unknown Asoka inscription from Kandahar is far more serious. (I am unfortunately unable to give the source of the story.) For a note of the Greek inscriptions found in Afghanistan other than here and at Aÿ Khanoum, cf. G. P. Carratelli in *East and West*, 1966, pp. 31 f, n. 16. Cf. also Paul Bernard, *The Proceedings of the British Academy*, 53 (1967), p. 88, n. 1. There are not many of them. As for the spread of Buddhism farther north and beyond the Hindu Kush, there are no archaeological traces of it in Sogdia, although there is some Gandaran artistic influence and even an Indian military colony at Toprak-kala in third and fourth centuries A.D. (cf. S. P. Tolstov in *Arts Asiatiques*, 1957).

14. It has been studied by D. Schlumberger and Louis Robert in *Journal Asiatique*, 1958. The date is shortly after 250. Robert concludes that 'l'hellénisme d'Arachosie . . . n'est pas confiné sans relations dans un coin perdu, ou il se ratatine et se sclérose . . .' For the second inscription, cf. *Comptes Rendus de l'Académie des Inscriptions*, 1964. The second inscription was only in Greek.

15. Cf. Tarn, *The Greeks in Bactria and India*, p. 388; the ambassador Heliodoros and the meridarch Theodoros. Greeks are listed as subjects of the Mauryan empire over which Asoka ruled (cf. *Journal Asiatique* (1958), p. 5).

16. It is hard to put a satisfactory date to the source of this information.

17. The earliest inscribed statues of Buddha anywhere as opposed to the first stupas (*c*. 255 B.C. at Sanchi) are not earlier than the first quarter of the first century A.D. (cf. M. Waliullah Khan in *East and West*, n.s., vol. 15, p. 53).

18. Buddhism before the time of its figurative art could be assimilated to a philosophy, and the Buddha to a great monotheistic religious teacher. The building of stupas from the third century on suggests the growing

sense of his divinity. The purity of primitive Buddhism did not survive, it gave way to Mahayana Buddhism, and it was Mahayana that made Gandaran art possible.

19. Several of Asoka's decrees inscribed on pillars travelled during the Middle Ages; one reached Allahabad perhaps under Akbar, and Diruz Shah took two to Delhi in the fourteenth century. It was one of these that a Catholic priest called Father Tieffenthaler saw and described in 1756. The most usual script of the inscriptions was deciphered only in 1836 by James Prinsep. The inscription in Greek at Kandahar was cut in rock, like the inscription at Sopara north of Bombay and the two inscriptions near Taxila.

20. Cf. D. Schlumberger in *Proc. Brit. Acad.*, 47 (1961), pp. 77f., and also cf. J. B. Ward-Perkins in the same journal, vol. 51, pp. 182f.

21. A hand-list was printed by Umberto Scerrato in *East and West*, 13 (1962), pp. 17f. Most of them are second or third century A.D., but towards the east, as in south India, there are some from the first century B.C. One denarius of Nero turned up in a Kushan context thirteen kilometres north of Termez, and there is a Nero bronze coin in an Uzbekistan museum. I bought in Kandahar a mysterious small brass coin which no one has yet been able to explain: someone is riding on (not standing by) a goat or a bull, in a fully Hellenized representation, and on the reverse a man is standing in a tunic holding something; he is not in Kushan dress, and the alphabet of the lettering is almost certainly Latin; the coin has been cast, not beaten. It seems to be a Roman provincial coin of some unknown kind, and was said to come from the big mound at Bhost, a trading station between Kandahar and Herat which I never visited.

22. *Ptolemy*, 6, 18, 4.

23. Ibn Haukal. In 1810 Ghazni was a stonewalled town of about 1,500 houses around the castle.

24. The first report was published in *East and West*, n.s. 18 (1969), by Maurizio Taddei, the director of the excavation (pp. 109f). The second has appeared by now but as I write I have not yet seen it.

25. In 1810 there were still Mullahs incessantly chanting the Koran over Mahmoud's grave and the shrine still had its doors. The carved teak doors were taken by the British to the Red fort at Agra; sandalwood doors were later returned. (Elphinstone, *Kingdom of Caubul*, vol. 2, pp. 141–2.)

26. No doubt I am prejudiced, because my father's birth certificate records my grandfather as an indigo merchant. But I cannot help feeling that peace, justice, democracy and the rule of law are all the product of commercial justice: the necessity for free and fair trade. Mommsen suggests this view in his explanation of the rise of the Roman republic, the later stages of which, as he also points out,

involve us in the whole problem of the history of capitalism and its nemesis.

27. Almost everything I say about the site comes from Maurizio Taddei, cf. note 24 above. Tepe or Tapa Sardar is a modern name; it refers to the Amir Habibullah who camped on this hill when he visited Ghazni. The old name was Tapa Naqqara, which means Kettledrum hill; there was a folk tale that the news of expeditionary armies leaving Ghazni for India used to be spread from place to place by musical instruments, and that the Sultan used to review his troops from this hill and the first drums were always sounded from it.

28. Pausanias 1. 21, 5f. We know also of tusk or tooth helmets from remote antiquity in Greece, but I doubt whether a scale-armour made of ordinary bone would be practicable or effective. Pausanias' Sarmatians are Russian nomadic horsemen who in his time used and presumably possessed no metal weapons. What Pausanias saw was a corselet, not a helmet, but I do not think this invalidates my suggestion.

29. *Memoirs*, p. 53 in the Beveridge translation. They were fighting against crossbowmen.

30. The old road in use until the asphalt mountain road was built about ten years ago was the historic Lataband Pass road, where the British Army perished in the nineteenth century. There is an excellent description of this road and its traffic in 1939 by Lt.-Gen. Molesworth in his *Afghanistan*, 1919 (pp. 175–6, published by Asia publishing house, London, 1962). General Molesworth's book gives exactly and fully the atmosphere, which already after so few years is almost impossible to imagine, of frontier operations between the two wars. There is an appealing and innocent distinction about his prose which makes it a perfect instrument for this task. The last case of a hold-up on the Kabul–Jellalabad road I heard about was six or seven years ago; all that was taken was petrol on that occasion.

31. The material from Hadda is mostly in the Musée Guimet at Paris, in Rome and in Kabul, but it has been widely dispersed since there was so much of it; it is to be found in many private collections, and is still bought in Kabul antique shops at excessive prices to be smuggled abroad. Nothing could be more obviously under classical influence than this style; the influence is specifically Alexandrian, cf. R. E. M. Wheeler in *Antiquity*, 28 (1949), pp. 1f.

32. The best treatment of Kushan dress is in Rosenfeld's *Dynastic Art of the Kushans*, pp. 183f. Cf. also the Hashtragar pedestal in the British Museum (*East and West*, 15, p. 58).

33. Published in an inadequate but indispensable form in English as a pamphlet, *The Fish Porch*, by Dr S. Mustamandi, by the Historical Society of Afghanistan. I bought my copy, which was secondhand, at the site, and never saw another. Clay models easily in this way: there

is a seventh-century figure from Fundukistan in the Kabul Museum, of a woman about to give birth under a tall, sailing wall of undulating flames in just the same convention. Cf. p. 22 in the French 1964 *Guide du visiteur*.

34. Macartney's map in Elphinstone's *Kingdom of Caubul*, 1839. The route from Kabul to Gardez (Guardaiz) swerves at the last moment to Ghazni, and no route goes from Gardez to the Indus except through Ghazni or by a roundabout route to the north-east.

CHAPTER SEVEN

1. There is an important map of these sites with the title *Sites de la Bactriane*, in *Monuments préislamiques de l'Afghanistan*, in the 19th volume of the Mem. D.A.F.A. (1964).

2. Cf. note 14.

3. Perhaps it is worth saying that to see the places makes the archaeological reports more intelligible, but places in themselves are hardly intelligible at all unless work has been already done and the reports written. Perhaps the least reliable method of all is to work from the objects one has seen in museums without reference first to the publications, and then to the places, although in practice museum collections are usually the stimulus and the starting-point of all archaeological inquiries. From this it follows that what is shown in museums should be presented whenever possible with a solid depth and range of materials and not as a series of isolated treasures of art. There is a story of a museum curator at Winchester locking away an ugly Saxon pin for fear of visitors crooning over it as a beautiful treasure; what he should have done was to present such a series of pins as to make their banality obvious, and other household goods as well. Art is a simple sign of human habitation, but it is never self-sufficient or self-explanatory.

4. Some elaborate capitals of the Kushan period were found at Cham Kala and published by French archaeologists in Mem. D.A.F.A.

5. Nancy Hatch Dupree, *The Road to Balkh* (1967), pp. 19–20; this story may come from a life of Abdur Rahman by Sultan Mahomed Khan (London 1900), which I have never seen. The road and fort referred to are not this one. There was some kind of sports pavilion perched on the north wall, hardly more than forty or so years old; the fortress appeared older than 1890, perhaps much older, but it may not be. There were a lot of fragments of plain pink and carmine pottery; the inner court was 142 paces across.

6. Surkh Kotal was excavated by the French archaeological mission under M. Daniel Schlumberger, at that time head of the mission. There have been a number of articles and preliminary reports, the best in *Journal Asiatique* (1964), pp. 303f., but no full report has yet been announced. Meanwhile the most important article in English is M.

Schlumberger's British lecture in 1961, published in the *Proc. Brit. Acad.*, vol. 47, pp. 77f. Cf. also J. B. Ward-Perkins, in *Proc. Brit. Acad.*, 51, pp. 175f. and Wheeler, *Flames over Persepolis* (1968), pp. 158f. and 171.

7. Now cf. Boethius and Ward-Perkins, *Etruscan and Roman Architecture* (1970), p. 441.

8. This is the only reasonable deduction from *Papers on the Date of Kanishka*, ed. A. L. Basham (Brill, 1968), which is a compendium of modern arguments about this subject.

9. The religious tolerance is typical of the Kushans and possibly of the Greeks before them. There are Jain as well as Buddhist Kushan inscriptions. On the Buddhist site at Surkh Kotal cf. *Journal Asiatique* (1964), p. 323, n. 2.

10. Cf. Fischer in *Artibus Asiae*, 21 (1958) on the Kunduz reliefs.

11. The authority is Hiuen Tsiang in A.D. 630 travelling near here from Balkh to Bamiyan, cf. Nancy Dupree, *The Road to Balkh* (1967), p. 21.

12. On the site cf. A. Foucher in *La Vieille route de l'Inde de Bactres à Taxila* (Mem. D.A.F.A., Paris, 1947), and more recently Professor Mizuno, *Haibak and Kashmire-smast*, Kyoto, 1962 (English summary).

13. Fitzroy Maclean's *Eastern Approaches* contains an excellent, dry account of an adventurous journey in Uzbekistan before the war.

14. Cf. Maclean, *Eastern Approaches*. He crossed the Oxus near Termez and travelled 60 miles through the desert ('dunes of sand and shrivelled tamarisk bushes') to Mazur. He saw marmots, the skeletons of horses and camels, and some ruined buildings which seem otherwise to be unknown.

15. For a more cheerful view of this awful place, cf. N. H. Dupree, *The Road to Balkh* (1967), pp. 48f. The hotel, which we tested again later, must surely be one of the worst in Afghanistan.

16. It has been suggested that it may be Greco-Iranian. There is one of these in the Kunduz Museum, and another in the Ashmolean Museum at Oxford. For a Russian example, cf. C. Trever, 'Terracottas from Afrasiab', in *Bulletin of the State Academy for History of Material Culture*, 93 (Moscow, 1934).

17. For the plan of this site and also of Amanullah's star-shaped suburbs, cf. Mem. D.A.F.A., vol. 19, fig. 10 (after plate 45).

CHAPTER EIGHT

1. Herodotos knew the Bactrians as a Persian frontier people (2, 92 cf. 1, 153, 4) and the city itself may well date from this period, even far earlier, since its position on a water source, and on important natural routes where there were water sources, must have made it an important site as early as the third millennium and the beginnings of the lapis lazuli trade to Mesopotamia. It has often been associated with the Aryan

migration and with King Yama who departed to the mighty streams and explored the way for many, but this is quite conjectural. There is no archaeological evidence at all before the Greek period at Balkh. It was the Arabs who first called it Mother of cities.

2. From a Zoroastrian document, the *Avesta* (*Vendidad*, 1, 7). Zoroaster (Zarathustra) is supposed to have been born and taught at Balkh. This takes the city back at least to the sixth or seventh century B.C. and there are earlier estimates.

3. Given by Artaxerxes of Persia in the early fourth century B.C. and described in the *Avesta*. It was at Balkh that Alexander introduced the practice of prostration before the sovereign to his Greek retinue, and probably here he married the satrap's daughter Roxane.

4. Firdausi in the *Shahnama* (tenth century A.D. from a mixture of lost Sassanian sources) says Zoroaster was killed there. There was a magnificent fire temple at Nau-Bahar outside the city with an enormous dome and a long silk banner. In general cf. G. Le Strange, *The Lands of the Eastern Caliphate* (Cambridge, 1930).

5. Described in detail in the seventh century A.D., when the practice of Buddhism was ebbing, by Hiuen Tsiang, cf. S. Beal, *Buddhist Records of the Western World* (reprinted by Paragon, New York, 1968). He says the richest Buddha 'has often been robbed', and that the priests 'are so irregular in their morning and night duties that it is hard to tell saints from sinners'. There was a stupa two hundred feet high, with a stuccoed dome of rock-like hardness.

6. Under the Samanids of Bokhara (872–999). The writers are Abul Shuqur, apparently the first writer of long literary narrative poems in Persian, Daqiqi, one of Firdausi's sources in the *Shahnama*, and Rabia of Balkh, who wrote an enchanting poem about flowers ending 'and the violet is dressed in blue like a monk, has it turned to Christianity?'

7. The source for this is Juvaini, writing thirty years afterwards. Two years later a Taoist monk passed by the ruins of Balkh and said, 'we heard the barking of dogs up and down the city.'

8. Ibn Battuta. The reference to Marco Polo is to Bk. 1, c. 23.

9. The study was by D. Schlumberger and M. Le Berre, in Mem. D.A.F.A. Dimensions of bricks vary even in one monument.

10. Mem. D.A.F.A., 15 (1957). J.-C. Gardin, *Céramiques de Bactres*. For example there is a reference to pre-Parthian and pre-Kushan white wares, about which it was hard to be more precise, being found *à proximité du sol vierge*. There were problems of the co-existence of earlier cruder types of pottery with later types on a baffling scale. For references to other pre-Kushan sites cf. p. 44, nn. 3–6. It is probable that the stratified finds from Ay Khanoum will make it easier to understand the Balkh pottery sequence.

11. Excavations in 1924–5, 1947–8, and 1955–6. For the critical

article by R. S. Young on the south wall (*American Journal of Archaeology*, 59, 1955) cf. Mem. D.A.F.A., 19, pp. 79–80.

12. The shrine of Khwaja Abu Nasr Parsa (died in 1597), also called the green mosque, Masjid-i Sabz. There is a tomb to the south of it supposed to belong to Rabia of Balkh, but there is no reason to suppose it is authentic; its discovery was announced in 1964.

13. No western archaeologist has seen Merv for a long time as it lies north of Herat not far from the frontier on the Russian side. The relevant culture is that of the Samanids at Bokhara (872–999). The mosque we were looking for was discovered by Pugachenkova. But cf. now Lisa Golombek in *Oriental Art*, autumn 1969. The reader should be warned that Mr J. M. Rogers, who has inspected the mosque since this was written, is firmly of the opinion that the correct date is eleventh century.

14. Tashkurghan has been renamed Khulm. In general cf. N. H. Dupree, *The Road to Balkh*, p. 36. The French 1969 Fodor guide to Afghanistan, which in general is so bad I have never mentioned it, expresses the general feeling about Khulm: 'Il n'est point de bourg de cette importance en Afghanistan qui ait a ce point gardé son caractère' (p. 207).

15. Bk. 1, c, 23–4.

16. Professor Mizuno of Kyoto. The result was included in a double publication with the Chardara site at Kunduz.

17. For the sites on the Swat river cf. Mark Aurel Stein's *Alexander's Track to the Indus*, pp. 36f. and pp. 52f. I am not suggesting any similarity between these sites and Aliabad Qala, which could for all we know to the contrary be an Islamic castle. I do not know any parallel in Afghanistan for the triple ditch and rampart; it is in Russia one should look for parallels. There was some pottery with a grey impressed net pattern, but we saw it later for sale in Kunduz bazaar.

18. Ria Hackim and Ahmad Ali Kohzad, *Légendes et coutumes Afghanes*, p. 201.

19. In the mid-nineteenth century, Kunduz was 'five or six hundred mud hovels' (Wood, *Journey to the Source of the River Oxus*, p. 138), 'and by its meanness, poverty, and filth, may be estimated the moral worth of its inhabitants.' What he hated was chiefly the slave trade (cf. p. 197 with Yule's note on slave prices later in the century). He may also have been angry about what Victorian boys' schoolmasters called 'vice'. Among the lunatic missions with the British Army at Kabul in 1841–2 there was a Society for the Suppression of Vice among the Uzbeks. The depopulations were big slave-raids; I thought I had read about it in Yule's notes to Wood's journey, but can no longer find the reference.

20. My informant was Mr Price. He was investigating the possibility of irrigation schemes in the same area. The ruins of the old canal are on 'terrace 3' level.

21. This mound is 8 kilometres away from Kunduz. The urn-base was

two feet across; there was also some finer white slip and a very dark red pottery.

22. Cf. Paul Bernard, 'Ay Khanoum', in *Proc. Brit. Acad.*, 53, p. 73. To be fair, the local people knew it as an ancient city and Wood thought there was a site of some kind, but he was possibly on the wrong side of the hill to see the more obvious part of it, and dismissed what he was shown as modern (*Journey to the Oxus*, p. 260), 'and to all our inquiries about coins and relics, they only vouchsafed a vacant stare and an idiotic laugh'. For the type of column cf. Bernard, 'Chapiteaux Corinthiens Hellénistiques d'Asie Centrale', in the periodical *Syria*, vol. 45 (1968), pp. 111f.

23. Sites include Shor Tepe (the ferry station due north of Balkh), Khisht Tepe or Qala-i Zal (north-east of Tashkurghan at the southernmost point of the Oxus), Khwaja Imam Sayid (due north of Kunduz), and on the Russian side, Kobadian, Tulkharskii, Qarawal Tepe and Faizabad Qala (north of Kunduz). The Japanese have explored Chaqal Tepe, and Durman Tepe at Chardara (cf. n. 25). For sites south of Kunduz cf. Mem. D.A.F.A. 19 (1964), the map of *Sites de la Bactriane*. Professor Mizuno's publication has an important list of sites and publications (pp. 5 and 8). No published or unpublished list I have seen (e.g. Klaus Fischer's map in the D.A.F.A. library at Kabul) has been at all complete.

24. Excavated by the Kyoto expedition; some of the material is in Kunduz, some under seal in the Kabul Museum awaiting further study, cf. Mizuno, *Durman Tepe and Lalma* (Kyoto, 1968, in Japanese and English).

25. These bases are common; they have been found at Surkh Kotal (four at Kunduz and six or more still *in situ*) at the Chardara tepes excavated by the Japanese (Durman Tepe, seven published, and Chaqal Tepe, four in Kabul) at Mazar and Baghlan, and in Russia, Almost no two bases have exactly the same combination of rings in the same proportion.

26. *Journey to the Source of the River Oxus*, p. 139.

27. But the whole supposition of a southern Greek kingdom which survived when the lands north of the Hindu Kush had already fallen to the Sakai has recently been brought in question; cf. the reviews of the D.A.F.A. publication of the Kunduz hoard of Greek coins (Mem. D.A.F.A. 20, 1965) by G. K. Jenkins in *J.H.S.* 88 (1968). The hoard was found at Khisht Tepe; the publication includes a map.

CHAPTER NINE

1. M. Casal dug the graves; the results were largely negative and have not yet been published.

2. Andrew Marvell, *Appleton House*, verse 55. I happened to be reading

Marvell on the same day. Both Bruce and I developed or rediscovered a passion for this poem during these weeks, and also for Lorca and above all for Basho.

3. The Cartographic Institute at Kabul was kind enough to show me air photographs of this region. The whole of Afghanistan has been photographed from the air, the north by the Russians (Technoexport) and the south by the Americans, and there are fine detailed air photographs of sites like Ghazni; but the Kunduz tumuli do not come out clearly enough to be worth reproducing in this book.

4. Cf. S. Puglisi, preliminary report in *East and West*, vol. 14 (1964). The drawings on the plaster may be later than the building, which seems to be Kushan.

5. Moorcroft and Trebeck, *Travels . . . from 1819 to 1825*, ed. H. H. Wilson, vol. 2, 1841; C. E. Yate, *Northern Afghanistan* (1888). Moorcraft was an unofficial traveller; he was a Lancashire vet, who lost money over a patent horse-shoe and went out to India as an army adviser. There he went loose and wandered as far as Bokhara with a young Englishman called Trebeck; he was murdered near Maimana and his body was brought back by camel and buried under the walls of Balkh. Trebeck died of fever at Mazar soon afterwards; their papers somehow reached the India Office, and finally the Royal Asiatic Society. Major Yate served on the Russo-Afghan border commission.

6. The source for the Han embassies is Ssu-ma Ch'ien, cf. C. G. F. Simkin, *Traditional Trade of Asia*, pp. 1–8 and 33. Hiuen Tsiang is in Beal's *Buddhist Records of the Western World* (reprinted 1968). For the horses cf. also Tarn, *The Greeks in Bactria and India*, p. 308.

7. Kwaja Muhammad; it was fifty miles away. The river was the Khanabad river, which consumes itself mostly in irrigation and meets the Kunduz river between Kunduz and the Oxus. We noted that the British maps for the area of Taliqan are wrong not only about rivers but about contours as well. The Taliqan plain is practically an island. Marco Polo (1, 24) suggests its importance was a supply of salt.

8. The undramatic pass between the streams was the watershed dividing the tributaries of the Kunduz river from those of the Kokcha. We had heard about this sheep-dip in Kabul; it was part of a new drive to persuade the nomads and transhumant herdsmen to improve their flocks by dipping. From Taliqan we were on Marco Polo's known route by Kishm and Badakhshan towards China, which is also the droving route. The tumuli suggest that as usual the ancient and modern movements of nomads were along the same route.

9. For the lapis lazuli mines, which are marked as 'azurite' on Macartney's map, cf. Georgina Herrmann, *Iraq*, 30 (1) 1968. The rubies are a deep rose-red spinel no harder than a topaz, called Badakhshan or balas (*balashan*) ruby. They were already known to Ibn Haukal in the tenth century and to Marco Polo (1, 26) and to Castillian envoys who

reached Samarkand in 1405. They probably reached China under the T'ang (cf. Schafter's *Golden Peaches of Samarkand*, p. 231), but there is no special word for this stone in medieval Chinese, any more than in Latin or Greek; still it seems probable that it must have been known before the Middle Ages. To Pliny it would be *carbunculus* and to Theophrastos *anthrax*. There are modern references to the ruby mines in Burnes's *Travels into Bokhara* (1834), which may I think be the same book as A. Born, *Reise in der Bucharei* (Moscow, 1849), and in Stein's *Innermost Asia* (vol. 2, p. 877). The best account of lapis and rubies is in Wood's *Journey to the Source of the River Oxus* (chaps. 17–19). The technique of extracting valuable stones by splitting rocks with fire is attested both in medieval England and in classical Greece; cf. R. J. Hopper in the annual of the British School of Athens, 1968.

10. 1, 25. We saw traces of an older road which no car could take, and the grave-mounds suggest and our experience confirmed that this is the natural route into the Wakan corridor. The route is still taken; the line is Taliqan, Kishm, Faizabad (= Badakhshan), Bahrak, then Zebak (although the modern road goes through Ishkashm). Marco Polo's southward excursus to Kashmir, etc., is based on travellers from the Anjuman Pass, that is at Faizabad. At some time he seems to have spent a year in Badakhshan, recovering from an illness (1, 26). He was cured by moving up to the pure and healthy air (and perhaps water) of the high mountain where he speaks of wild flocks of goats. They are not the same as the famous Marco Polo sheep with the curling horns, which he describes elsewhere, and which still exist where he describes them, in Wakan.

11. The Frantz family: never underestimate a midwesterner; they were a kind of Swiss Family Robinson, and the parents were as cool as cucumbers. They were all very sweet and gentle, practical and funny. She was the image of a nineteenth-century pioneer with no fuss and absolutely no nonsense; he was a successful American doctor working for two years as a volunteer in Afghanistan, and this journey had been planned for two years. He spoke of his ideal books being by Voltaire, Gibbon and Montaigne, and his conversation was full of the *New Scientist*. We all fell hopelessly in love with the whole family, but the one we really worshipped was Mrs Frantz, who was funniest.

12. Ibn Haukal mentions such a mosque in the tenth century. Mr Barakzai of the Kabul Museum had once attempted to reach this very important site but he was blocked by snow in the pass or a swollen river, and failed to reach it. No archaeologist has ever seen it.

13. At the risk of being tedious, I would like to underline that this surely was Marco Polo's route, and the route of the Kushan Army that crossed the Pamirs and attacked China in A.D. 90. (Teggart, *Rome and China*, 1969, p. 143), and that the originals of the many purely Greek types of terracotta animal figures which are found in Han and T'ang

Chinese graves, and which revolutionized Chinese art, very probably travelled up this valley. For the alternative northern route cf. Stein's Khotan and his map; for the terracottas, which I first saw in the Princeton University Museum, cf. in general, B. Laufer's *Chinese Pottery of the Han Dynasty* (1909) and his *Chinese Clay Figures* (1919).

14. The rivers were almost at their highest at this time and the edges of fields beside the Warduj were under water. In winter the streams are lower and freeze altogether. Wood records the freezing of the Oxus, and *The Lata'if al Mara'if of Tha'libi* has a lot to say about it in connection with the Chorasmian winter (ed. C. E. Bosworth, Edinburgh, 1968, p. 143). 'Elephants, caravans and armies can pass over it. It remains thus frozen for a period of forty days to two months.' Ibn Fadlan claimed that in the winter of 921–2 the ice on the Oxus was five and a half feet thick. (Togan, Ibn Fadlan's *Reisebericht* text 7–8 tr. 13–14, quoted by Bosworth.) The glaciers in the Hindu Kush are still two-thirds of their original size.

15. This is an Italian delicacy Elizabeth had brought from England. It is a concentrated compound of fruit and spice supposed to date from the thirteenth century. It was the last food we had; it is even better than Kendal mint cake (our usual hard rations) and as indestructible, but harder to come by in England. The Afghans used a compounded mulberry cake for winter travelling, but we were unable to find any. I did find a sort of apricot and mulberry fudge in Kabul but that was mere confectionery.

16. There is a police conspiracy at Faizabad to keep people to a particular van from the town to the airfield, for which the fare is artificially high. We felt rightly or wrongly that we had to fight this as a matter of principle. It is nothing to what goes on at the Kunduz airline office, where you not only pay double as a foreigner according to the law, but they try to make you pay in dollars, in which you pay fourteen dollars more than the true dollar equivalent of the double charge. No doubt both these arrangements are unofficial.

17. From the Kushan capital city at Kapisa, now in the Kabul Museum.

18. Obviously he could have seen them; they are quite common in the Western Isles of Scotland and they enter the Channel. But to Yeats they are Byzantine ornaments. If he were more interested in the real nature of everything I would find him a more necessary poet. Even Marvell would never have spoken about dolphins in such dismissive praises.

CHAPTER TEN

1. The books and articles on Nuristan are listed with brief descriptions by Schuyler Jones, *An Annotated Bibliography of Nuristan* (Copenhagen, 1966). The best single book is certainly Robertson's *Kafirs of the Hindu*

Kush (1896); cf. also E. Newby, *A Short Walk in the Hindu Kush*, and F. Maraini, *Where Four Worlds Meet*.

2. Cf. in general Colonel Durand's *Making of a Frontier* (1899) and Schuyler Jones, No. 58 (Gen. Chamberlain in *Saturday Review*, 1896), and No. 174.

3. Schuyler Jones, No. 191 and No. 185 (T. G. Montgomerie in *Journ. Roy. Geog. Soc.*, 41 (1871) and H. C. Marsh in *Journ. As. Soc. Bengal*, 45, 1876).

4. Later Sir George Scott Robinson and political agent and Resident at Chitral, where he was murdered. He had a hard time in Kafiristan, and on the whole his description is level and convincing. Testing it with our own experiences we were astonished by its accuracy and the excellence of the drawings. But Robinson was not an anthropologist or a comparative religionist, and he never forgave the villagers for laughing at him in his inflatable rubber bath. (Curzon also travelled with one, a cheering thought.)

5. The last native ruler of Chitral and the last ruler of Swat were deposed by the central government of Pakistan and their positions abolished only in August 1969, about a fortnight after our journey. The position of the rulers was guaranteed by the settlement at the division of India, but of course their power had been much eroded. Still, when they were abolished certain areas refused to pay their taxes, and an important village in Swat was destroyed from the air. On the way authority used to function in Chitral cf. John Clark, *Hunza* (1957).

6. This invasion was described by the Amir Abdur Rahman himself in his English autobiography (London, 1900). Cf. also Schuyler Jones, No. 190.

7. Robertson's account of religion is invaluable but terribly inadequate. There is more material with modern photographs in Maraini's *Where Four Worlds Meet* (1964), specially plates 152–63. The principal Kafir gods were Imra the sky and weather god, Gish the war god, and Moni the devil-killer and god of prophecy, who was worshipped as a big rock. The religion was shamanistic with some strong Siberian overtones in the mythology. In general, cf. Morgenstierne in *Acta Orientalia*, 21 (1951), pp. 161f. and Karl Jettmar, *Die Religionen des Hindukusch*, published in the seventies. Peers Carter walked up the Pech and Kantiwa rivers in 1972. He was shown a large boulder just below Kantiwa as an ex-god.

8. Schuyler Jones, No. 196; the article discusses a number of Kafir genealogies but is written in Norwegian.

9. The annual letter to Rome for 1678 (cf. MacLagan, *The Jesuits and the Great Mogul*, 1932) reports this mission, which was a reconnaissance following a report by Armenian traders that the Kafirs had once been Christian. The result of the mission was the information that the Kafirs were pagans who worshipped a stone called Mahdeu and lived in independent villages. Mahdeu may refer to Mahandeo, a god reported by

Maraini as still worshipped in Chitral in 1959 (*Where Four Worlds Meet*, 1964, pp. 261f.). He is the equivalent of Gish. The first Jesuit traveller to report on Kafiristan is Brother Benedict Goes, who reached China from India by Jellalabad and Kabul; he met a hermit who told him about the Kafirs but had the commonsense to keep out of their mountains (cf. H. Bernard, *Biento de Goes*, Tientsin, 1934). Two Catholic missionaries seem to have died in Kafiristan in the seventeen seventies (*Memoirs of Alexander Gardner*, ed. Pearse, 1898, p. 159) and there seems to have been some Catholic missionary activity there in the twenties of this century; perhaps this is the source of a number of French Catholic crucifixes from Kafiristan for sale in Kabul in 1969. The crucifixes seemed to be from about 1880 and were mass-produced.

10. Sir George Grierson in *Journ. Roy. As. Soc.*, London, 1900, and *The Pisaca Languages*, 1906, Asiatic Soc. monographs vol. 8. The truth about the racial origins of the Nuristanis is that they do have close affinities tribe to tribe and dialect to dialect; Sir Aurel Stein, who was in Chitral in 1906—8, speaks of the pure *homo alpinus* of the high Oxus valleys. The legend that the last Buddha of the past had predicted the Gautama Buddha at Nagarahara (Jellalabad), which was popular in local art, particularly at Shotorak, is another phenomenon of the same kind.

11. Marco Polo, 1, 26, on Badakhshan. Also in Abufazl (historian to Akbar), in Macartney's appendix to Elphinstone's *Kingdom of Caubul*, and in many nineteenth-century writers.

12. Marco Polo links it with the descent of rulers from Alexander by his marriage with Darius' daughter (1, 26, supposed to have taken place at Balkh, 1, 23). The word used for Alexander is not Iskander but Zulgarnayn, which means 'two-horned' and seems to refer to Alexander's coins. The same kind of assimilation of real to more famous and glamorous legendary beginnings resulted in the name of Ayuthia, the capital of Thailand, being changed to Ayodhya, the legendary capital of Rama's kingdom in the *Ramayana*.

13. This also was current at least as early as 1836 (G. T. Vigne, *Visit to Ghazni, Kabul and Afghanistan*, 1840, Schuyler Jones No. 269). There are relics of an even stranger story told somewhere among the mountains. Lt. Wood met a Russian Jew who had come to Afghanistan to make contact with the ten lost tribes of Israel. The claim to Jewish origin in Afghanistan goes back at least to the Makhzan-i Afghani of Nematullah, secretary to the Mogul emperor Jahangir in the early seventeenth century. This work was translated (into English) by Professor Dorn of Kharkov in 1829. No doubt it was Dorn who was responsible for the journey of Wood's Russian Jew.

14. Sir Aurel Stein believed that T'ang Chinese power crossed the Pamirs and extended south of the Hindu Kush in the eighth century; he found the claims of Chinese annalists confirmed by local Chitrali

traditions about ancient sites, and by an occasional place name. In 749 the Chinese are supposed to have invaded over the Baroghil and Darkot passes (about 12,400 and 15,400 feet) in the course of the war with Tibet. Tamburlaine left an inscription which has been visited, most recently in 1951 by Mackenzie I believe (Newby, *A Short Walk in the Hindu Kush*, p. 92), but not photographed. He crossed the Khawak Pass in 1398.

15. The fullest account of these wooden statues is by Lennart Edelberg, 'Statues de Bois rapportées par l'Emir Abdur Rahman', in *Arts Asiatiques*, 7 (1960), pp. 243f. There are also two in the Ashmolean Museum, Oxford, and probably some in private collections. Almost all or all of the many small Nuristan carvings we saw for sale in Kabul in 1969 were modern fakes.

16. 'Fragments d'un Stupa', in *Arts Asiatiques*, 4 (1957), with two sketch-maps and fourteen photographs.

17. An ancient Hindu temple, *Oriental Art*, 5, new series, 1959. By spending an extra day we could easily have walked from Chagaserai and spent time at this site.

18. Recorded by A. L. Lloyd; I once heard them broadcast. The people in the fields in Afghanistan sometimes sing impromptu antiphonal songs of the same kind; if you understand what is being sung you sometimes discover you are being talked about.

CHAPTER ELEVEN

1. The old Stevgrom where Robertson took refuge from Kamdesh. There are said to be the ruins of two other villages higher up in the Pech valley, both abandoned before the eighteen nineties. We did not find them. Kamdeh is not the same as Kamdesh.

2. Maraini (*Where Four Worlds Meet*) produces photographs of a lorry being washed away by one of these terrifying sudden floods. Bruce had met two Frenchmen who ran uphill in the nick of time to avoid a great uncontrolled mass of water and rocks and earth that came sweeping down a steep valley. They had been sheltering in a car, which they later found crushed flat. In June 1969 the *Kabul Times* reported the death of forty people in Badakhshan through 'the collapse of a mountain'.

3. Nuristani music has more than one tone system. Polyphony depends on a leader improvising a two, three or four beat theme, which he keeps repeating, while a second lead singer sings in counter point with different timing, and other singers add their own themes each improvising more or less in the same way. When there are four voices and the four parts are well started and can be recognized, everyone present follows the four themes, first the leader's, then they transfer together to the second, and so on. The words are often meaningless, and exist only to mark the rhythm. There are special Nuristani instruments, including a harp played with a wooden plectrum; its soundbox is the shape of a boat and covered

in gooseskin. There are different kinds of drum, reed-flutes and flutes made of bird-bone, like the bird-bone flutes still used in Sardinia. Gooseskin is interesting because the nomadic route down into Chitral follows the migration route of wild geese, just as the geese follow the Milky Way.

4. Unrecorded by Heath in his rather full typewritten account of this valley, which is in the library of the British Embassy at Kabul. Mr Christopher Rundle has also written an account, more accurate than mine, which will be kept there.

5. Heath's Chitas.

6. Por qui duermes solo, pastor?

En mi colcha di lana

dormirias mejor.

Tu colcha de oscura piedra,

pastor,

y tu camisa de escarcha,

pastor.

7. The chief source of hallucinogenic drugs at this level. The use of hallucinogenic drugs of one kind or another is very ancient in Asia; 'hashish' inhalers have been recovered from the Altai kurgans of the fifth and fourth centuries B.C. Cf. Jettmar, *Mitteilungen der Anthropologischen Gesellschaft in Wien*, 92 (1962), and in general Jettmar's *Die frühen Steppenvölker* (Baden Baden, 1964).

8. Photographs in *Folk Tales of Swat* by Inayat-ur-Rahman, pt. 1 (Rome, 1968), plates 12, 32-3, 43-6 and 50.

9. The same reference, p. 10, etc. The stories also contain a seeker after foreign wisdom like Herodotos' Solon (Herod. 1, 30, 2, *Swat Volk Tales*, p. 34), a classical lamia (p. 22), Rokshana the Tibetan princess with a crystal ball (pp. 32-3) who seems to be Alexander the Great's Roxane from the Alexander romance, and a reference to the worship of air, water and fire, with fire supreme (pp. 29-30). The photographs include what looks like a curious survival of Hellenistic pottery shapes at Mingora in Swat (fig. 43). Hellenistic pottery shapes occur in China under the T'ang at about the same time as the small terracotta grave figures from Hellenistic originals, and the pottery shapes of Swat might be learned from China. I have not studied this question properly and must be forgiven if my conjecture appears romantic; it seems to me slightly likelier to be true than to be untrue.

10. Inayat-ur-Rahman, *Folk Tales of Swat* (Rome, 1968), plate 45 (Madyan), plate 32-3 (Kalam).

CHAPTER TWELVE

1. But the Fairchild survey marks the Kunjenida Pass at 4,400 metres, which is above 14,400 feet. Heath marks the Kungani Pass as lower. Chris had seen his leopard at about 4,092 metres. Robertson's Kungani

Pass is north of the source of the Nichingul (or Nechingal), the river that runs down to Kamdesh, but Heath's Kungani Pass, which he marks as Robertson's route, follows the river from its source. We know that Robertson crossed his pass in a panic, fleeing from Kamdesh, and his topographic observation during these few days was certainly not as good as usual. We know that the two-day route to Kamdesh followed the right bank of the Pech at least longer than our own. It must be assumed there was an easy way up to the Kungani Pass from near the source of the Pech, and then a swift route down one of the left bank tributaries of the Nichingul.

2. The heights given by the Fairchild survey (Cartographic Institute at Kabul) are 5,160 m. (c. 17,028 ft.) for the peak, and 4,765 m. (c. 16,384 ft.) for the lowest point of the col. If I have made a great fuss about this tiresome but simple route, the reader should remember we were not travelling under ideal circumstances, and we had no idea where we were being taken. But the Uchuk route to Kamdesh will always take at least three days. We could hardly have climbed this mountain and got down the other side before dark in one day from Ishtiwi.

3. The upper valleys of Nuristan communicate more easily with the north than they do with the south, if only because horses and baggage animals can enter only from the north. In a country where the axe is so important both as an instrument and as a symbol, it is at least curious that the Nuristani word is *tabar* and the Russian word *topor*. Still more curiously, both forms derive from the Arabic.

4. It was the dance *Attane Meli Kaschana*, or one very like it. H. Pressl collected this dance, which he calls the national dance of the Petsch tribe, in the Nichingul valley (*Kabul Times*, 20 July 1969). When it is properly performed the dancers carry weapons and wear animal skins.

5. The Nichingul is also called the Weigal and (wrongly) the Boralkut; the Kamdesh river is also called the Kamus and the Bashgal; the Bashgali language was the language of this valley, and Kamdesh was the central town and meeting-place of the confederated tribes.

CHAPTER THIRTEEN

1. Ptolemy, 1, 12, 6; a city belonging to Sogdia (cf. Bernard, *Proc. Brit. Acad.* 53, p. 92, n. 4). Tarn thought its existence dubious (*The Greeks in Bactria and India*, p. 118, n. 6), probably because no one but Ptolemy mentions it. The only other known site which is a rival candidate to the name is Termez on the Russian bank of the Oxus north of Kunduz, but Tarn shows that Termez was probably called Demetrias and was founded later (*ibid.*, pp. 118-19). One would expect a Sogdian city to be on the north bank. No inscription has yet been found at Ay Khanoum giving its Greek name, but no likelier name for Ay Khanoum than Alexandria on

the Oxus can be suggested on the existing evidence. The Sogdian Alexandria mentioned by Pliny *in ultimis eorum finibus* is *Alexandria-Eschate* (Chodjend) and a reference to Pliny (6, 49) should be added to Tarn, p. 118, n. 5. There were four or five cities in central Asia called Alexandria; the first Alexandria was in Thrace, founded in 340 B.C. after Alexander's first victories, in his father's lifetime.

2. Ssu-ma Ch'ien, letter to Jen-an about 100 B.C. Cf. Penguin anthology of Chinese literature, ed. C. Birth, p. 122 (translation by J. R. Hightower).

3. Ptolemy on the Sakai (6, 13). The Sakai first met the Greeks at Gaugamela where they fought on the Persian side. Later they invaded and overwhelmed Greek Bactria; they are probably among the ancestors of the Pathans (cf. Olaf Caroe, *The Pathans*, ch. 4).

4. 'Babylon was his difficulty and also the Bactrian people and the Sakai . . .' (1, 153, 4; cf. also 1, 201f. on the Massagetai and 4, 11f.). Darius took Sogdia and Bactria; Sind seems to have been conquered very early in his reign, before the terrace at Sousa was begun. Cf. Herzfeld, *Persian Empire*, 1968, p. 282.

5. Heketaios, fr. 299, quoting Skylax and quoted by Stephanos s.v. Opiai.

6. It is quite likely, since he makes no mention of Kunduz, that Marco Polo travelled this track (1, 23–24). But I do not understand how he can have covered over a hundred miles from Balkh in two days, unless he galloped through the desert all day with good guides and good horses. How did he cross the Kunduz river? From Taliqan to Kishm he took three days, but admittedly that track was stony and mountainous. One must suspect that either his memory was at fault or the text of his memoirs was wrong about the two days.

7. For example at the Göksür oasis, cf. G. N. Lisitsina, 'The Earliest Irrigation in Turkmenia', in *Antiquity*, 43 (1969), pp. 279f., particularly p. 282, and compare in general R. Adams, *Land Behind Baghdad*, 1965.

8. The roofspans were seventeen, fourteen and fifteen metres. The only building in mainland Greece with a roofspan like this was the Odeion in the Athenian agora (twenty-five metres) called the Odeion of Agrippa, built about 15 B.C. Its roof collapsed and it was rebuilt about A.D. 150, on a less ambitious scale (cf. *The Athenian Agora*, 1962, American School of Classical Studies, Athens, pp. 72–4). There is also an analogy at Priene, but less systematic and smaller. The groundplan of Persepolis, with its tent-like forest of interior pillars, shows up clearly on the airview reproduced in Wheeler's *Flames over Persepolis* (1968, p. 34). But Persepolis has no front court. The porch of the palace at Ay Khanoum was held up by sixteen unfluted Corinthian columns with very delicate volutes on which nothing can have rested, so that the cornice must have been raised from the centres of the capitals and the pediment must have seemed to float in the air above the columns. The courtyard in front of this porch was 110 metres by 120 metres. Its outer gate is off-centre, evidently

because the hero-shrine on its mound already existed where its centre should have been. For the Corinthian capitals cf. Bernard, 'Chapiteaux Corinthiens à Ai Khanoum', *Syria* 45, 1968.

9. Pronaos.

10. For Rhea and Kybele cf. Nilsson, *Gesch. Griech Relig.*, vol. 1 (1967), p. 298; for the Mother at Athens cf. Judeich, *Topographie von Athen* (1931), p. 345, *The Athenian Agora*, vol. 3 (*testimonia*) pp. 150f., *The Athenian Agora* (1962), pp. 48f.

11. Cf. H. Graillot, *Le culte de Cybèle* (Paris, 1912), p. 21 and cf. p. 518. The Orgeones of the Metroon at the Piraeus seem to have been a foreign group.

12. The head of a herm. Photograph in Wheeler, *Flames over Persepolis*, p. 85. He is mistaken about the find-spot (cf. Bernard, *Proc. Brit. Acad.* 53, pl. 19–20). I have seen it in Kabul. The head has an old, flat, athlete's face and a spade beard with curls; the pillar wears an athlete's cloak.

13. Columns *in antis*. For the groundplan cf. Wheeler, *Flames over Persepolis*, p. 81.

14. Temenos.

15. The famous men are the Seven Wise Men. The inscriptions were due to be published by M. Louis Robert, and perhaps have been, but I do not remember seeing the publication.

16. Professor Bernard suggested this, with the important observation that this Klearchos wrote on Iranian, Indian and Jewish religion.

17. Professor Bernard has already shown an influence of the kind of architectural element found at Ay Khanoum on Cham Qala (*Proc. Brit. Acad.* 53, p. 95). If there is really a Buddhist or Kushan site a few hundred yards from Ay Khanoum it is very important indeed.

POEMS WRITTEN IN AFGHANISTAN

June–September 1969

PETER LEVI

I

Trees of roses. The water crashed headlong
Tearing the darkness out of the stone face.
A god of war might be a god of song,
The sign of faith is a physical grace:
Thinness colour and smell like Asian clover,
The informal appearance of a lover.
Water is religion, it has no voice,
But drowns the silence of God in its noise.
There is no life to be had in the pure air,
And passion for goodness not having it
Is rank swan-music and water-spirit,
Ice and a hundred moving points of fire.
The monks in the illuminated cave
Only love what cannot love, and will save.

In England morning colours like fruit-skin,
It darkens again with a whisp of light:
Apple-trees to work at, grass to play in,
The blossom in the deepest woods is white.
That sun is cultivated, the sky even:
The god of song can love nothing but heaven.
He is exploding stars, the piston-rod
In the sky's dying engine, true and good.
His sudden, light drumming in a back street:
What passes is love, it is not belief,
Love's religion is destructive of life,
It is the heavy seed in the pale wheat.
Death shakes out the last words, what they release
Is the old god of nature and of peace.

Living in the religion of peace
Where God is outward, the world ingrowing,
I break my life to pieces in my voice,
To be like God in his imagining:
The origin of goodness was a fable,
Piety cast off made it available:
Passion for goodness is love in the end,
It is broken language nothing can mend.

The throaty agitation of the trees
Snow-infected, colourstained by the air
Expresses green nature like a despair:
Whatever lives has inward boundaries.
God has none, he is natured like a stone
Frosteaten and sunbitten and alone.

II

RIDDLE ABOUT A DESERT

Without me there is no person.
You would die by what I live on.
Thistles can be a skeleton.
The element of rock is height,
The broken rocks I cannot eat are my delight.

My limbs are chaos in motion
The dusty coat, the dead lion,
My breath was sugar, it is gone.
The element is dry and bright,
The broken rocks I cannot eat are my delight.

The blue immense murdered my swan
My yellow and my green and brown.
Blind I am cold, my eye is sun,
I have voices that live on light,
The broken rocks I cannot eat are my delight.

III

Wooroo of wild birds in a ragged garden.
A gunshot hardly motions them at all
Banging away at sixpence in the wall.
I choose peace, and the dumbness of this season.

The pink weeds in mid-river on the island
And the thin poplar woods are without weight,
Air scored with branches, branches scored with light,
Walnut and willow give the sun day-shadow.

It has a house maybe of a green texture,
Hollyhocks and great sarsens of granite
(Splashed ochre and a kind of silver-white)
Decorate the rough hills time hardly grazes.

Things pile up in analogous confusion;
These old sunflowers hallooing the sun
Extend themselves as if death were someone,
Or snowy quiet not the one dimension.

IV

Bushroses hanging crumpled a leaf drops,
Time is new extent, minute by minute,
Lives easily in wet, dark middle air,
Green fruit will hang stains of colour on it.

Age-ease is no profound intuition,
It is dark extent, future memory,
Can move freely in the horizon of one hour:
Spirit is breath, lighter than time can be.

Buddha is in nature, in my nature,
And silver and solid as a time-piece:
The richness in the Victorian dark;
The sun's whisper troubles Buddha's increase.

Fierce snow-rivers tear away the whole track,
Rock-dust withers and it is sediment.
Poplar and willow make light architecture
And green embroidery on the blue tent.

V

You lose the sense of time's development,
The stones the fleas the hailstorm the dung fires
Have no ambition
It is the spirit that has no ambition.
I want to hang two pieces of fruit
Their colour is their history.

I want them to be in the tree and the air
The fruit creates the tree that it hangs in
The tree creates the air.
The sources of time are in childhood.
Mountain thunder annihilating spirit,
Give me two pieces of fruit in the tree,
Let them hang. Then let them drop.

VI

The stain is in my liver and my brains
And my strength is a carcase of soupbones.
Heaven is swirling like a summer cloud,
There is no salt in the weak taste of blood,
The spirit blows to tatters in thin trees
And whines and cannot reach the provinces;
The angry mewing of the party chief
Sours the bloodbath by indicating 'if'.
He will become paper, become God,
A paper taste alternative to blood.

VII

*Some fragments of translations
from Afghan Poetry*

(i)

On this terrace not one leaf of the roses will survive
In the bitter breaths of autumn.
Let them be glad of a few days of peace in my garden
When the nightingales yell and tear their breasts.
When those lamentations are silent
The dignity and glory of this garden do not survive.

> (KHUSHAL KHAN, b. 1613.
> Khushal Khan produced in his
> lifetime 57 sons and 350 books;
> he did not number his daughters)

(ii)

Where does the spring come from?
Anemone, basil, lily, thyme,
Jasmine, white rose, narcissus, pomegranate,
But the best and groundtone is the dark red tulip.

(KHUSHAL KHAN)

(iii)

They are shooting at me
While I, fool that I am,
Carry a glass shield in front of my face
With no other defence through the world.

(KHUSHAL KHAN)

INDEX